Pelican Books
Power Politics

Martin Wight was Professor of History at Sussex
University when he died in 1972. A colleague of
Arnold Toynbee at the Royal Institute of
International Affairs as a young man, he spent the
war years working in Margery Perham's team at
Oxford on colonial constitutions, and for some years
taught in the International Relations Department of
the London School of Economics. Martin Wight was
one of the most distinguished scholars to have worked
in the field of international relations and brought to it
unusual qualities of intellectual depth and erudition.
Little of his work in the field of international
relations was published in his lifetime. His works
include *Diplomatic Investigations*, which he edited
together with Herbert Butterfield; *Systems of States*,
edited by Hedley Bull; and *Power Politics*, of which the
present work is a revision and expansion.

Martin Wight

Power Politics

Edited by
Hedley Bull and Carsten Holbraad

Penguin Books
Royal Institute of International Affairs

Penguin Books Ltd, Harmondsworth,
Middlesex, England
Penguin Books, 625 Madison Avenue,
New York, New York 10022, U.S.A.
Penguin Books Australia Ltd, Ringwood,
Victoria, Australia
Penguin Books Canada Ltd, 2801 John Street,
Markham, Ontario, Canada L3R 1B4
Penguin Books (N.Z.) Ltd, 182–190 Wairau Road,
Auckland 10, New Zealand

First published by Pelican Books 1979

Published simultaneously by Leicester University Press

Set, printed and bound in Great Britain by
Cox & Wyman Ltd, London, Reading and Fakenham
Set in Monotype Ehrhardt

Tanton placuit concurrere motu,
Iuppiter, aeterna gentis in pace futuras?
Aeneid, xii, 503–4

Civil knowledge is conversant about a
subject which of all others is most
immersed in matter, and hardliest
reduced to axiom.
Francis Bacon, *The Advancement of
Learning*, Book II, xxiii, 1

Contents

Introduction

The original version of Martin Wight's *Power Politics* was published by the Royal Institute of International Affairs in 1946 as one of its 'Looking Forward' Pamphlets.[1] Although a slender essay of sixty-eight pages and long out of print, it has had a deep influence on the study of international relations in universities, especially in Britain. In the last twenty years of his life – he was born in 1913 and died in 1972 – Martin Wight saw the revision and expansion of this essay as his principal scholarly task.

Unfortunately, he did not complete it. The question had to be considered whether the unfinished manuscript of the new *Power Politics* should be published. On the one hand it had to be recognized that some of the chapters existed only in draft form, that different chapters were written at different times from the 1950s to the 1970s, and that unlike the original version the new manuscript did not have the unity of one man's view of the world at a particular time. There was also a need to respect the very high standards Martin Wight set himself for publication. On the other hand it was apparent that all the chapters foreshadowed in the author's table of contents existed at least in draft, with the exception of the concluding one. The fact that different parts of the book were written at different times could not be considered a serious defect if it was borne in mind that the whole emphasis of Martin Wight's work is on the elements of continuity in international relations rather than on the elements of change, and that references to contemporary events are only illustrations, not essential to the central theme. Above all, it was not possible to doubt that publication of the manuscript would be of immense value to students of the subject.

1. Martin Wight, *Power Politics*, 'Looking Forward' Pamphlet No. 8, Royal Institute of International Affairs, London, 1946.

The reader will find in this book a classical account of the system of international politics that emerged in Europe at the beginning of modern times, spread itself over the other continents and today still provides the political framework of the world. The author is concerned not to provide a guide to the ephemera of international politics today, but to set out those features of international politics that are fundamental and enduring. He notes in the first chapter that the political writings of the Greeks have remained classical because their relevance and topicality have been experienced afresh by each succeeding generation. This is the kind of relevance and topicality to which the present work can lay claim.

Much of the book is devoted to definition, to stating the essence of such fundamental and enduring features of the international political landscape as powers, dominant powers, great powers, international revolutions, international anarchy, the balance of power, war and intervention. But while the author's purpose is thus to distil from historical experience he does not lose sight of historical experience itself; the argument never becomes abstract but is rich in historical illustration. It is not a work of history but of reflection about history, but the solidity of the historical knowledge on which it rests is not in doubt. Its language is not pretentious or obscure but simple and clear. It provides no methodological prolegomena or personal apologia but addresses itself directly to the substance of international politics. The view it presents is intensely realistic but at the same time deeply humane, the fruit of a scholar's regard for the truth but also of a passionate moral concern and questioning, that is not paraded but which the reader cannot fail to sense. There is in this book an innocence of purpose, an absence of academic mannerism and an intellectual authenticity that are unusual in works of its kind.

The new *Power Politics* is much longer than the original version of thirty years ago. Is it also markedly different in substance? The new version, unlike the original, reflects awareness of the debate about the impact of military technology on international politics, and includes chapters on the arms race, disarmament and arms control. The concentration of the original essay on the theme of conflict among states is modified by the inclusion of chapters on international society, and its institutions – alliances, diplomacy and war – dealing with the theme of cooperation among states. There is also a chapter on international revolutions, concerned with 'horizontal' or transnational conflict and cooperation. By contrast with the original version the present text takes seriously the concept of a middle power – a change reflected in the substitution of a chapter on minor powers (including both middle and small powers) for the original chapter on small powers.

But if we consider how much international politics, and fashions in the academic study of it, have changed since 1946, what is remarkable about the new *Power Politics* is how little it differs either in style or in substance from the original one. Thirty years of the passage of international events – the rise and decline of the cold war, the spread of nuclear weapons, the dissolution of European empires and the emergence of the Third World – have caused the author to supply new illustrations but his underlying preoccupations, the basic thrusts of his argument, are the same. Nor have thirty years of prolific growth in the academic study of international relations caused the author to alter his position or to change his approach to any noticeable degree: he sets aside the writings of the behaviourists and (apart from some scattered references) of the strategic analysts, and of the political economists – that loom so large in what is taken to be standard literature of the subject today.

How far is this imperviousness to change and to intellectual fashion a weakness of the analysis presented in the present volume and how far is it a source of strength? If we compare the new *Power Politics* with the bulk of introductory studies of international relations published in the Western world today there are perhaps five respects in which it may strike us as expressing a view of the subject which has great clarity, depth and scholarship but is hardly in the contemporary fashion.

First, it may be said that the underlying perspective of the new *Power Politics*, as of the old one, is Eurocentric. It is true that the author notes the emergence, after Japan's achievement of great power status, of an international system which is no longer European but global or inclusive; the decline, within that system, of European ascendancy; the rise of the ex-colonial states using the United Nations as their instrument; and 'the beginning of the contemporary phase of international history' in the collective intervention of the European powers and Japan against the Boxer Rising in China in 1900.[2]

But the author seems to overlook the passing of European ascendancy when he states that 'we might define a world power as a great power which can exert effectively *inside* Europe a strength that is derived from sources *outside* Europe',[3] a definition that could be acceptable only if it were applied retrospectively to the international system before the end of the Second World War. There are points in the argument – as in the chapter on the United Nations – at which Wight appears to accept uncritically the value premises underlying the policies of the Western states, and to fail to take seriously the claims of the Third World states that they are involved in a just struggle against domination. The author's account of 'power politics' is a distillation of the experience of the Western states-system, but he does not ask how far we can rely on this experience in seeking to understand a states-system whose members are predominantly non-Western.

An analysis which, unlike Martin Wight's, sprang directly from the preoccupations of the present time, would be bound to treat the latter question as central. Given that the historical experience of non-Western peoples has been for the most part outside the bounds of the Western, or indeed any other, states-system, how far can their behaviour today be understood on the basis of a series of generalizations about power politics drawn from the history of the West? Given that the norms and institutions of modern international society were evolved by Western states to promote Western objectives, how far are they binding on the new states of Asia, Africa and Oceania, which played no part in shaping them?

But it should not be forgotten that while the states-system of today is global and a majority of its members are non-Western, it is itself a Western institution, or series of related institutions: the diplomatic procedures, the forms of international law, the international organizations, even the methods of war and espionage in terms of which the new members of international society conduct

2. p. 57.
3. p. 56.

their external relations are those which have been inherited from the period of Western dominance. In this sense the global states-system of today is still Eurocentric, an impressive monument to the Western impact on the rest of the world. The expansion of the society of states in Asia, Africa and Oceania marks the decline of European or Western political domination of the world, but it also marks the triumph, for the time being at least, of European or Western conceptions of universal political organization.

In his study of *Systems of States*, to which reference is made below, Martin Wight maintains that all historical states-systems have presupposed a common culture, and he explicitly defends (against the challenge to it presented by the late Professor C. H. Alexandrowicz) the thesis that the modern states-system is the product of specifically Western or European experience.[4] If this is so it must lead us to ask whether or not the global states-system of today is founded upon any common culture, and if not whether it has any prospect of survival. Is the states-system of today in process of disintegration because it has expanded beyond its originally European cultural base? Or is it finding a new base in the cosmopolitan culture of so-called modernity? These are questions which Martin Wight's work helps us to tackle, even though he does not address them directly himself.

Secondly, the new *Power Politics* – again, like the old one – presents world politics as comprising chiefly the relations among powers, or states in their external aspect, whereas most studies today assert that states share the stage of world politics with 'other actors' such as classes, political parties or business corporations, and that transnational or trans-state relations among these various groups are no less central to the subject than international or interstate relations. 'Modern man in general', the author maintains, 'has shown a stronger loyalty to the state than to church or class or any other international bond'.[5] This may or may not be so, it may be said, but surely the student today will need at least to examine the claims of, say, the European Economic

4. See *Systems of States*, especially Chapters 1 and 4; and C. H. Alexandrowicz, *An Introduction to the History of the Law of Nations in the East Indies*, Clarendon Press, Oxford, 1967.

5. p. 25.

Community, the world communist movement, the pan-African, pan-Arab or pan-Islamic movements, or of national or ethnic groups in many parts of the world, to provide alternative foci of loyalty.

But while the author does not discuss the role of non-state actors in specifically contemporary terms there does run through all his work a vivid consciousness that the position of the state, and hence of the system of states, is contingent. He notes that in the broad sweep of history the states-system is an exceptional form of universal political organization, that the idea of its normalcy is an illusion.[6] He contends that while states are the prime and immediate members of international society, its ultimate members are individual men.[7] In the chapter on international revolutions he notes that the three great revolutionary conflagrations of modern times – those of the Reformation, the French Revolution and the Russian Revolution – have brought to light a degree of unity in human society, whilst also creating fissures in it that cut across the divisions among states. He argues against the assumption that periods of revolutionary international politics, in which these 'horizontal' divisions are uppermost, are exceptional or abnormal, whereas periods of non-revolutionary international politics, in which the 'vertical' divisions among states have primacy, are the rule. He points out that modern international history has been about equally divided between the former and the latter, and that to say one or the other state of affairs is 'normal' is merely to express a preference about the future.[8]

In *Systems of States* Martin Wight explores the historical and geographical boundaries of the modern states-system, and considers some of the alternative forms of universal political organization that have existed outside them.[9] In his unpublished lectures on the theory of international relations he treats transnational or 'horizontal' relations as one of the three basic elements in world politics, alongside conflict among states and cooperation or inter-

6. p. 23.
7. p. 106.
8. p. 94.
9. See *Systems of States*, Chapters 4 and 5.

course among states.[10] His work does not in fact underrate the importance of transnational or 'horizontal' relations in world politics; moreover, it helps us to see that the role of these relationships in world politics at present is not new or unprecedented, that it may not be as great as it has been at some periods in the past, and that the present exponents of the primacy of transnational over international links and cleavages are airing a theme that has been a recurrent one throughout modern times.

Thirdly, the new *Power Politics* is like the original one in dealing essentially with the political relations among states, and saying very little about the economic relations among them, or more generally about the economic aspects of world affairs; in this respect also it is out of step with approaches to the subject that prevail today. It is obvious that at the present time much of the content of dealings among states, or more generally among actors in world politics, is economic in character – whether we consider the network of trade and monetary and investment relationships that involve the rich countries with one another, the place of development assistance and redistribution of wealth in negotiations between rich and poor, or the heightened concern of countries both rich and poor with access to or exploitation of scarce resources. What is more, it is often argued today that within the field of relations among states political matters have become less important relatively to economic matters. Or it is argued (perhaps more elegantly) that while international politics remains the central theme, economic matters have become an inseparable part of international politics, and have grown in importance in the political relations of states relatively to military or strategic matters; that in the competition among states for power and influence (if that is what we mean by international politics) economic objectives and economic means have become more prominent, military objectives and military means less prominent.

We have also to note the influence commanded today by accounts of world politics which assert not merely the importance

10. See Hedley Bull, 'Martin Wight and the Theory of International Relations. The Second Martin Wight Memorial Lecture', *British Journal of International Studies*, July 1976.

of economic factors in international politics but the primacy of these factors over others in the determination of events. Here we may instance not only the classical Leninist explanation of rivalries between the capitalist powers in terms of economic imperialism, but neo-Marxist or neo-Leninist explanations of the relationships between rich and poor states and societies in terms of 'structural dependence' or 'neo-colonialism', and also theories emanating from the capitalist world which explain the regional, political integration of states in terms of economic factors, or which present economic or technological interdependence as a new and revolutionary force in the world that is leading to the transformation of the states-system, and perhaps to its decline or obsolescence.

It is true that in this book Martin Wight does not attempt to engage these arguments; we may only speculate as to what answer he would have given them. He undoubtedly saw the political theme in international relations as the central one, and would have rejected suggestions that the economic theme is displacing it. In the same way he certainly believed in what has been called the autonomy of international politics, and would not have countenanced interpretations that treat economic processes as fundamental in international history and political processes as subordinate or derivative.

It is not necessary to his thesis to deny that economic gain can figure as an objective of political struggle (as when wars are fought to establish control of resources or access to raw materials), or that economic means are used as instruments of such struggle (as when energy or food or raw materials are withheld to exact political concessions). Nor is the doctrine of the primacy of political considerations in any way compromised by the recognition that whereas during much of the nineteenth century, under the influence of *laissez-faire* economic doctrines, international politics and international economics were in large measure separated, in the twentieth century they have come to be closely connected – just as they were in the seventeenth and eighteenth centuries in the era of mercantilist thinking.

However, the notion – sometimes adumbrated in the Western countries in recent years – that international economics is in some sense taking the place of international politics, that the struggle for power and influence in world affairs can somehow be by-passed or set aside, is one which Wight would be bound to regard as resting on a shallow and unhistorical view of the human predicament. Moreover, it would be open to him to point out that the idea of the triumph of international economics over international politics has been a recurrent one in modern thinking about international relations, and one which – as in its Cobdenite form in Britain in the last century – has only been made plausible by temporary and local circumstances which, when they disappear, give rise to a return to international politics with a vengeance.

Fourthly, *Power Politics* is a work which – partly because of its title, but also because of its content – is bound to be associated with the so-called realist school of writing about international politics that had its chief vogue in the late 1930s and 1940s but has fallen out of fashion since that time. The realist writers, who were a school only in the loosest of senses, formulated their views in reaction to the so-called idealist or progressivist thinking of the 1920s and early 1930s, which centred upon the hopes then invested in the League of Nations. Where the earlier thinkers had spoken of 'power politics' as an unfortunate feature of past international practice that now could and should be repudiated, or as a feature only of the foreign policies of certain malevolent or recalcitrant states, the realists saw 'power politics' as a necessary or inherent feature of all relationships among sovereign states.

In the course of the last three decades a great deal of criticism has been directed at accounts of world politics of this nature. The doctrine that the international behaviour of all states can be interpreted in terms of the pursuit of power, not only as a means but as the end of foreign policy, can easily be shown to be a reductionist one. The idea that the behaviour of a particular power in foreign policy – say, the United States – can be understood in terms of general laws concerning the behaviour of powers, great powers, dominant powers or world powers, overlooks the fact that the United States has a unique character, that its policy is the outcome of domestic as well as of international circumstances, that the number of states in the states-system (by comparison, for example, with the number of citizens in any state) is quite small, and hence that it may not be through generalizations that they can be best understood, but rather through specific knowledge of the individual character of each state.

Explanations of international relations in terms of 'power politics' cannot readily accommodate the fact that certain groupings of states (as today in their different ways the English-speaking states, the Nordic countries, the European Economic Community, the Socialist Commonwealth) reflect the existence not merely of diplomatic combinations against external antagonists but of multi-state political communities, each one of which induces the states within it to behave towards one another according to laws other than those simply of 'power politics'. The theory of international politics as 'power politics', moreover, may also be dependent on the assumption, today widely questioned, that foreign policy is conducted 'rationally' and purposively. The doctrines of international progress or improvement, against which the writings of the realists were originally directed, have had a rebirth today in 'policy-oriented' studies of future world order, in which attacks are made on the views of the realists on moral grounds and also on the grounds that they draw too sharp a distinction between description and prescription, between understanding the world and changing it. We need not consider here whether or not these and other criticisms of the theory of international politics as 'power politics' are necessarily fatal to it. What we can say, however, is that these are criticisms which need to be met by any deliberate attempt today to restate or rehabilitate what we have called a realist position.

But it may be doubted whether Martin Wight's position is properly described as realist. In calling his work *Power Politics* what he has in mind is that it deals with the politics of powers, or independent political units acknowledging no political superior.[11] He explicitly disavows the idea that such politics can be equated with *Machtpolitik* or the politics of force, or with '"power politics" in the popular sense of the term'.[12] Unlike Hans Morgenthau – whose *Politics Among Nations* (1948) was the most

11. p. 23.
12. p. 29.

18

influential of the realist works, at least in academic circles – he does not claim to present a comprehensive theory of international politics, based on the proposition that all foreign policy is concerned with the pursuit of national interest defined as power. Unlike E. H. Carr – whose *The Twenty Years' Crisis* (1939) influenced him – Wight does not describe his position as a realist one, or present it as an alternative to utopianism, or seek to make use of the Marxist analysis of ideology. Unlike George Kennan – whose *American Diplomacy* (1952) employed realist perspectives in the attempt to provide guidance to the foreign policy of the United States – Wight does not attack 'moralism', or maintain that his analysis gives rise to practical lessons.

The idea that the politics of powers takes the form of a struggle for power is one which Wight presents only in a tentative and interrogative fashion. In the first chapter he introduces the idea as a kind of working hypothesis, that 'has the merit of pointing to a central truth about international relations, even if it gets certain other things out of focus';[13] and in the last chapter he returns to the idea, to show that the things which it gets out of focus are the common interests of states and the tradition of their common moral obligations.[14] In his as yet unpublished lectures on international theory Wight presents international politics in terms of a debate between the realist or Machiavellian interpretation, which emphasizes conflict among states, the rationalist or Grotian interpretation, which emphasizes cooperation or intercourse among states, and the revolutionist or Kantian interpretation, which emphasizes the unity or solidarity of mankind. In these lectures he clearly does not embrace a realist position, but rather contends that the truth has to be sought not in any one of the three interpretations, but in the argument and contention among them.[15]

Wight's attitude to the realist position, then, is an ambivalent one; and in *Power Politics* he does not so much formulate or expound it as suggest that it is food for thought. In doing so he does not purport to present a rigorous or systematic theory;

13. p. 23.
14. pp. 289–94.
15. See Hedley Bull, 'Martin Wight and the Theory of International Relations', *supra*.

indeed, he regarded all such theories in the field of international politics with scepticism and distaste.

Fifthly, it may be said, the new *Power Politics* makes little or no attempt to come to terms with the academic literature of the subject that has accumulated in the years since the original version appeared. We have seen that the author does not seek to anticipate certain obvious charges that would naturally occur to anyone familiar with this literature, and defend himself against them. He does not acknowledge any need to relate his arguments to recent writings, with which students can be expected to be familiar. He takes no account of the debate that has taken place about the methodology of studies of international relations, and in particular does not seek to engage the so-called behaviourist or social scientific school, whose critique has been directed against the methodological premises of precisely such a work as *Power Politics*.

Martin Wight's indifference to the recent literature of the subject may be held to be a shortcoming of the present work, but from another point of view it is a source of strength. International relations is not one of those subjects in which it can be assumed that new studies represent an advance on old ones, that the multiplication of books and journals is a sign of intellectual progress, or that a master of the subject is a person steeped in the latest writings about it. Particularly in a work which, like the present one, seeks to provide an account not of the international political system as it is at the present moment, but of those features of it that are fundamental and enduring, the need is to build one's exposition not on what has been said recently, but on those statements about the subject that are classical, in the sense that they are the standard or most excellent expressions of a particular view of it.

In judging that little of the recent academic literature of international relations is classical in this sense, Martin Wight, we believe, was correct. Had he devoted a substantial part of the present study to a discussion of the work of the American strategic analysts, or of recent theories of international law, or of the exponents of the 'structural dependence' theory, this would have had the advantage of enabling him to define his position in relation to current discussion, but it would also have carried the danger that he would have been deflected from his main purpose. In particular, the behaviourist school – with its calculated exclusion of moral or ethical questions, its lack of attention to historical inquiry and its underlying utilitarianism of purpose – was one whose claims he was not able to take seriously.

The student embarking upon the study of international politics will need to consult many other books besides this one: there are issues with which it does not deal, questions to which it does not supply answers. But he will find in it an historical introduction to the cardinal principles at work in international politics today, that will provide him with a steady point of reference. In contrast to many other works on the subject its theme is not change, but continuity. Basic changes occur in the structure of international politics, and are occurring in our own times, but it is only against the background of an understanding of what is permanent in that structure that we can recognize changes when they come or assess claims that they are basic.

Whereas the original *Power Politics* contained only fifteen chapters the present text contains twenty-four. Of these only one chapter is unaltered (the last, Chapter 24); thirteen have been revised (Chapters 1, 2, 3, 4, 5, 8, 9, 14, 16, 17, 18, 19 and 20); and ten are wholly new (Chapters 6, 7, 10, 11, 12, 13, 15, 21, 22 and 23). The editors have followed the principle that nothing should be included in the text that was not written by the author himself. They have felt free, however, to determine the arrangement of chapters, to delete passages and to make minor stylistic corrections, and they have had in some cases to choose between alternative drafts of chapters.

In the case of Chapter 13, dealing with war, only a fragmentary draft existed, and in its place the editors have included a reprint, with minor editorial changes, of a talk given by the author on the BBC Third Programme and published in *The Listener*.[16] Chapter 20 on the United Nations includes, in addition to the author's draft on this subject, edited extracts from a paper on 'The Power Struggle Within the United Nations' read to the Institute

16. 'War and International Politics', *The Listener*, Vol. LIV, No. 1389, 13 October 1955.

of World Affairs in Pasadena, California, and subsequently published in its Proceedings.[17] Two fragments – on the grading of powers and on international doctrines – are included as appendices. At the end of each chapter the editors have supplied a footnote estimating the time at which it was written.

The manuscripts left by Martin Wight also included a series of essays on historical states-systems written in the last eight years of his life for meetings of the British Committee on the Theory of International Politics. These have been published separately under the title *Systems of States*; a brief account of Martin Wight's life and thought – and, more particularly, of his contribution to the study of international relations – is given in the Introduction to this volume, together with a list of his publications.[18]

The editors wish to express their gratitude to Gabriele Wight, who has been constantly helpful, and to Harry Pitt of Worcester College, Oxford, who first sorted the papers left by the author and has provided guidance and criticism throughout. They must also thank Hélène Mitchell for her help in checking the text and footnotes and Hermia Oliver for preparing the index.

The editors

17. *Institute of World Affairs Conference Proceedings*, 33rd Session, 1956.
18. Martin Wight, *Systems of States*, edited with an Introduction by Hedley Bull, Leicester University Press in association with the London School of Economics, 1977. A further discussion of Wight's ideas, dealing more particularly with his lectures on international theory, is provided in Hedley Bull, 'Martin Wight and the Theory of International Relations. The Second Martin Wight Memorial Lecture', *supra*.

1 : Powers

Power politics is a colloquial phrase for international politics. We shall have occasion later in this book to consider how far it is an appropriate phrase, but let us begin by taking it at its face value. It has the merit of pointing to a central truth about international relations, even if it gets certain other things out of focus. For, whatever else it may suggest, 'power politics' suggests the relationship between independent powers, and we take such a state of affairs for granted. It implies two conditions. First, there are independent political units acknowledging no political superior, and claiming to be 'sovereign'; and secondly, there are continuous and organized relations between them. This is the modern states-system.[1] We have the independent units, which we call states, nations, countries or *powers*, and we have a highly organized system of continuous relationships between them, political and economic, diplomacy and commerce, now peace, now war.

It will help us to understand this state of affairs if we recall that it is by no means the rule in history. The present states-system has existed roughly since the early sixteenth century, and we have the illusion that it is normal. But looking further back, we can see it was preceded by something different. In the eleventh or twelfth centuries there were no sovereign states repudiating any political superior, for the conception of sovereignty was unknown. There was instead, in theory, a single juridical unit, known as Christendom, and presided over in ecclesiastical affairs (which included much of what today passes as 'politics') by the successor of St Peter at Rome. The innumerable kingdoms, fiefs and cities which

1. The author defines the states-system at greater length in *Systems of States*, Leicester University Press and the London School of Economics, 1977, Chapter 1, 'De Systematibus Civitatum'. Eds.

composed medieval Christendom did not assert (perhaps because they were too imperfectly organized to assert) their political independence in the absolute terms of the modern sovereign state. Again, Christendom had external relationships of trade and war with the Mohammedan powers across the Mediterranean and with the Byzantine Empire across the Ionian Sea; and these relationships showed much the same principles as those of the modern states-system; but they were not in the same degree continuous and organized. If we look still further back, across an interval of confusion and migrations, we see something different again: another single juridical unit, occupying a rather different geographical position from Christendom – the Roman Empire. This was a centralized state with a single, absolute, divine ruler instead of a loose confederation, with limited authorities. It too had diplomatic relations and wars with the Parthian and Persian Empires across the Euphrates, and it even traded with distant China; but these contacts were still more intermittent and irregular than those of Christendom with the Byzantines and the Moslems.

But looking back once more beyond the Roman Empire, we see the familiar sight of a warring family of independent states, brilliant cities and broad kingdoms, each jealous of its freedom and ambitious to expand, fighting and intriguing, making alliances and holding conferences, and all of them at last conquered, pacified and swallowed up by the strongest among them, the Roman Republic. This political kaleidoscope of the Greek and Hellenistic ages looks modern to our eyes, while the immense majesty of the Roman peace, and the Christian unity of the medieval world, seem remote and alien. The political writings of the Greek period of antiquity have remained classical because their relevance and topicality have been experienced afresh by each succeeding generation. One of the supreme books on power politics is the history by Thucydides of the great war between Athens and Sparta, commonly called the Peloponnesian War. It was this that General Marshall had in mind when he spoke at Princeton University in 1947:

It has been said that one should be interested in the past only as a guide to the future. I do not fully concur with this. One usually emerges from an intimate understanding of the past, with its lessons and its wisdom, with convictions which put fire in the soul. I doubt seriously whether a man can think with full wisdom and with deep convictions regarding certain of the basic international issues of today who has not at least reviewed in his mind the period of the Peloponnesian War and the fall of Athens.[2]

Power politics in the sense of international politics, then, came into existence when medieval Christendom dissolved and the modern sovereign state was born. In the medieval world there were growing up tribal and national authorities which shaped the modern nations of Europe, and they fought constantly among themselves. At the zenith of the Middle Ages the two highest potentates, the Pope and the Emperor, waged a two hundred years' war for supremacy (1076–1268). This conflict itself destroyed the balance of medieval society, and led to a revolution in politics that culminated in the Reformation.

Most obviously, it was a revolution in loyalties. Medieval man had a customary loyalty to his immediate feudal superior, with whose authority he was in regular contact, and a customary religious obedience to the Church under the Pope, which governed every aspect of his life; but his loyalty to the King, whom he probably never saw and was seldom aware of, was weaker than either. In due course the King suppressed the feudal barons and challenged the Pope, becoming the protector and champion against oppression and disorder at home and against a corrupt and exacting ecclesiastical system whose headquarters was abroad. The common man's inner circle of loyalty expanded, his outer circle of loyalty shrank, and the two met and coincided in a doubly definite circle between, where loyalty before had been vague. Thus the modern state came into existence; a narrower and at the same time a stronger unit of loyalty than medieval Christendom. Modern man in general has shown a stronger loyalty to the state than to church or class or any other international bond. A power is a modern sovereign state in its external aspect, and it might almost be defined as the ultimate loyalty for which men today will fight.

2. Speech of 22 February 1947 in *Department of State Bulletin*, Vol. 16, p. 391.

More fundamentally, there was a change in the moral frame-work of politics. Medieval politics were grounded in a deep sense of religious and social unity, which emphasized the whole rather than the part: they were mainly concerned with defining or interpreting a hierarchy where everyone in theory had his place, from the Pope and the Emperor down to the meanest feudal baron. 'Medieval history', said the historian Stubbs, 'is a history of rights and wrongs; modern history as contrasted with medieval is a history of powers, forces, dynasties and ideas ... Medieval wars are, as a rule, wars of rights; they are seldom wars of un-provoked, never wars of absolutely unjustifiable aggression; they are not wars of idea, or liberation, or of glory, or of nationality, or of propagandism.'[3] In the modern states-system the sense of unity has become rarefied as a multitude of powers have developed their independence of one another, and agreement on moral standards has been weakened by doctrinal strife within Europe and the expansion of the states-system beyond Europe. It seems that 'international society' is only the tally of sovereign states, that the whole is nothing but the sum of the parts. The medieval political outlook saw the gulf between ideals and facts as a condemnation of the facts, not of the ideals. The modern political attitude is expressed rather in the saying of Bacon: 'So that we are much beholden to Machiavel and others, that write what men do and not what they ought to do.'[4]

The power that makes a 'power' is composed of many elements. Its basic components are size of population, strategic position and geographical extent, and economic resources and industrial pro-duction. To these must be added less tangible elements like administrative and financial efficiency, education and techno-logical skill, and above all moral cohesion. Powers which have declined from former greatness, like Britain or France, or which have not attained great power, like India, naturally emphasize the value of political maturity and moral leadership, though these phrases are more likely to carry weight within their own frontiers than beyond. In times of international tranquillity these im-

3. W. Stubbs, *Seventeen Lectures on the Study of Medieval and Modern History*, Clarendon Press, Oxford, 1886, pp. 209, 217.

4. Francis Bacon, *Advancement of Learning*, Book II, XXI, 9.

ponderables can have great influence. Nevertheless, just as in domestic politics influence is not government, so in international politics influence is not power. It is concrete power in the end that settles great international issues.

When men dislike Bismarck for his realism, what they really dislike is reality. Take his most famous sentence: 'The great questions of our time will not be settled by resolutions and majority votes – that was the mistake of the men of 1848 and 1849 – but by blood and iron.' Who can deny that this is true as a statement of fact? What settled the question of Nazi domination of Europe – resolutions or the allied armies? What will settle the question of Korea – majority votes at Lake Success or American strength? This is a very different matter from saying that principles and beliefs are ineffective. They can be extremely effective if translated into blood and iron and not simply into resolutions and majority votes.[5]

The moral cohesion of powers is often spoken of in terms of nationality or nationalism. But this can cause confusion, since these words have several meanings. First, in its oldest sense, a nation means a people supposed to have a common descent and organized under a common government. Here the word nation is almost interchangeable with the words state or power; it was formerly possible to speak of the republic of Venice or the kingdom of Prussia as nations. The sense is illustrated by the phrase 'the law of nations', and survives in the adjective 'international'. Secondly, after the French Revolution the word nation came to mean in Europe a *nationality*, a people with a consciousness of historic identity expressed in a distinct language. Italy or Germany or Poland were nations in this sense, though each was divided among many states, and the Habsburg and Russian Empires were 'multinational' powers. The principle of national self-determination asserts the right of every nationality to form a state and become a power, and the peace settlement of 1919 attempted to reorganize Europe in accordance with it. Thirdly, in Asia and Africa, since the First World War, the word nation has come to mean a political unit asserting its right of independent statehood against European domination. Some of these units are

5. A. J. P. Taylor, *Rumours of War*, Hamish Hamilton, London, 1952, p. 44.

ancient civilizations, like India and China; some are historic kingdoms, like Ethiopia and Persia; some, like the Arab states, are fragments of a wider linguistic group and most perhaps have been created by European colonial administrators, like Indonesia and Ghana. But in terms of nationality more of them resemble the Habsburg Empire than Ireland or Denmark. They combine the passions of the second kind of nation with the social diversity of the first kind. Of the five surviving nominal great powers today, France alone comes near to being a homogeneous nationality. The Soviet Union and China are multinational states; the United Kingdom is the political union of the English, Welsh, Scottish and Northern Irish nations; and the United States is a unique attempt to create a new nation from immigrants of all European nationalities.

The word 'nationalism' describes the collective self-assertion of a nation in any of these three senses, but especially in the second and third. This compels us to speak of conflicting nationalisms within a single state: there is both a Scottish nationalism and a British, a Sikh nationalism and an Indian, a Ukrainian and a Soviet nationalism. (The word 'patriotism' is generally reserved by the ruling class for the larger and inclusive loyalty.) The student of power politics will not be misled by nationalist claims, and will remember that in most cases the freedom or rights of one nation or nationality have been purchased only by the oppression of another nation or nationality. Every power that is a going concern will in course of time generate loyalties which it will be proper to call nationalist, but powers are less the embodiment of national right than the product of historical accident.

It is a consequence of nineteenth-century nationalism that we personify a power, calling it 'she', and saying that *Britain* does this, *America* demands that, and the *Soviet Union*'s policy is something else. This is mythological language, as much as if we speak of John Bull, Uncle Sam or the Russian Bear. 'Britain' in such a context is a symbol for an immensely complex political agent, formed by the permanent officials of the Foreign Office, the Foreign Service, the Foreign Secretary, the Prime Minister, the Cabinet, the House of Commons, the living electorate, and the dead generations who have made the national tradition, combining and interacting in an infinitude of variations of mutual influence. These shorthand terms are of course unavoidable in political writing, but they are dangerous if they lead us into thinking that powers are inscrutable and awesome monsters following predestined laws of their own. A power is simply a collection of human beings following certain traditional ways of action, and it is possible that if enough of them chose to alter their collective behaviour they might succeed in doing so. There is reason to suppose, however, that the deeper changes in political behaviour can only be produced by a concern for non-political ends.

We must note in conclusion that the phrase 'power politics' in common usage means, not only the relations between independent powers, but something more sinister. Indeed, it is a translation of the German word *Machtpolitik*, which means the politics of force – the conduct of international relations by force or the threat of force, without consideration of right and justice. (About the time of the First World War, 'power politics' in this sense superseded an older and more elegant phrase, *raison d'état*, which implied that statesmen cannot be bound in public affairs by the morality they would respect in private life, that there is a 'reason of state' justifying unscrupulous action in defence of the public interest.) As Franklin Roosevelt said in his last Annual Message to Congress, 'In the future world the misuse of power as implied in the term "power politics" must not be the controlling factor in international relations.'[6] It would be foolish to suppose that statesmen are not moved by considerations of right and justice, and that international relations are governed exclusively by force. But it is wisest to start from the recognition that power politics as we defined them at the outset are always inexorably approximating to 'power politics' in the immoral sense, and to analyse them in this light. When we have done this we can more usefully assess the moral problem. It will be all the time at our elbow, and we will consider it in the last chapter.[7]

6. 6 January 1945 in S. I. Rosenman (ed.), *The Public Papers and Addresses of Franklin D. Roosevelt*, Vol. IV, Harper & Brothers, New York, 1950, pp. 483–507.

7. This draft was apparently written in the late 1960s, probably in 1967. Eds.

2 : Dominant Powers

The most conspicuous theme in international history is not the growth of internationalism. It is the series of efforts, by one power after another, to gain mastery of the states-system – efforts that have been defeated only by a coalition of the majority of other powers at the cost of an exhausting general war. 'Life', as the President of the United Nations General Assembly once said, 'is a continuous sequence of dominations . . .'[1]

There are hints of the theme before the end of the Middle Ages. France enjoyed a European hegemony after the collapse of the Empire, and made the papacy during its Avignonese Captivity (1305–77) to some extent her political tool. England undertook a great war of aggrandizement in the Hundred Years War (1337–1453), transforming a feudal dispute about Aquitaine into a struggle to unite the English and French crowns, first under Edward III and then more brilliantly and ephemerally under Henry V. But it was among the Italian powers that feudal relationships first disappeared and the efficient, self-sufficient, secular state was evolved, and the Italian powers invented the diplomatic system. The French invasion of Italy in 1494 is the conventional beginning of modern international history because it dramatically marks the point from which the European powers at large begin to adopt the habits of Italian power politics.

Spain, not France, is the earliest power to dominate the states-system as a whole. When the Habsburg King of Spain inherited the Austrian dominions and was elected Emperor as Charles V, he became the greatest power in Europe, and quickly supplanted the French in Italy. On his abdicating Spain was separated from Austria, but the two branches of the Habsburg family continued

1. O. Aranha (of Brazil), 16 September 1947, UN General Assembly *Verbatim Record of the Plenary Meetings*, Second Session, 1947, p. 4.

to work together as a dynastic axis, and occasioned two general wars. The first was fought by Philip II from 1572 to 1598 against a growing coalition of the Dutch (for whom it was their war of independence), the French and the English. The second raged from 1618 to 1659, beginning with the Thirty Years War (1618–48), which was an attempt by Austria to unify Central Europe in the name of the principles of the Counter-Reformation, and continuing in the Franco-Spanish War of 1635–59.

In the seventeenth century there were two systems of international relations in Europe, partially independent of one another. In Western Europe the chief powers were Spain, France, Holland and England; in the north round the Baltic the chief powers were Sweden, Denmark, Poland and Russia; and the two systems overlapped in Germany, where Austria was predominant. Their wars were separate but interlocking, like the European and Pacific wars which together made up the Second World War. Sweden became the dominant power in northern Europe when Gustavus Adolphus launched her into the Thirty Years War, and she lost her ascendancy in the Great Northern War of 1700–21, when Charles XII fought against a coalition led by Russia and including at one time or another Poland, Saxony, Denmark and Prussia.

While Sweden was the dominant power in the Baltic, the predominance in Western Europe was passing from Spain to France, and French ascendancy in its turn caused two general wars. The first was the war of 1688–1713, in which Louis XIV was defeated by a coalition of Holland, England and Austria. The second was the war of 1792–1815, by which time Western and northern Europe had merged into a single system, and Revolutionary and Napoleonic France fought against Britain, Russia, Austria and Prussia. Continental predominance passed to Germany with her defeat of France in 1870–71, and in the twentieth century Germany in her turn has waged two general wars against coalitions of the majority of other powers. As a result of the second of these wars continental predominance passed to Russia.

This sequence provides the political skeleton of international relations. But to complete the picture we must notice that on the oceans there has been a different succession of dominant powers from that on the Continent. Spain alone has had the dominion both of the land and of the sea, and the vast responsibilities destroyed her. France inherited the continental ascendancy, but the maritime predominance fell to Holland.

> Trade, which like Blood should circularly flow,
> Stopp'd in their Channels, found its Freedom lost:
> Thither the Wealth of all the World did go,
> And seem'd but Shipwrack'd on so base a Coast.[2]

For this reason England waged her three Dutch Wars, and Louis XIV launched his destructive attack upon the Dutch in 1672, a war which permanently reduced the relative power of the United Provinces.

Holland was supplanted in the maritime predominance by England. The Anglo-Dutch alliance (which under William III was virtually a personal union of the two powers) is the clearest example of what has regularly occurred in these successions, the predecessor becoming a satellite of the successor. It was for the prize of maritime supremacy, as much as to prevent French domination of the continent, that Britain was regularly at war with France from Louis XIV's time to Napoleon's. 'The miseries resulting from the overweening power of Spain in days long gone by seemed to be forgotten,' wrote the American historian Mahan; 'forgotten also the more recent lesson of the bloody and costly wars provoked by the ambition and exaggerated power of Louis XIV. Under the eyes of the statesmen of Europe there was steadily and visibly being built up a third overwhelming power, destined to be used as selfishly, as aggressively, though not as cruelly, and much more successfully than any that had preceded it.'[3]

Britain's history of predominance, like that of most other dominant powers, went through two cycles. The first ran from the defeat of Louis XIV to the American Revolution. It rose to its zenith in the Seven Years War (1756–63), when Canada and India were conquered, and Britain reached a greater height of relative

2. John Dryden, 'Annus Mirabilis: The Year of Wonders 1666', in E. N. Hooker and H. T. Swedenberg (eds.), *The Works of John Dryden*, Vol. I, University of California Press, 1956, pp. 59–60.
3. A. T. Mahan, *The Influence of Sea Power upon History 1660–1783*, Sampson Low, London, 1890, p. 63.

power than she ever afterwards attained. But her naval and commercial supremacy evoked foreign enmity as well as colonial rebellion; and in the War of American Independence (1775–83) she had to fight a coalition of the United States, France, Spain and Holland, with Russia, Sweden, Denmark, Prussia and Austria in a hostile Armed Neutrality to uphold the rights of neutral powers. Britain was isolated and defeated, and her first empire was shattered. She recovered her oceanic predominance in the Revolutionary and Napoleonic Wars. To English eyes this was a generous struggle to free Europe from the tyranny of Napoleon. From the detached standpoint of the American President it looked different. 'Two nations of overgrown power', wrote Jefferson in 1807, 'are endeavouring to establish, the one an universal dominion by sea, the other by land';[4] and it was against the former not the latter that the United States eventually joined the war. The nineteenth century was the golden age of British economic and naval supremacy. British manufactures and capital, and the example of British institutions, spread all over the globe, and the British navy maintained a rudimentary world order almost everywhere outside the European continent. But the second phase of predominance ended, like the first, in diplomatic isolation. The British conquest of the Boer Republics in the South African War (1899–1902) aroused universal hostility in Europe, and France, Germany and Russia toyed with the project of a continental league to put limits to the British Empire.

They lacked, however, both the naval strength to challenge Britain and a strong common interest against her. For the Pax Britannica had bridged the transition from French to German hegemony on the Continent, and it was to collapse, not in a second general war against British predominance, but in two general wars against German predominance. Already the dominant power on land, in 1898 Germany began building a great navy, to challenge Britain at sea as well. Britain defeated her in the First World War, at the price of losing her own naval predominance. The American diplomatist Colonel House, President Wilson's personal envoy, used language in 1918 resembling that of Jefferson

4. Letter to James Maury, 21 November 1807, in A. E. Bergh (ed.), *The Writings of Thomas Jefferson*, Vol. XI, Washington DC, 1907, p. 397.

in 1807 when he wrote: 'I did not believe the United States and other countries would willingly submit to Great Britain's complete domination of the seas any more than to Germany's domination of the land, and the sooner the English recognize this fact, the better it would be for them.'[5] At the Washington Conference in 1922 the United States, Britain and Japan agreed on a 5:5:3 ratio of naval strength, Britain accepting parity with America. The Washington Treaty expired in 1936 in consequence of Japan herself demanding parity, and in the succeeding years the United States' vast resources enabled her to assume a naval superiority which was only temporarily shaken by Pearl Harbor in 1941. The Second World War confirmed the United States as dominant sea-power, as it made Russia dominant land-power.

If we remember that a political definition describes a pattern to which every historical example only approximates, we might define a dominant power as a power that can measure strength against all its rivals combined. Pericles said that the strength of imperial Athens at the beginning of the Peloponnesian War lay in her possessing naval forces more numerous and efficient than those of all the rest of Hellas.[6] Thus Louis XIV took over from Philip II the proud device, *Nec Pluribus Impar*: a match for many.[7] At the end of the seventeenth century, just before the War of the Spanish Succession broke out, 'France had been constantly in arms, and her arms had been successful. She had sustained a war, without any confederates, against the principal powers of Europe confederated against her, and had finished it with advantage on every side . . .'[8] When Holland was at the height of her power in the same century, it was 'generally esteemed, that they have more shipping belongs to them, than there does to all the rest of

5. C. Seymour, *The Intimate Papers of Colonel House*, Vol. IV, Ernest Benn, London, 1928, p. 165. But House, unlike Jefferson, was able to say it to the British to their faces.

6. B. Jowett (trans.), *Thucydides*, Book 1, 143, i, Clarendon Press, Oxford, 1900, p. 99. Cf. the Corinthians' admission in Book I, 122, ii, p. 81.

7. Voltaire, *The Age of Louis XIV*, J. M. Dent & Sons, London, 1935, p. 269.

8. Bolingbroke, *Letters on the Study and Use of History*, Vol. II, Millar, London, 1752, p. 55.

Europe'.[9] Perhaps the most perfect specimens of dominant power are Britain in the mid eighteenth century, who won her oceanic triumphs single-handed against the combined navies of France and Spain; and Revolutionary and Napoleonic France, which with no allies of importance overthrew three military coalitions within fifteen years, before the fourth brought her to her knees. But 'however great France may be', said Pitt in 1802, 'we had a revenue equal to all Europe, . . . a navy superior to all Europe, and a commerce as great as that of all Europe, – and he added, laughingly, to make us *quite gentlemen*, a *debt* as large as that of all Europe . . .'[10]

It is singular that Abraham Lincoln, in his first important speech, long before he or anyone could foresee that he would preside over the war that would make the United States momentarily the greatest military power on earth, described her in similar language:

At what point shall we expect the approach of danger? By what means shall we fortify against it? Shall we expect some transatlantic military giant to step the ocean and crush us at a blow? Never! All the armies of Europe, Asia, and Africa combined, with all the treasure of the earth (our own excepted) in their military chest, with a Buonaparte for a commander, could not by force take a drink from the Ohio or make a track on the Blue Ridge in a trial of a thousand years.[11]

In the later nineteenth century, when the rapid changes in naval construction were making the traditional wooden walls of England obsolete, Britain formally adopted a two-power standard, aiming at a fleet equal in strength to the next two largest navies

9. Sir William Temple, 'Observations upon the United Provinces of the Netherlands', in *The Works of Sir William Temple*, Vol. 1, Round, London, 1740, p. 60.

10. *Diaries and Correspondence of the Earl of Malmesbury*, Vol. IV, Richard Bentley, London, 1844, p. 147.

11. Address before the Young Men's Lyceum of Springfield, 27 January 1838, in P. van Doren Stern (ed.), *The Life and Writings of Abraham Lincoln*, Random House, New York, 1940, p. 232. This passage is the kind of thing immortalized by Dickens in the Pogram Defiance (see *Martin Chuzzlewit*, Ch. 34); but the rest of the speech is very different.

combined. Germany in her turn indulged in this kind of self-comparison. The German ambassador remarked to the British Foreign Secretary in 1906 'that Germany felt herself too strong a nation and in too strong a position to be overawed by a combination even of two other great powers'.[12] The foundation of Hitler's triumphs was that, in a Europe organized on the principle of nationality, the Germans were twice as numerous as the next largest nation apart from the Russians. In the transitory moment between the defeat of Japan in 1945 and the first Russian atomic explosion in 1949, the position of the United States could be described in similar terms of quantitative superiority. The Russians, said a British Member of Parliament in 1947, 'know that there are not two great powers in the world, there is only one. The largest air force in the world, the biggest navy afloat, £9,000,000,000 of gold, the atom bomb, the largest productive capacity in the world concentrate in the United States, the greatest financial, military and economic power that has ever resided in one country'.[13]

But a dominant power must be described by purpose as well as by power. Each dominant power is engaged in straightforward aggrandizement, but it generally also appeals to some design of international unity and solidarity. Henry V dreamed, like most later medieval conquerors, of leading a reunited Christendom in a last crusade against the Turks. The House of Habsburg was itself a kind of international organization, a dynastic confederation of many states (Austria, the Netherlands, Spain, Naples, Milan, Bohemia, Hungary, Portugal), asserting the principles of international Catholicism. Gustavus Adolphus sought to make himself protector of all Protestant states. Napoleon carried the benefits of the French Revolution throughout Europe, and gave a new life to the ancient title of Emperor. So effective was the Pax Britannica in the nineteenth century that it was easy to mistake its fragile and temporary nature, and even to compare it with the Roman Empire, as if it denoted a monopoly of power. Of all the dominant powers,

12. Grey of Fallodon, *Twenty-Five Years*, Vol. I, Hodder & Stoughton, London, 1925, p. 83.

13. S. N. Evans, 19 June 1947, in the House of Commons, *Parliamentary Debates*, Fifth Series, Vol. 438, Col. 2266.

Louis XIV and Hitler had least to offer mankind, yet Louis was the exemplar of Catholic monarchism, and Hitler (beside whom the arrogance of Louis XIV shines as a kingly sense of duty) persuaded many people even outside Germany that his savage designs would lead, not only to a new order in Europe, but to a reconstitution of the world on biological principles. Every dominant power aspires, by giving political unification to the whole of international society, to become a universal empire.

The coalitions that overthrow the dominant powers, however, describe their struggle in terms of freedom and independence. Their policy is the balance of power; their classic appeals are 'the liberties of Europe' and 'the freedom of the seas'. They have usually sought to re-establish these liberties, at the end of a general war, by holding an international congress and drawing up a general peace treaty, which remains the legal basis of international politics until the next general war. These congresses have their ancestry in the Oecumenical Councils of the Church. The Council of Constance (1414–18) shows the modern states-system embryonically within the womb of medieval Christendom. Meeting to end the Great Schism, it was concerned with political issues as much as religious; 'the last occasion on which the whole of Latin Christendom met to deliberate and act as a single commonwealth'[14] was also the first occasion on which Christendom organized itself procedurally as nations. The Council of Constance was the last occasion when an Emperor presided in an international gathering; the last occasion when the Pope presided was the Congress of Mantua (1459–60), which dismally failed in its purpose of organizing a crusade to liberate Constantinople from the Turks. The congress that made the Treaties of Westphalia between 1644 and 1648 at the end of the Thirty Years War was afterwards reckoned as the first of the great diplomatic peace settlements. It concluded what is still the longest unbroken period of war that the states-system has known; by ending Habsburg predominance it gave independence to the states of Germany, and by ending the religious wars and taking the Pope and the Emperor out of international politics it was thought to

14. J. Bryce, *The Holy Roman Empire*, National Book Company, New York, 1886, pp. 250–51.

place international politics on a rational footing. But it had had a precedent in the Treaty of Cateau-Cambrésis (1559), which concluded the wars against the hegemony of Charles V, and even in the general pacification of 1516–18, which ended the first round of the Italian Wars. It was followed by the Congress and Treaty of Utrecht (1713) after the defeat of Louis XIV; the Congress of Vienna and Treaty of Paris (1814–15) after the overthrow of Napoleon; and the Paris Conference and Treaty of Versailles (1919) at the end of Germany's first effort at predominance. There was no general peace settlement at the conclusion of the Second World War for the same reason that there was none after the defeat of Philip II: in each case the end of the war was only a political incident in a profound doctrinal conflict, which divided the states-system, made general agreement about reorganizing it impossible, and left room only for piecemeal settlements.

The shifts in predominance between the powers have generally been registered in matters of diplomatic etiquette and practice – in precedence and recognition, in the titles of rulers, in the places chosen for conferences and in the official language of diplomacy. Some of the perennial themes of international politics are already visible in the Council of Constance. The Italian bishops were by far the largest voting bloc; to counteract their numerical superiority, the English delegation proposed voting by nations. Four nations were constituted, the Italians, the Germans (including the other peoples of central and northern Europe), the English (including the other peoples of the British Isles) and the French. When a delegation arrived from Aragon, the Spanish were constituted a fifth nation. The French, who were suffering under the aggression of Henry V, thereupon proposed that, since four was the 'natural' number of nations, and since the English were clearly inferior to all the others, who were themselves multinational nations, the English ought therefore to be thrown in with the Germans, or voting by nations should be abandoned. The argument was put forward for propaganda reasons, and was not effective.

By the time of Louis XIV, the object of French diplomacy was precedence over Spain; in 1661 there was a battle in the streets of London between the rival followers of the French and Spanish ambassadors; the French were worsted; Louis sent an ultimatum to the Spanish court, and obtained a solemn declaration of French primacy; but the dispute continued throughout his reign. In 1721 Peter the Great celebrated the final triumph of Russia over Sweden by assuming the title of Emperor, hitherto reserved to the Holy Roman Emperor alone; but France did not recognize the diplomatic equality of Russia until the Treaty of Tilsit in 1807, when she too flaunted the imperial title, and these two were the only great powers left on the Continent.

In the earlier days of the states-system, conferences were usually held in some neutral town on the borders of the warring states: Noyon, Cambrai, Cateau-Cambrésis, Verrins, the Island of Pheasants in the River Bidassoa, which was the scene of the Treaty of the Pyrenees, Oliva, Carlowitz, Passarowitz. This was mainly due to convenience of communication, partly due to prestige. The Swedes in the 1640s proposed that the peace conference to end the Thirty Years War should meet at Munster and Osnabrück, when the Emperor would have preferred the Rhineland towns of Speier and Worms.[15] This practice has recurred in more recent times: the Russo-Japanese War ended with a treaty negotiated at Portsmouth, New Hampshire; and the peace talks between the United States and North Vietnam in the 1960s and 1970s were held in Paris, as a neutral place. Louis XIV's diplomacy, arrogant in other matters, did not insist on not negotiating on enemy soil. All Louis XIV's wars ended with a conference on enemy soil: Aix-la-Chapelle, Nijmwegen, Rijswijck, Utrecht; so did Napoleon's – Campo Formio, Amiens. It was not until the nineteenth century that the practice became regular of holding a peace conference in the capital city of one of the victorious great powers.

In the nineteenth century, Napoleon III repeatedly sought the prestige of an international conference at Paris; but after 1871, when Germany succeeded France as dominant power, Berlin for the first time became the seat of international gatherings – the Congress of 1878 on the Eastern Question and the Conference of 1884–5 on the partition of Africa. Washington became the seat of a great conference for the first time in 1922, with the conference

15. A. de Wicquefort, *L'Ambassadeur et ses fonctions*, J. and D. Steucker, The Hague, 1680, Book II, pp. 266–7.

that marked the formal end of British naval supremacy. Stalin refused to travel abroad, insisting that other heads of government should come to meet him, either on Russian soil (as at Moscow and Yalta) or (as at Teheran and Potsdam) in a city under Soviet occupation.

The official language of diplomacy has similarly followed the movement of power. Latin was the ordinary language of international intercourse until the mid-seventeenth century. French replaced it, and reigned unchallenged for two hundred and fifty years: Prussian ambassadors even wrote their reports to their own king in French till Bismarck put an end to it after 1862. In 1919 the predominance of the United States and Britain at the Paris Conference made English for the first time an official language equally with French. (Italy, the other of the Big Four Powers, was defeated in a similar claim for Italian.) The competition among languages is now based on wide usage rather than tradition, and the most widely used languages are those with powerful and populous states to back their claims. If we reckon wide usage of a language by the number of states that speak it, Spanish (the chief Pan-American language) and English come first today; if by the number of individuals who have it as mother-tongue, the order is probably Chinese, English and Russian. The *reductio ad absurdum* of the competition among diplomatic languages was reached at the San Francisco Conference in 1945. It was intended at first that the official languages of the conference should be English, Spanish and Russian. In the event the traditional claims of French could not be disregarded, since it is probably still next to English the best known of all languages in non-French-speaking countries; and the claims of Chinese had to be admitted. Thus all the languages of the five nominal great powers were given equal rights. The disadvantage of multiplying official languages is in the labour of translating official resolutions and the danger of conflicting versions and interpretations. The United Nations has had to flatter its most powerful members by acknowledging these five official languages, but has got along in practice with English and French as 'working' languages.[16]

16. This draft was apparently written in the early 1970s. Eds.

3 : Great Powers

'Dominant power' is not an accepted phrase of diplomacy. The other states in the states-system recognize a dominant power in fact, either by collaborating with it or by uniting in resistance to it; but hegemony has never been accepted in theory, except within the dominant power's limited range of influence, as Philip II and Louis XIV, Napoleon and Hitler were accorded a primacy by their satellites at the height of their success, or as the 'leading role' of the Soviet Union has been recognized among Communist countries since 1945. The only distinction in normal diplomatic intercourse is that between great powers and other powers. What is a great power?

This is one of the central questions of international politics. It is easier to answer it historically, by enumerating the great powers at any date, than by giving a definition, for there is always broad agreement about the existing great powers. Since the Second World War they have been the United States, Russia, Britain, France and China. In 1939 they were the United States, Britain, France, Germany, Italy, Russia and Japan. In 1914 they were Britain, France, Germany, Austria-Hungary, Russia, Italy, the United States and Japan. In 1815 they were Britain, Russia, Austria, Prussia and France.

The phrase 'great power' can be found in political writings from the beginning of the international system, and five great powers were recognized in fifteenth-century Italy: Venice, Milan, Florence, the Papal State and Naples. But it was not until the Congress of Vienna that great-power status became regularly established in international politics. This congress marked a double development. It abandoned the old order of precedence among sovereigns, based on the antiquity of their title, which had been made obsolete by the American Revolution and the French

Revolution and Napoleon's abolition of the Holy Roman Empire. Henceforward empires, kingdoms and republics were all equal in diplomatic rank, and a doctrine became generally accepted among international lawyers of the equality of states, with a corollary that later became known as the unanimity rule, viz. that a state cannot legally be bound by decisions to which it has not consented. But in terms of politics, as contrasted with those of diplomatic theory and international law, the Congress of Vienna replaced the old system based on tradition by a new system based on power. Castlereagh planned that the control of the congress should be in the hands of 'the six powers most considerable in population and weight'. These were Britain, Russia, Austria, Prussia, Spain and defeated France, but in the event Spain dropped out of the running. The four Allies in practice managed the congress, and the minor powers, after making protests, acquiesced in their decisions. For the next hundred years 'the powers' meant the great powers, and the Concert of the Powers fitfully ruled the world.

This is the most famous example in international history of the great powers' tendency to club together as a kind of directorate and impose their will on the states-system. They usually justify their action as enforcing peace and security. But these are among the ambiguous words of power politics: we must ask whose security is in question, and at whose expense it is purchased. The Partition of Poland by Prussia, Russia and Austria (1772–95) was excused on the grounds that it preserved peace between the partitioning powers. The partition of Czechoslovakia with British and French consent at Munich in 1938 was described by Chamberlain as 'peace with honour'. When Germany and Russia made the Fourth Partition of Poland in 1939 they signed a treaty of friendship announcing that they had created 'a sure basis for a durable peace in Eastern Europe'. When Britain and France attacked Egypt in 1956, they excused themselves variously as separating the Israeli and Egyptian forces, protecting the Suez Canal, and preventing the Israeli-Egyptian war from spreading. History affords little support for the assertion the great powers like to make that they are more restrained and responsible than minor powers. It suggests, rather, that they wish to monopolize the right to create international conflict. The Concert of the Powers is often given the credit for there having been no general war in Europe from 1815 to 1914; and it would be foolish to deprecate the standards of diplomatic moderation and good faith which the Concert developed. But the pacification of Europe was due less to the working of the Concert than to there being at that time apparently limitless opportunities of independent expansion outside Europe for Britain, Russia and France, while Prussia was busy conquering Germany. When the outward expansion began to come to an end, the great powers were thrown back upon one another in Europe, and the Concert broke down in the crises that led to the First World War.

The Paris Peace Conference in 1919 repeated the experience of the Vienna Congress. The Principal Allied and Associated Powers (as the United States, Britain, France, Italy and Japan were styled) made the chief decisions before these were submitted to the conference as a whole; otherwise, if thirty powers had wrangled instead of five, there would have been no decisions at all. At the first plenary session the minor powers protested, and Sir Robert Borden, the Canadian Prime Minister, asked on their behalf, 'By whom have these decisions been reached, and by what authority?' Clemenceau, the President of the Conference, replied to their complaints with relish. He reminded them, first, that it was the great powers who had decided that there should be a peace conference at all and had invited the nations interested, and secondly, that on the day the war ended the great powers had twelve million men under arms. 'This entitles them to consideration.'[1] To justify the procedure, a distinction was made between powers with 'general interests', viz., the great powers, and those with 'limited interests', viz., the rest. At the same time the status of great power first obtained *legal* recognition, with the possession of a permanent seat on the Council of the League of Nations. For since great powers have wider interests and greater resources than small powers, the main duty of settling international affairs must

1. Lord Hankey, *The Supreme Command*, Allen & Unwin, London, 1963, p. 46; H. W. V. Temperley (ed.), *A History of the Peace Conference of Paris*, Vol. 1, O.U.P., Oxford, 1920, p. 249n.; also H. J. Mackinder, *Democratic Ideals and Reality*, Holt, New York, 1950, Appendix, pp. 207–8.

fall upon them; and it was hoped that they would develop, as it has been said, from great powers into Great Responsibles. Therefore the League of Nations had two organs: the Assembly in which all member-states were represented, and the Council, which was intended primarily as an executive committee of the great powers. But besides the permanent seats for the great powers there were four non-permanent seats for minor powers to be elected by the Assembly. These were the object of much diplomatic jealousy, since after the Peace Settlement of 1919 there were several semi-great powers, each seeking to be recognized as great. Poland with a population of over thirty millions regarded itself as being closer to Britain, France and Italy with their forty-odd millions than to a Lithuania with its two millions. Brazil, with a population of similar size to Poland's, was the leading American power at Geneva once the United States had not joined the League. Spain was an ex-great power, and in some sense the leader of the Spanish American states. When the entry of Germany into the League was arranged at Locarno in 1925, with the promise of a permanent seat on the Council as befitted an undoubted great power, Poland, Spain and Brazil announced that they would oppose the admission of the ex-enemy unless they too were given permanent seats; and China, with an eye to the future, put forward the argument that 'in considering a nation as a great power we should take into account solely its economic potentialities and geographical position'. This undignified wrangle ended with Brazil resigning from the League, Spain withdrawing from its work, and Poland being pacified by the creation of quasi-permanent seats on the Council, of which she occupied the first. But within a few years Germany transferred the tests for great-power status from the conference room to the battlefield, and inflated claims were quickly blown away – including, in the upshot, her own.

The Second World War enhanced the diplomatic and legal pre-eminence of the great powers. During the war the United States, Russia and Britain agreed to erect a new international organization when it ended. They invited China to the Dumbarton Oaks Conference in 1944 at which the United Nations Charter was drafted, and invited both China and France to join them as sponsoring powers for the San Francisco Conference in 1945 at which the Charter was signed. France refused on a point of prestige to be a sponsoring power, but along with the other four powers accepted a permanent seat on the Security Council. The United Nations gives the great powers a stronger position than did the League, and abrogates the unanimity rule, which had been retained in the League to conciliate American opinion. The United Nations Charter establishes majority voting in both the Security Council and the General Assembly, and by giving each of the great powers a veto in the Security Council restricts to them alone the protection of the unanimity rule.[2] The doctrines of equality and unanimity were always fictitious, but they were morally superior to a doctrine placing the great powers above the law they are to impose on others.

But there is equally a good deal of fiction in speaking of great powers today in terms of the permanent members of the Security Council. In the first place, it is obvious that the great powers are not great powers because they have a veto in the Security Council, but that they were able to give themselves the veto because they were great powers. In the second place, it is obvious that they are not all of comparable strength. The man in the street makes the practical judgement that there are only two great powers in the world, the United States and the Soviet Union, and gets round the formal classification by inventing new phrases, such as 'super-power', to describe the powers which seem to him indubitably great. For it is only part of the truth to say that a great power is a power that is recognized as great by its contemporaries. Such recognition may contain an element of the wishful or the con-ventional, as when the Big Three coopted China and France at the end of the Second World War. The complementary truth was expressed by the young Napoleon, when he said that the Revo-lutionary French Republic at the height of its victories needed

2. The Covenant slightly modified the unanimity rule by depriving a party to a dispute of a vote in certain circumstances: see Articles 15 and 16 of the Covenant, and contrast Articles 3, 4 and 11. In the United Nations, the Security Council decides by a majority of seven out of eleven, with the con-curring votes of the permanent members; the General Assembly by a two-thirds majority. See Articles 18 (2) and 27 (3) of the Charter.

'recognition as little as the sun requires it',[3] and by the nineteenth-century Russian statesman who said that 'a great power does not wait for recognition, it reveals itself'.[4] Thus Khrushchev remarked, after a visit to Peking in 1958, that the policy of ignoring China made no sense: 'This great power exists, grows stronger, and is developing independently of whether it is recognized or not by certain governments.'[5] The existence of what is recognized determines the act of recognition, and not the other way round. So the class of great powers presents a double focus, according to whether we consider it formally or substantively; because at any time there are likely to be some powers climbing into it and others declining from it, and in a time of revolutionary changes, formal recognition will lag behind the growth or decay of power.

The self-revelation of a great power is completed by war. If we ask when the older great powers achieved their rank, such as France, Spain and Austria, we may find the most satisfactory answer in the slow processes of territorial amalgamation through dynastic inheritance. But at least since the Peace of Westphalia it has been true that, as the head-hunters of Borneo entered into manhood by taking their first head, so a power becomes a great power by a successful war against another great power. England had played the part of a great power under Elizabeth I and under Cromwell, but she sank into dependence on France under the restored Stuarts, until in 1688 William III drove them out and put England at the head of the coalition against Louis XIV. The Glorious Revolution did not only establish English liberties: it began the war that made Britain a great power. Russia became a great power through the defeat of Sweden in the Great Northern War. Prussia became a great power through Frederick the Great's attack on Austria in 1740 and his successful defence of his gains in the Seven Years War (1756–63). Italy became a great power by courtesy after her unification (1859–60), and developed a national

3. Hegel, *Philosophy of Right*, Additions, T. M. Knox (trans.), Clarendon Press, Oxford, 1942, paragraph 331, p. 297.

4. Gortchakov, 'une grande puissance ne se reconnaît pas, elle se révèle', in O. von Bismarck, *Reflections and Reminiscences*, Vol. 1, A. J. Butler (trans.), Smith Elder, London, 1898, p. 302.

5. *The Guardian*, 6 August 1958, p. 1.

inferiority complex through never having proved her place among her peers by war. (As Bismarck said of her, 'she has such poor teeth and such a large appetite'.) The conquest of Abyssinia in 1935–6 was a desperate act of self-assertion, and Mussolini's emphasis on the 'siege by the fifty sanctionist states' was an attempt to put Italy's great-power status beyond further question by the prestige of having defied a coalition of the world. The coalition and the prestige, however, proved equally spurious. Japan became a great power through her defeat of Russia in the Russo-Japanese War (1904–5). China became a great power through her indomitable resistance to Japan in the long struggle from 1931 to 1945, and confirmed her rank by the defeats she inflicted on the United States in the Korean War (1950–53).

The United States, in this respect as in others, is exceptional. Her attainment of great-power status is sometimes reckoned from the Spanish-American War of 1898, with the extension of a protectorate over Cuba and the annexation of Puerto Rico and the Philippines. But the mouldering Spanish Empire was scarcely an adequate victim, and a truer judgement dates the event from the titanic internal conflict of the Civil War a generation earlier (1861–5). Years afterwards the greatest of American historians, who during the Civil War was a private secretary in the American legation in London, remembered with romantic emotion the turning-point of the war at Gettysburg and Vicksburg in July 1863.

Little by little, at first only as a shadowy chance of what might be, if things could be rightly done, one began to feel that, somewhere behind the chaos in Washington power was taking shape; that it was massed and guided as it had not been before . . . As the first great blows began to fall, one curled up in bed in the silence of night, to listen with incredulous hope. As the huge masses struck, one after another, with the precision of machinery, the opposing mass, the world shivered. Such development of power was unknown. The magnificent resistance and the return shocks heightened the suspense. During the July days Londoners were stupid with unbelief. They were learning from the Yankees how to fight.[6]

6. *The Education of Henry Adams*, Constable, London, 1919, p. 169. Also L. Oppenheim, *International Law*, Longmans, 1912, Vol. 1, pp. 48 and 70, and subsequent editions.

The Civil War left the United States momentarily the greatest military power in the world; and before the power was dispersed, it had compelled Napoleon III to abandon his attempt to build a Catholic empire in Mexico.

Great-power status is lost, as it is won, by violence. A great power does not die in its bed. Sometimes it can lose its position in a war which, though victorious, leaves it outstripped by a more powerful ally. This was the case with Holland after the war against Louis XIV, when she sank into dependence upon Britain, as Britain after the war against Hitler has sunk into dependence upon the United States. But usually a great power succumbs through defeat. Sweden ceased to be a great power after her overthrow by Russia in the Great Northern War; Turkey, after her defeat by Russia in the war of 1767–74. Spain was never again a great power after her subjection by Napoleon in 1808, and history will probably record the same verdict on France after her subjection by Hitler in 1940. Italy has abandoned any claim to be a great power since the Second World War.

It is however possible to cease to be a great power temporarily. Prussia lost her standing in the catastrophe of Jena in 1806, but regained it in the War of Liberation in 1813–14. France lost hers in 1815, but regained it when she was admitted to the Concert of the Powers at the Congress of Aix-la-Chapelle in 1818. Russia was put out of action by her defeat in 1917, and Germany by her defeat in 1918; Germany resumed her rank at the Locarno Conference in 1925, and Russia when she entered the League in 1934. Japan forfeited her great-power status, and Germany hers for the second time, as the result of their disastrous defeat in the Second World War. It has sometimes been thought that they may recover their position; but it seems clear that Japan will never again be a match for China, nor Germany for Russia. There are no examples of a second resurrection after total defeat.

The truest definition of a great power must be a historical one, which lays down that a great power is a power which has done such and such. A scientific definition, laying down the attributes that a great power may be supposed to possess, will be an abstraction in some degree removed from our complicated and unmanageable political experience. It may be thought obvious that a great power is stronger than the average state in respect of some at least of the components of power – in population, extent of territory, industrial resources, social organization, historical tradition and will to greatness. But in respect of some of them, or most, or all? And how much stronger? And what is the average state? The military criteria of a great power have constantly changed. At the Yalta Conference in 1945 Churchill supported Stalin's objection to admitting France to the discussions of the Big Three, saying jovially that the Big Three were 'a very exclusive club, the entrance fee being at least 5,000,000 soldiers or the equivalent'.[7] Britain scarcely possessed such an entrance fee even then, and since then the entrance fee has been increased with bewildering rapidity. In the disarmament negotiations in 1955 the Western powers proposed that the United States, Russia and China should alone have 1,500,000 men under arms in peacetime, Britain and France coming far behind with no more than 750,000 and Mr Calvocoressi suggested that the three 'millionaire' powers, as he called them, were now the great powers.[8] Harold Macmillan said that Britain must confirm her place as a great power by making the H-bomb.[9] Others have said that the test of a great power is the ability to launch a sputnik.

Such statements as these tell us the military force and mechanical equipment that a great power may be expected to possess today, but not what the abiding quality of a great power is – not why Germany was a great power in 1914, or France in the eighteenth century, or Venice when, in 1508, she stood against the combined forces of the papacy and France and Spain and the Empire. In the same way, it is only partially satisfying to be told that China has become a great power on the grounds that the Communist Revolution has provided her for the first time in the past hundred years with a centralized administration capable of organizing all her resources; for the same could be said of Tito's Yugoslavia or Peron's Argentina, and these are not accounted great powers.

7. J. F. Byrnes, *Speaking Frankly*, Heinemann, London, 1947, p. 25.

8. P. Calvocoressi, *The Listener*, 28 July 1955, p. 132.

9. Speech in the House of Commons, 23 February 1958, in *Parliamentary Debates*, Fifth Series, Vol. 582, col. 2305.

It seems, then, that if we are to seek for a scientific definition of a great power, we must meet two requirements. We must satisfy the exact appreciation of power rather than (or as well as) its conventional recognition. And we must find it in terms, not of the quantity or ingredients of power, but of relationship to the states-system as a whole.

Probably the most satisfactory definition, therefore, is one which embodies the distinction made at the Paris Conference in 1919 between powers with general interests and powers with limited interests. Great powers are powers with general interests, i.e. whose interests are as wide as the states-system itself, which today means world-wide. Professor Toynbee formulated it a few years later in a way which avoids an ambiguity in the word 'interests': 'A great power may be defined as a political force exerting an effect coextensive with the widest range of the society in which it operates.'[10] Sir Alfred Zimmern has put the same idea in a different way: '... every Foreign Minister of a great power is concerned with all the world all the time'.[11] Such a definition accords with many observations of great-power status behaviour that can be made. Doubt about the position of France since 1945 (in the minds of Frenchmen no less than others) has been caused primarily by France's inability to maintain her former world-wide interests. Her age-long connection with the Levant ended against her will when Syria and Lebanon finally became independent in 1946; she was forced out of the Far East when she left Indo-China in 1954; the independence of Morocco, Tunis and Algeria has ended her power (though not her influence) in North Africa. Conversely, the accession to great-power status of China has been quickly manifested in an assertion of a universality of interests. So long as China was represented by Chiang Kai-shek, the United States and Britain sought to introduce China into general discussions of the international situation, since it would give them a supporter; and Russia correspondingly opposed it. Since the Communist Revolution in China, they have changed roles. The

10. A. J. Toynbee, *The World after the Peace Conference*, O.U.P., Oxford, 1926, p. 4.

11. *Spiritual Values and World Affairs*, Clarendon Press, Oxford, 1939, p. 32.

first meeting of the Council of Foreign Ministers, in London in September 1945, broke down on the issue of whether China should take part in discussing the peace treaties for Eastern Europe. But ironically it was the momentary weakness of Russia at the time of the Hungarian Revolt in 1956 that enabled China to assert an influence in European affairs as arbiter of ideological disputes within the Communist camp, and sent Chou En-lai journeying to Warsaw and Budapest in January 1957. And the Suez Crisis, which occurred at the same time, gave China the opportunity for the first time to thrust herself into the Middle East, with threats (however empty – but in power politics a threat itself is an act) of military intervention. This criterion of great-power status was appealed to long before it was formulated in 1919. It was in these terms that Napoleon III justified, in the smaller world of 1859, a French concern with Rumania. 'If I were asked what interest France has in those distant countries which the Danube waters, I should reply that the interest of France is everywhere where there is a just and civilizing cause to promote.'[12] And it is amusing to recall that Britain used the same argument in trying to persuade Russia to come to her aid against France and Spain in the American Revolutionary War. After being kept at arm's length for six months, the British minister in St Petersburg was at last admitted to a discussion on policy with Catherine the Great, and asked her to intervene.

'Admitting what you say,' replied she, 'what right have I, after all, to interfere in a quarrel foreign to my own concerns, on a subject I am not supposed to understand, and with Courts at such a distance from me?' I answered Her Imperial Majesty by saying, that if, in the last century, a Sovereign of Russia had held this language to me, I should have been puzzled for a reply; but since Russia was become a leading power in Europe, the answer was obvious; she was too great to see any great events with indifference; the concerns of Europe were now the concerns of Russia.[13]

The Empress, who had never dissented from such arguments, did subsequently intervene in the war, but against Britain. But it

12. Address to the French Legislative Body, 7 February 1859, in R. W. Seton-Watson, *History of the Roumanians*, C.U.P., Cambridge, 1934, p. 267.
13. *Diaries and Correspondence of the Earl of Malmesbury*, Vol. 1, p. 253.

is not simply the possession of wide interests that marks a great power. Holland before 1947, with her empire in the East Indies as well as Dutch Guiana and Curaçao in America; or Portugal with her vast colonies in Africa, Goa in India, half the island of Timor in the East Indies and Macao in the China Sea, were examples of minor powers with almost world-wide interests. We must add an ability to protect or advance those interests by force. And this means a readiness to go to war.

'The great powers', A. J. P. Taylor has said of nineteenth-century Europe, 'were, as their name implies, organizations for power, that is, in the last resort for war. They might have other objects – the welfare of their inhabitants or the grandeur of their rulers. But the basic test for them was their ability to wage war.'[14]

Another definition that meets our two requirements was given by the Prussian historian Treitschke: 'A state may be defined as a great power if its total destruction would require a coalition of other states to accomplish.'[15] It will be noted that this definition resembles that which we gave in the preceding chapter for a dominant power, and it is possible that Treitschke, when he wrote this, was generalizing from the European hegemony of Germany to which he himself, by preaching German nationalism, had largely contributed. Moreover, the definition is untrue to historical fact if 'total destruction' means the kind of defeat imposed by Napoleon upon Prussia in 1806 or by Hitler upon France in 1940, since these were single-handed exploits.[16] It might be an ideal definition that, as a dominant power is a power that can confidently contemplate war against any likely combination of other powers, so a great power is a power that can confi-

14. A. J. P. Taylor, *The Struggle for Mastery in Europe*, Clarendon Press, Oxford, 1954, p. xxiv.
15. H. von Treitschke, *Politics*, Vol. II, B. Dugdale and T. de Bille (trans.), Constable, London, 1916, p. 607.
16. The most memorable example in Western history of a literal 'total destruction' is the extinction of Carthage by Rome in 146 BC. There was no coalition here, since Rome had only the most uncertain assistance from the Numidians. But Carthage had lost the status of a great power with her defeat in the Second Punic War of 218–201 BC, which made her tributary and gave Rome control of her foreign policy.

dently contemplate war against any other existing single power. But history does not conform to ideal definitions, and there are many examples of declining great powers (like Holland after 1676, and Austria-Hungary after 1866, and France after 1871, and Britain after 1945) whose continued great-power status depends upon an alliance, sometimes with a stronger partner. Nevertheless, Treitschke's definition is useful, because it illustrates the difficulty of distinguishing exactly between dominant powers and great powers. Most great powers have been dominant powers in decline. And we may say that every great power aspires to be a dominant power, as every dominant power aspires to be a universal empire.[17]

17. This draft was apparently written in the late 1950s. Eds.

4 : World Powers

The discussion in the last chapter has brought us to a point where we must consider a striking characteristic of the great powers. They have tended to decrease in number and increase in size. The process occurred first of all on the small stage of Europe. In 1500 there were a number of great powers, some like Portugal which afterwards ceased to be a great power, and some like Venice which afterwards ceased to be a power at all; but at last they were reduced to the Big Five of the Congress of Vienna. Since 1815 the process has been re-enacted on the world stage. In 1914 there were eight great powers. In 1939 there were seven. By the end of the Second World War there were a nominal five but a substantive two. (Edward Crankshaw once described it as 'the Law of Diminishing Nigger Boys'.)[1] And the Potsdam Conference powers of 1945 were as much bigger in calibre than the Congress of Vienna powers as the Congress of Vienna powers were bigger than Venice and Portugal.

This decrease in number and increase in size is a result of the expansion of the European states-system to cover the earth, which has accompanied the development of international politics through every stage since the break-up of medieval Christendom. The powers on the circumference of Europe have reached out and encircled the globe. Since the ships of Portugal first sailed round the Cape of Good Hope (1487–8) and crossed the Indian Ocean (1497–9), since the ships of Spain first discovered America (1492) and crossed the Pacific to circumnavigate the world (1519–22), every general war in Europe has sent vibrations round the earth. Even the Thirty Years War, which began with a disputed succession to the throne of Bohemia and is the most exclusively European in its military operations of all the great wars, had in

1. *The Spectator*, 28 June 1946, p. 668.

the margin of the picture the transfer of colonial power from Spain and Portugal to Holland. Macaulay has a famous description of the repercussions of a conflict between the King of Prussia and the Queen of Hungary about a central European province in 1740: 'The whole world sprang to arms . . . The evils produced by his wickedness were felt in lands where the name of Prussia was unknown; and in order that he might rob a neighbour whom he had promised to defend, black men fought on the coast of Coromandel, and red men scalped each other by the Great Lakes of North America.'[2] In order that Hitler might destroy a neighbour with whom he had signed a non-aggression pact, Sudanese troops fought Italians in Somaliland and Australians hunted Japanese through the jungles of New Guinea.

In this expansion the European powers have conquered and exploited the other civilizations of mankind, in Mexico, Peru, India, Islam and China, and aroused a sleeping dragon when they disturbed the hermit kingdom of Japan. They have used these vast and distant resources to settle their own quarrels in the battle-ground of Europe, and conversely they have fought in Europe to settle the ownership of these distant resources. Thus the English and Dutch in the sixteenth century attacked the Spanish Empire in America, for they hoped 'by bearding the King of Spain in his treasure-house to cut the sinews by which he sustained his wars in Europe';[3] Pitt in the Seven Years War, when by containing French military power on the continent he secured North America between the Alleghanies and the Mississippi for the English-speaking world, said in a famous phrase, 'America has been conquered in Germany.'[4] Thus Napoleon sought in vain to reconquer with his armies in Europe the Cape of Good Hope, and the East Indies, which Britain had taken from the Dutch; and Canning, when the French in 1823 invaded Spain, in reply recognized the independence of the Spanish American colonies and placed them under the protection of the British navy, later saying:

2. *Frederic the Great*, Clarendon Press, Oxford, 1918, p. 22.

3. Quoted in G. Edmundson, 'Frederick Henry, Prince of Orange', *Cambridge Modern History*, Vol. IV, C.U.P., Cambridge, 1906, p. 703.

4. B. Williams, *The Life of William Pitt*, Vol. II, Longmans, London, 1913, p. 131 (speech in House of Commons, 13 November 1761).

'. . . I resolved that if France had Spain, it should not be Spain *with the Indies.* I called the New World into existence, to redress the balance of the Old.'[5] And history has examples of grotesque miscalculations of the relative value of European and overseas possessions. When Spain in 1800 ceded to France the vast territory of Louisiana which Jefferson purchased three years later, the return she exacted was a central Italian principality for the Queen of Spain's son-in-law. Conversely when Napoleon III failed to understand the significance of the Prussian unification of North Germany in 1866, it was partly because he had been distracted by the will-o'-the-wisp of a Catholic empire in Mexico.

The phrase world power is often used to mean a power with interests in the world at large. With more precision we might define a world power as a great power which can exert effectively *inside* Europe a strength that is derived from resources *outside* Europe. One of the chief reasons why Spain was the first dominant power to overshadow Europe was that she was the first effective world power. By the beginning of the nineteenth century, when the Spanish Empire was dissolving and France had been decisively defeated in America and India, Britain was the only remaining world power of Western Europe. But another world power was arising on the further edge of Europe. Russia had reached the Pacific by a colonizing expansion over land; and throughout the nineteenth century the world's debate was between Britain and Russia as throughout the eighteenth it had been between Britain and France. The Industrial Revolution, moreover, brought a world market into existence, and European expansion was accelerated in the later nineteenth century by the discovery of many new materials of modern industry (which means also of modern war) such as petroleum and rubber, situated mainly outside Europe. This was a principal reason for the partition of Africa and the Near East, and the semi-partition of the Far East. It was an unintended political consequence that the international states-system became world-wide. The Second Hague Conference in 1907 was the first international gathering at which European states were outnumbered by non-European.

5. R. Therry, *The Speeches of George Canning*, Vol. VI, James Ridgeway, London, 1828, p. 111 (speech in House of Commons, 12 December 1826).

But it was becoming accepted that a great power must make pretensions to being a world power, by acquiring colonial possessions. Lenin in his theory of imperialism used the two terms great power and world power interchangeably. France entered upon a second and more successful career as a world power after 1871 in order to offset her loss of European predominance, acquiring Indo-China and the largest of all territorial empires in Africa. Italy lost a shadowy protectorate over Abyssinia in the disaster of Adowa (1896), and recouped herself by seizing Tripoli from Turkey in 1911–12. By 1914 Austria-Hungary was the sole great power with no overseas colonial possessions. The world power claims of the great powers might be symbolized by the action they took to suppress the Boxer Rising in China in 1900. A popular unofficial movement of Chinese patriots, infuriated by Western humiliations, murdered Europeans and attacked the foreign legations in Peking. The great powers replied with an international force under German command. On 28 August 1900 they entered the Forbidden City of Peking in the following order: 800 Russians, 800 Japanese, 400 British, 400 Americans, 400 French, 250 Germans, 60 Austrians, 60 Italians. The Austrians and Italians had no interests in China, but since they were great powers they claimed universal interests and had to join the parade. This unique example of the collective military action by all the great powers of the world before 1914, marking the deepest humiliation of the oldest non-European civilization, might be taken as the dramatic beginning of the contemporary phase of international history, which continues to put down so many of the mighty from their seats.

The United States and Japan were the first great powers whose resources were situated wholly outside Europe. Japan never became a world power in the sense of our definition, though the conquest of Europe was the ultimate objective of the Japanese imperialists between the World Wars. Japan had less influence on European politics in forty years than Communist China, her successor as the great power of Asia, has had in a much shorter period. Britain and France declined the offer of Japanese troops on the western front in the First World War, though Japanese submarines operated in the Mediterranean. Japan was a signatory to the Montreux Convention of 1936 regulating the Black Sea Straits, but this was a formal assertion of great-power status like the Austrian troops in the march into the Forbidden City. But the United States was historically and strategically dependent upon Europe, despite her traditional repudiation of all its concerns. The Civil War engendered her vast industrial strength,

> The great metallic beast
> Expanding West and East,

and from then on she was forced almost against her will, the sole reluctant dragon among the great powers, to take control of the Americas and to take part in international affairs outside them. She established a quasi-protectorate over Samoa in 1878; she took part in the Berlin Conference on Africa in 1885–6; she founded the Pan-American Conference in 1889. Considerably less reluctant under Theodore Roosevelt, she brought Russia and Japan to end their war in 1905 by a peace treaty signed on American soil, and the Moroccan crisis of 1905–6, when she helped to bring about the Algeciras Conference and to save it from collapse, was her first diplomatic intervention in the affairs of the Concert of Europe. She was led inexorably to exert her strength inside Europe by the rise there of a new dominant power. A hundred years earlier she had been brought near to war with a preponderant France. When Napoleon was planning a colonial empire in Louisiana, Jefferson wrote that the day France took possession of New Orleans 'seals the union of two nations, who, in conjunction, can maintain exclusive possession of the ocean. From that moment, we must marry ourselves to the British fleet and nation'.[6] The danger was averted when Napoleon instead sold Louisiana to the United States (1803). When Germany's unrestricted submarine campaign in 1917 threatened to starve Britain and transfer to Germany herself the command of the Atlantic, Jefferson's prophecy became fulfilled.

Germany was the first dominant power which, because of her position at the centre and not on the circumference of Europe, and because of her late unification, was not a world power. The

6. Letter to Robert R. Livingston, 18 April 1802, in *The Writings of Thomas Jefferson*, Vol. IX, p. 313.

two World Wars arose from her attempts to become one. Bismarck's successors sought 'a place in the sun' and 'a future upon the water' by building a great navy, and thus came into conflict with Britain. Hitler afterwards described the two issues of the First World War from the German point of view when he wrote: 'England did not want Germany to be a world power, but France did not want Germany to be a power at all.'[7] He himself, when he became German ruler, sought a colonial empire on the Eurasian steppes. His aim was a trans-continental expansion to the Urals and the Caucasus, which would make the greater German Reich as large and as full of natural resources as the United States. 'Germany will either become a world power or will cease to exist altogether,' he had said.[8] And this was the theme of the Second World War. It destroyed Germany as a power altogether. It brought this about by the application in Europe of resources situated outside Europe – of Soviet industrial power in the Urals and American industrial power in the Ohio valley and the Great Lakes and the Pacific coast. And it eliminated all the great powers whose main strength was in Europe, leaving none but world powers. In the twentieth century the world powers are the only great powers that can stand the pace.

Is it possible that this tendency to the combination and monopoly of international power will be carried to its conclusion, and that all the competitors for international power will be reduced to a single universal world power, a new Roman Empire? This seems to have been the way in which every other period of power politics known to us in history has ended. 'A Roman peace,' said Walter Lippmann in 1943, 'in which one state absorbs and governs all the others, is so completely impossible in our time that we need not stop to argue whether it would be inferno or utopia.'[9] Whether subsequent events have confirmed this judgement, whether it would still be true after a Third World War waged with nuclear energy, are among the largest questions which

7. A. Hitler, *Mein Kampf*, Zentralverlag der NSDAP, Frz. Eher Nachf., Munich, 1934, p. 699.
8. ibid., p. 742.
9. W. Lippmann, *US Foreign Policy*, Hamish Hamilton, London, 1943, p. 64.

5 : Minor Powers

The great powers have always been a minority in the society of states. They reached their highest proportion of the membership of the states-system in the 1870s. The principle of nationality had then drastically reduced the number of small states by unifying Italy and Germany, without having yet had the contrary effect in Eastern Europe; it was dubious moreover whether the international system included any states outside Europe except those of the Americas, if indeed those. At that time the great powers numbered nearly a quarter of the whole. As one goes back before that time, one finds an increasing number of small principalities (the debris of feudalism) steadily reducing the relative number of the great powers. Coming forward from that time, one finds their relative number steadily reduced by the increasing number of small states which are the debris of colonial empires. In 1972 there were nominally five great powers, 125 other members of the United Nations, and perhaps ten more states which were members of the states-system, though outside the United Nations.[1]

Thus the vast majority of states are not great powers. These are the minor powers. Great powers, as we have seen, are not of uniform strength; and the range of minor powers is far wider, stretching from powers on the fringes of the great to states so small and lacking in military strength, like Luxembourg or Costa Rica, that they scarcely deserve the name of *powers*. Yet we must always bear in mind that this multitude of members of international society do not *ipso facto* speak for the majority of the human race, since they mostly have exiguous populations compared to those of the great powers.

The smallness we are talking about when we speak of small

1. In 1975 the figures are 142 states in the United Nations and approximately 15 which are not members. Eds.

powers is smallness relative to the international society they belong to. It has often been argued that the highest and most lasting culture has been produced only by small political units. 'It is a fact that the great things in the heritage of the West have often been the work of the little peoples – an Athens or a Florence, Elizabethan England, or the seventeenth-century United Netherlands.'[2] These are unfortunate examples. Each was a great people, in terms of power or wealth or population, relative to the states-system of which it was a part. Athens at her cultural zenith under Pericles was the dominant power of Hellas, territorially much larger than any state except her rival Sparta, and vastly superior to Sparta in population, social energy and economic strength. Florence under the Medici was one of the five great powers of fifteenth-century Italy, industrially the most advanced and financially the strongest if militarily the weakest. England established her rank as a great power under Elizabeth if she had not done so before. Though less populous than Spain or France, she was the wealthiest and most secure of Protestant powers and the recognized champion of the Protestant cause internationally. The United Provinces in the seventeenth century were, as we have already seen, the maritime dominant power of Europe, and an object of bitter jealousy to England and France:

> Crouching at home, and cruel when abroad:
> Scarce leaving us the means to claim our own.

It is certainly a vulgar error to see intrinsic value in political size. Small states may well be the happiest and most civilized members of the international community. Some very small states, Geneva in the sixteenth century, Weimar in the later eighteenth, Switzerland in the nineteenth and twentieth (the shining example of multinational democracy and internationalist philanthropy) have had a culturally stimulating or beneficent influence on the whole states-system. But there is an unhistorical sentimentalism in the assertion that 'All the great things have been done by the little nations'.[3] Any generalization about cul-

2. A. Cobban, *National Self Determination*, O.U.P., London, 1944, p. 139.
3. B. Disraeli, *Tancred*, Longmans, London, 1871, p. 229; this is a sparkling cadenza on the theme. See also R. Cobden, Speech at Rochdale, 29

tural values will seem dubious if it does not take account of the Grand Siècle of France, the baroque of Austria under Charles VI and Maria Theresa, the science of Victorian Britain, the literature of nineteenth-century Russia – not to speak of the imperial Rome of Cicero and Virgil, Gaius and Ulpian. It may well be that at any period there is an optimum political size for cultural efflorescence, but the examples mentioned suggest that this optimum size increases through the centuries. And it seems that high culture is fostered by certain concentrations of political and perhaps more clearly economic power, relative to the international community in which the phenomenon occurs.

Two kinds of minor power achieve an eminence which distinguishes them from the common run: regional great powers, and middle powers. Political pressures do not operate uniformly throughout the states-system, and in certain regions which are culturally united but politically divided, a subordinate international society comes into being, with a states-system reproducing in miniature the features of the general states-system. Italy and Germany before they were unified are examples in Europe; the Arab world and South America are examples in the wider world. In such sub-systems as these, there will be some states with general interests relative to the limited region and a capacity to act alone, which gives them the appearance of local great powers. Egypt, Iraq and perhaps Saudi Arabia have been great powers in the Arab world; Argentina and Brazil have played a similar role in South America. Similarly, South Africa may be regarded as a great power relative to Black Africa. Such regional great powers will probably be candidates, in the states-system at large, for the rank of middle power.

The grading of powers, as distinct from the older questions of precedence, first became a subject of diplomatic discussion at the peace settlement of 1815.[4] It was then that a class of middle powers was first formally recognized, among the states of Germany. The history of Germany has in several ways provided a microcosm of

October 1862, in J. Bright and T. Rogers (eds.), *Speeches by Richard Cobden MP*, Vol. II, Macmillan, London, 1870, pp. 305–37, for a duller treatment.
    4. For earlier attempts to grade powers, see Appendix I. Eds.

the whole European states-system, and in this case Germany set a precedent which the states-system has so far not followed. In the ordinary assembly of the Diet of the German Confederation, eleven of its thirty-nine members had a separate delegate: the remaining twenty-eight states were grouped into six *curiae*, with a delegate for each *curia*. The eleven were: Austria and Prussia, which were great powers of the European system, and only entered the German Confederation with an express reservation of their superior rights; Hanover, whose sovereign was the King of Great Britain, Holstein, whose sovereign was the King of Denmark, and Luxembourg whose sovereign was the King of the Netherlands; and Bavaria, Saxony, Württemberg, Baden, Electoral Hesse and Grand-Ducal Hesse. It was the last group that was usually meant by the term middle states. But among them there were gradations of influence and differences of interest. The South German states, Bavaria, Württemberg and Baden, sometimes tried to pursue together a policy independent of Austria and Prussia, and were considered the middle states *par excellence*.

During the San Francisco Conference in 1945 there was some demand that powers of the second rank should be recognized in the United Nations by giving them priority in election to the non-permanent seats of the Security Council. Those pointed out as middle powers were Canada, Australia, Brazil, Mexico, Poland, Holland and Belgium. A similar list today would probably omit the last two, and certainly include a number of powers which since have enhanced their status, such as India, which in 1945 was not yet independent (if indeed India be not granted an honorary rank as great power), Sweden (which in 1945 was in the twilight of disesteem surrounding all neutrals at the end of a great war), Yugoslavia and Egypt. Middle powers, indeed, are more difficult to distinguish than great powers, and they were not given a place in the United Nations arrangements. Diplomatic recognition of such a class would create many jealousies; as with the middle class in England, it would be invidious to show that any individual did not belong to it. It might be argued that a middle power reveals itself, no less than a great power, by the successful assertion of independence of a Tito or a Nasser, by the diplomacy of a Lester Pearson or a Krishna Menon, by the beneficent role of a Count

Bernadotte or a General Burns. With more precision, it might be argued that a middle power is a power with such military strength, resources and strategic position that in peacetime the great powers bid for its support, and in wartime, while it has no hope of winning a war against a great power, it can hope to inflict costs on a great power out of proportion to what the great power can hope to gain by attacking it. It is a calculation of this kind that governs the defence policy of Sweden, and may lead it to produce its own atomic weapons.

Middle powers appear when the qualifications for great-power status are being revised. The number of middle powers varies inversely with the number of great. In the nineteenth century, when the great powers were a stable and relatively numerous group, there were no recognized middle powers. (But in the German Confederation between 1815 and 1866, as we have seen, there were two great powers – Austria and Prussia, nine recognized as middle states, and twenty-eight small states.) Claimants to middle-power status reappeared in 1919, when the aristocracy of the great powers had been gravely shaken. The most obvious middle powers today are the powers which have lost the status of great power as a result of the two World Wars: Britain, France, Germany and Japan.

Nevertheless there is usually a greater gulf between great powers and minor powers (middle powers included) than there is between middle powers and other minor powers. Minor powers (middle powers included) have the means of defending only limited interests, and of most of them it is true that they possess only limited interests. They have territorial or maritime disputes with their neighbours, as Yugoslavia has with Bulgaria and Greece over Macedonia; or their livelihood depends on fisheries, like Iceland; or they have to sell their raw materials, like the oil-producing Arab states. But they cannot unify continents, or rule the high seas, or control the international market. Of some small powers, however, it may be said that the range of their foreign policy is so contracted that they have no interest except the preservation of their independence.

As great-power status has become increasingly hardened and defined, so has the status of the minor powers. The opposite side of the Concert of Europe was that the minor powers had no role internationally. The Hague Conferences of 1899 and 1907 were the first international gatherings at which the minor powers were generally represented – it was another aspect of the inclusion of non-European states in the international community – and the Balkan Wars of 1912–13, when Montenegro, Bulgaria, Serbia and Greece first dismembered European Turkey and then with Rumania fought among themselves about the spoils, against the will of the Concert, are a rare example of a group of small powers successfully defying the combined great powers. The League of Nations brought what might be called the formal enfranchisement of the minor powers. They now had a regular means of making their voice heard in the Assembly, where all were represented equally. And here by a paradox it was seen that the powers who by definition were without 'general interests' were more capable than the great powers of pursuing consistently what might be regarded as the universal interest of upholding international law and order. The League Assembly (unlike its successor in the United Nations) had equal rights with the Council to deal 'with any matter within the sphere of action of the League or affecting the peace of the world', and under the early leadership of men like Hymans of Belgium, Branting of Sweden, Nansen of Norway, Beneš of Czechoslovakia, Politis of Greece, Motta of Switzerland and Lord Robert Cecil for South Africa, it resembled in the 1920s an embryonic international parliament. When sanctions were imposed on Italy in 1935–6 to restrain her aggression against Abyssinia, the small powers showed a resolution and readiness for sacrifice, which do much to answer the argument that they can afford to champion international ideals because they do not have the responsibility for enforcing them. It was the great powers who destroyed the League system, by a combination of aggressions and defections.

The General Assembly of the United Nations has had a less impressive history than its predecessor. This is partly because it is less powerful, partly because the character of the small powers has changed. In the League the small powers were predominantly conservative in international outlook, in the United Nations they are predominantly discontented and revolutionary. The League was still a predominantly European institution, and the small powers were predominantly the satisfied and sedentary small powers of Western Europe, together with the satisfied and victorious small powers of Eastern Europe who were concerned to maintain the hard-won freedom of the Versailles settlement. In the United Nations the small powers are predominantly the Asian, African and Latin American powers, who see themselves as the first-fruits of a continuing revolution which has to be extended to all non-self-governing peoples and deepened so as to achieve a redistribution of the world's wealth at the expense of the Western great powers.[5]

5. This draft was apparently completed in 1972. Eds.

6 : Sea Power and Land Power

It has often been remarked that the states-system came into being in the second half of the fifteenth century at about the same time as the Great Discoveries, which showed that European sea power could encircle the world's continents. The history of international politics down to 1945 has been the history of the ascendancy of sea power. An Indian historian has called it 'the Vasco da Gama epoch'.[1] He implied that with the dismantling of the European overseas empires after 1945, the epoch of European supremacy came to an end. Has the epoch of the ascendancy of sea power come to an end too?

The beginning of the states-system also came at about the same time as the regular adoption of artillery in warfare. (The effects of the double coincidence have been working out in politics ever since.) The sea power of the Great Discoveries was already a matter of guns. The sea made artillery mobile. At a time when on land guns had to be dragged laboriously across country, ships carried their cannon around the world. When Vasco da Gama bombarded Calicut on the Malabar coast in 1502, on his second voyage, to punish the Hindu ruler for the murder of Portuguese merchants, he began the long development of sea power that culminated on 6 August 1945, when the aeroplane *Enola Gay* set off from the island of Tinian in the Marianas for the 1,400 mile flight to Hiroshima. For this too was an exercise of sea power. If the Americans had not first conquered the Pacific they could not have bombed Japan; and they too were visiting retribution on an Asiatic power for having violated Western standards of international conduct.

It was the Portuguese who invented the use of ships as artillery

1. K. M. Panikkar, *Asia and Western Dominance*, Allen & Unwin, London, 1959, title page.

carriers, rather than as military transports for boarding other ships, and of guns for sinking other ships, rather than helping boarding parties. The English followed, and perhaps invented the broadside.[2] They developed the political uses of sea power. The guns of Winter's fleet could play a prime part in driving the French out of Edinburgh in 1560 and ending the Auld Alliance for ever; Drake's guns could range the Pacific coast of the Spanish Empire and insult the King of Spain in his home ports; Blake could overpower the shore-batteries of the Bey of Tunis in 1655 by direct gunfire from the sea, and secure the release of captives. Seventy-one per cent of the earth's surface is water, only twenty-nine per cent land; so that a power with access to the sea has been able to live in contact with most of the globe, while a land power, with little or no serviceable coastline, has depended upon crossing territory controlled by others. 'To call a country with a fleet like England's "distant" from a small maritime nation like Portugal is an absurdity. England is, and yet more in those days was, wherever her fleet could go.'[3] And command of the sea, the ability to send one's own trade and troops over the water and to prevent one's opponent from doing so, enabled a power to bring pressure on any country with a coastline, in peace or war. 'A fleet of British ships of war', said Nelson, 'are the best negotiators in Europe.' The US Sixth and Seventh Fleets showed the same character after 1945 in Mediterranean and East Asian waters.

'He that commands the sea', wrote Bacon, reflecting on the Elizabethan war with Spain, 'is at great liberty, and may take as much and as little of the war as he will. Whereas those that be strongest by land are many times, nevertheless, in great straits.'[4]

2. 'It is likely that the firing of the first English broadsides, which was as revolutionary an occasion as the successful launching of the first guided missile, took place against the French fleet off Shoreham on 15th August 1545; and thereafter the broadside remained the principal instrument of maritime power right down to recent times.' S. W. Roskill, *The Strategy of Sea Power*, Collins, London, 1962, pp. 24-5.

3. A. T. Mahan, *The Influence of Seapower upon History*, p. 320.

4. 'The Essays: Of the True Greatness of Kingdoms & Estates', in Basil Montagu (ed.), *The Works of Francis Bacon*, Pickering, London, 1834, pp. 107-8.

Command of the sea has enabled a power to land and maintain military forces where it chose on enemy territory, as Britain maintained Wellington's army in the Peninsula for over four years in a campaign that crippled Napoleon, and as the United States and Britain together could pour their armies into North Africa in 1942 and into Normandy in 1944. It has allowed a power to withdraw military forces if necessary to fight again elsewhere, as the British did Sir John Moore's army from Corunna in 1809, and more dramatically the Anglo-French troops from Dunkirk in 1940. Command of the sea has seemed the decisive military factor in the defeat of successive dominant continental powers by successive grand alliances led by maritime powers. 'Those far distant, storm-beaten ships, upon which the Grand Army never looked, stood between it and the dominion of the world.'[5] Sea power has enabled its possessors not only to wage war at chosen places round the periphery of opposing land powers, but also to cut off all their maritime trade. The Dutch invented the naval blockade of an enemy coastline during their War of Independence against Spain (1572–1609). Here guns, coupled with naval improvements that increased the sea-endurance of ships, became the weapon of economic warfare, to be used by the maritime powers against Louis XIV, Napoleon, and perhaps most effectively against Germany in the First World War.

Of all implements of mass murder, wrote a German after that war, [a fleet] is the most sophisticated. The striking force, the drive of will and the destructive skill of entire nations are concentrated in a couple of gigantic hulls. Millions of warriors can annihilate provinces, but hardly destroy a whole nation: a dozen grey dreadnoughts, besieging a country, invisible in the far distance, can spread hunger and misery over an entire continent.[6]

After the United States entered the war, the Allied control of international commerce became complete. The remaining neutrals had to apply to the Allied and Associated Powers for the commodities they wanted, and were rationed. Their merchant fleets were commandeered, and by the end of the war almost all

5. A. T. Mahan, *The Influence of Seapower upon the French Revolution and Empire*, Vol. II, Sampson Low, London (no date), p. 118.
6. Wilhelm Dibelius, *England*, Cape, London, 1930 p. 103.

shipping on the world's oceans was sailing by Allied leave. The success of the blockade in strangulating the central powers was in the minds of the statesmen who drafted the Covenant of the League of Nations. It prompted their belief in the sufficiency of economic sanctions, because they assumed that the British and American fleets would in future cooperate to maintain peace.

Both the wielders and the victims of sea power, however, tended to exaggerate its effectiveness, crediting it with results which were due rather to propitious circumstances. Blockade was decisive in war only when all other weapons were being employed successfully at the same time. Powers have had a naval superiority and been decisively defeated on land: the French fleet could virtually blockade the North German coast in the Franco-Prussian War, but it did not offset France's military inferiority. Moreover, the exercise of sea power always assumed the maintenance of secure and productive bases. It seemed that sea power, in the last analysis, required the possession of some land power, in a way in which the reverse was not true. There were European statesmen between the sixteenth and nineteenth centuries, educated in a knowledge of classical history, who remembered that it was not Athens, the naval empire, but Sparta, the continental power, that won the Peloponnesian War; that Alexander destroyed the Persian fleet's principal base at Tyre, and went on to conquer the central dominions of Persia; and that Carthage was in the end destroyed by Rome. The English themselves in the seventeenth century, as they contemplated the detested Dutch masters of the sea, like the French revolutionaries and the German Kaiser when they in later times looked at the detested England, adopted for their own encouragement the old Roman saying, *Carthago delenda est*. An English publicist wrote in 1701 of the ancient Athenians, 'Their navy indeed was the occasion of their greatness, but whatever nation has the chief dominion at land, will in time have the dominion of the seas . . .'[7] To continental statesmen there seemed something parasitical and unnatural about sea power. Napoleon believed, like Hitler after him, that if he could march his armies far enough, occupy enough coastline or

7. C. Davenant, 'Universal Monarchy', in *Essays*, James Knapton, London, 1701, p. 287.

conquer enough economic resources, he would break the strangle-hold of the maritime octopus. The logic of land power was to grow until all the shores of the Old World were held by one and the same continental power.

It is often the case that historical developments come to flower, and formulate their ideal, at the moment when far-sighted observers can see that decay has set in. Thus sea power found its classic description at the end of the nineteenth century in the writings of the American naval officer Mahan; but it was in the last two decades of Mahan's lifetime that it began to be apparent that the industrial growth of powers other than Britain and the revolution in mechanical transport on land might undermine the superiority of sea power over land power. One of the earliest to expound this view was the British geographer Mackinder, and the First World War confirmed his reasonings.

It may be helpful to expound and illustrate Mackinder's argument. It was put forward first in 1904, and elaborated in 1919 when he believed the First World War had confirmed it. It[8] may be reduced to the following points:

1. The mobility and pervasiveness of sea power has obscured its inability to exist without territorial roots. It is fundamentally a matter of secure and productive bases, and above all a fertile home-base. 'The productive base is needed for the support of men not only for the manning of ships, but for all the land services in connection with shipping . . .'[9] 'The manpower of the sea must be nourished by land-fertility somewhere, and other things being equal – such as security of the home and energy of the people – that power will control the sea which is based on the greater resources.'[10]

2. Sea power in history has regularly succumbed through the conquest of its bases by land power. Thus, in the classical world, Alexander reduced Tyre, the Persian fleet's main base, after a seven months' siege, one of his greatest feats of arms, before he marched into the central dominions of Persia. Moreover, it was

8. H. J. Mackinder, 'The Geographical Pivot of History', *The Geographical Journal*, Vol. XXIII, 1904, pp. 421–44; and *Democratic Ideals and Reality*.
9. *Democratic Ideals and Reality*, p. 139.
10. ibid., p. 34.

the core of Mackinder's doctrine that it is easier for land power to take to the sea than for sea power to take to the land. Thus in the classical world, by the end of the Peloponnesian War Sparta, the continental power, had built a fleet and defeated Athens, the naval empire; and as early as the First Punic War the Romans, a nation of farmers, built a fleet, learned its use, and defeated Carthage at sea.

3. The outward expansion of Europe, 'the Columbian epoch', of which sea power had been the great instrument, had now come to an end. In the half-generation after the American frontier had closed (officially in 1890), the world's moving frontier too had closed. Africa had been partitioned; Russia had failed to conquer China between 1895 and 1905 and her defeat by Japan had thrust her back upon Europe; the North Pole had been reached in 1909, the South Pole in 1911. 'From the present time forth, in the post-Columbian age, we shall again have to deal with a closed political system, and none the less that it will be one of world-wide scope. Every explosion of social forces, instead of being dissipated in a surrounding circuit of unknown space and barbaric chaos, will be sharply re-echoed from the far side of the globe, and weak elements in the political and economic organism of the world will be shattered in consequence.'[11]

4. The closing of the world's frontier brought a new geographical perspective. The Old World, the joint continent of Europe, Asia and Africa, could now be seen as a strategic unit, a world-island, with promontories guarded by Cape Town and Singapore. 'There is one ocean covering nine-twelfths of the globe; there is one continent – the world-island – covering two-twelfths of the globe; and there are many smaller islands, whereof North America and South America are for effective purposes two, which together cover the remaining one-twelfth.'[12]

5. Two developments had made the world-island, the 'Old World', into a strategic unit for the first time since the nomad empires of the Huns and Mongols, but far more effectively. The first was the revolution in land communications. 'It was an unprecedented thing in the year 1900 that Britain should maintain

11. 'The Geographical Pivot of History', p. 422.
12. *Democratic Ideals and Reality*, p. 65.

a quarter of a million men in her war with the Boers at a distance of six thousand miles over the ocean; but it was as remarkable a feat for Russia to place an army of more than a quarter of a million men against the Japanese in Manchuria in 1904 at a distance of four thousand miles by rail.'[13] The effects of the railway had been confirmed by mechanized road transport and the aeroplane. The second development was the growth of population, above all of the Russian peasantry. 'In regard to land power we have seen that the camel-men and horsemen of past history failed to maintain lasting empires, from lack of adequate manpower, and that Russia was the first tenant of the heartland with a really menacing manpower.'[14]

6. The core of the world-island is the vast lowland drained by great rivers either northwards to the Arctic coast or southwards to salt inland seas. This was the region, covering half Asia and a quarter of Europe, that Mackinder called the world's 'pivot area', or the heartland. It is inaccessible to navigation from the ocean. 'The heartland, for the purposes of strategical thinking, includes the Baltic Sea, the navigable Middle and Lower Danube, the Black Sea, Asia Minor, Armenia, Persia, Tibet and Mongolia. Within it, therefore, were Brandenburg-Prussia, and Austria-Hungary, as well as Russia – a vast triple base of manpower, which was lacking to the horse riders of history. The heartland is the region to which, under modern conditions, sea power can be refused access.'[15]

7. The triumph of sea power in the First World War was accidental and in a sense illusory, because the political strategy of the war had been unique in European history. It was the first general war in which the dominant power had not been overthrown by the combined pressure of sea power on the Atlantic flank and of a rival land power on the Continent, imposing a war on two fronts. Thus Philip II had been worn down by the combination of Anglo-Dutch sea power and Franco-Dutch military power; Louis XIV by the combination of Britain and Austria, the partnership of Marlborough and Eugène; Napoleon by the com-

13. ibid., p. 115.
14. ibid., pp. 139-40.
15. ibid., p. 110.

74

bination of Britain and Russia. But in the First World War Russia had collapsed, and Germany had been able to dictate peace on her own terms on the eastern front; the role of rival continental power had been played by the American troops, brought to bear upon Germany at the decisive crisis of 1918 in the Atlantic bridgehead maintained by sea power; and this seemed to give sea power a predominant role. The Second World War was to revert to the general pattern, and illustrate again the successful combination of sea power and land power that overthrew Napoleon.

8. The real lesson of the First World War was rather the reverse: a warning of the 'ever-increasing strategical opportunities to land power as against sea power'.[16] During the year between the collapse of Russia in 1917 and Germany's own defeat on the western front, Germany had come within sight of control of the Eurasian continent. 'Had Prussia won this war it was her intention that Continental Europe from [Cape] St Vincent to Kazan, with the addition of the Asiatic heartland, should have become the naval base from which she would have fought Britain and America in the next war.'[17] 'What if the Great Continent, the whole world-island or a large part of it, were at some future time to become a single and united base of sea power? Would not the other insular bases be outbuilt as regards ships and outmanned as regards seamen? Their fleets would no doubt fight with all the heroism begotten of their histories, but the end would be fated. Even in the present war, insular America has had to come to the aid of insular Britain, not because the British fleet could not have held the seas for the time being, but lest such a building and manning base were to be assured to Germany at the peace, or rather truce, that Britain would inevitably be outbuilt and outmanned a few years later.'[18]

9. A final geographical point about the heartland needs to be made. The heartland has little natural frontier with Europe on the west. The Baltic and Black Seas and the Danube valley belong to it. Thus, command of Eastern Europe leads towards command of the heartland itself, and in 1919 it was essential to establish a

16. ibid., p. 111.
17. ibid., p. 120.
18. ibid., p. 70.

stable 'middle tier' of independent states between defeated Germany and Russia.[19] But in sharp contrast to the open passage from the heartland into Europe is the system of mighty mountain barriers that separate the heartland on the south and east from India, South-east Asia, Indonesia and China.[20] And in these coastlands or rimlands there live more than half the population of the globe.[21] 'What part may ultimately be played by that half of the human race which lives in 'the Indies' no man can yet foresee, but it is the plain duty of the insular peoples to protect the Indians and Chinese from heartland conquest.'[22]

Mackinder's ideas (like Mahan's) had a great influence on the German thinkers who invented the pseudo-science of geopolitics. Geopolitics was world political geography studied as an instrument of militaristic expansion. It aimed sometimes at redividing the world into great continental aggregations of power, each seeking self-sufficiency, sometimes at bringing Mackinder's heartland into political life through a German domination of Russia, either through alliance or through subjugation. Hitler's conquests seemed to confirm Mackinder's warning, and still more so did Stalin's. In the early years of the Cold War, the Western powers were faced by a potential dominant power that had brought half Europe under its control, and stretched out beyond Europe to the limits of Asia. Now for the first time Britain had no chance of an alliance with a power standing in the rear of the dominant power. Now there was no rear. The situation at the Peace of Brest-Litovsk in March 1918 had reappeared in a more menacing and permanent form. The Soviet Union was conterminous with the heartland of the world-island. And the Communist conquest of China added the world's largest and most disciplined population to the central continental monolithic bloc. When Khrushchev declared early in 1958 that it was no longer the capitalist powers that were encircling the socialist world, but the socialists who were encircling the capitalists; when he told Nasser that the US Sixth Fleet in the Mediterranean was nothing more than steel

19. ibid., pp. 158–66.
20. ibid., p. 106.
21. ibid., p. 83.
22. ibid., p. 175.

76

coffins for its sailors, and told Eisenhower that surface navies have become fit for nothing but courtesy visits and targets for rockets;[23] he was displaying the strategic self-confidence of the first great power in history to occupy the role that Mackinder had feared.

But Mackinder's theory of land power, despite its air of providing a geographical explanation of universal history, rested on a more selective foundation of historical evidence than did the corresponding theories of sea power. In arguing that land power in general possesses a long-term strategic advantage over sea power, it gave the impression that sea powers have always or usually been conquered by land powers. It ignored the examples of a sea power succumbing to assault by superior naval power, as Byzantium succumbed to Venetian aggression in 1204 (and as Japan was later to succumb to American assault in the Second World War); it ignored the example of a dominant power on land and sea losing its maritime position through internal decay and defeat by more vigorous maritime powers, as Spain was defeated at sea by England and the Dutch; it ignored the examples of a maritime great power declining into a satellite of a still mightier maritime ally, as the Dutch Republic became dependent on Britain (and as Britain afterwards became dependent on the United States). It ignored the strange case of Venice, the dominant maritime power of Christendom in the Middle Ages, which in the end succumbed to the land power of Bonaparte (1797) it is true, but had ceased to be a naval power a hundred years before, and had nevertheless kept her mainland territory in North Italy intact for nearly three hundred years. Mackinder's most cogent examples of the ultimate superiority of land power are drawn from classical history. Perhaps he did not sufficiently consider that the states-system of classical antiquity grew up round a sea enclosed by land, while the modern states-system has grown up on a continent surrounded by the ocean.

The First World War did not only produce or confirm the geopolitical theories of land power. It also saw the birth of air power. The advocates of air power became a third party to the dialogue. If sea power was more pervasive than land power

23. *The Guardian*, 26 July 1958, p. 5; A. E. Sokol, *Seapower in the Nuclear Age*, Public Affairs Press, Washington DC, 1961, p. 234.

because of the great preponderance of ocean over land on the earth's surface, then air power must be more pervasive than either, because aircraft could fly more impartially over sea and land, and at greater speeds than could be attained on sea or land.

During the First World War, air forces were used mainly in tactical roles, for reconnaissance and liaison. But Germany initiated their use for strategic bombing, against the 'home front', with the Zeppelin and Gotha raids on London. These raids showed British civilians that they were no longer immune from attack on an invulnerable island. Britain established the first independent air force in 1917, and carried out a bombing offensive against military targets in the Rhineland in 1918; and if the war had lasted another week the RAF was under orders to drop giant bombs weighing a ton on Berlin.

Between the World Wars, Britain developed the use of air power in the Middle East and on the north-west frontier of India, to maintain order on the marches of the Empire. It was an economical and perhaps humane exercise of force, comparable to the use of gunboats in the preceding century. But what was effective against Kurdish and Wazir tribesmen might be effective, *mutatis mutandis*, against European great powers. A theory of air power was now being developed by Douhet in Italy, Trenchard in Britain and Mitchell in the United States, which claimed that this new arm would be decisive in future war, because it could strike with crushing effect at the cities, the industries and the economic life of every country.

This became the orthodox doctrine of all national air forces. Baldwin put its central idea in simple form when he said, 'I think it is well also for the man in the street to realize that there is no power on earth that can protect him from being bombed. Whatever people may tell him, the bomber will always get through...'[24] And he was expressing the misgivings of a country which believed its traditional immunity from invasion to have passed away. Strategically, Britain's ability to defend the Empire or to act in concert with other powers was now qualified by a sense that the heart of the Empire had become its most vulnerable organ;

24. Speech in the House of Commons, 10 November 1932, *Parliamentary Debates*, Fifth Series, Vol. 270, col. 632.

politically, her influence was at a minimum when she dared not run risks through unpreparedness against the weapon that every civilian dreaded most. The menace of air bombardment was latent in Hitler's diplomacy and enabled him to intimidate Europe. The destruction of Guernica in the Spanish Civil War by German aircraft (1937) was a demonstration to the watching nations. As Chamberlain flew back to London from his visits to Germany in the Czechoslovak crisis of September 1938, he looked down on the flimsy streets of the East End and could not bear to think of them lying a prey to enemy bombers. In March 1939 Hitler compelled President Hacha to surrender the independence of Czechoslovakia by the threat of the immediate destruction of Prague from the air.

The Second World War brilliantly confirmed the tactical use of air power. But it put to the test the orthodox theory of strategic air power, the use of air power independently of military and naval forces, in an attempt to destroy the industry and resources on which the enemy's economic life depended. The Western powers put more effort into this than the Axis, partly because between Dunkirk and the invasion of North Africa the strategic air offensive was the only offensive they could take, more because of the hope that air bombardment was the way to get a military decision without the vast casualties of the First World War. If we compare the contribution of strategic bombing to the defeat of Germany in the Second World War with the part played by the economic blockade in the First World War, we may see that the first was less decisive. The 'hunger blockade' ground down the endurance of Germany, and still more of the other central powers, in a way that aerial bombing did not. The blockade compelled Germany to the fatal move of declaring unrestricted submarine warfare and produced a disintegration of morale on the home front in strikes and revolutionary discontent that preceded military surrender. Neither of these had a counterpart in the Second World War; though the reason for the second may have been that governments, democratic as well as totalitarian, had meanwhile attained a higher degree of control and management of their population. Strategic bombing, as is now well known, did not prevent an increase in German armaments production until the last twelve months of the Second World War, and strengthened rather than undermined civilian morale. This is not to say that concentration on better objectives might not have made it more effective. The strategic air offensive against Japan was much more decisive, more concentrated both in time and in targets.

The steady unification of the world by faster communications has made the old argument between sea power, land power and air power obsolete. The three arms have become increasingly interdependent. It is only service pride that can say, 'It was our sea power that had caused the downfall of Napoleon; it was our sea power that caused the downfall of the Axis powers.'[25] The internal arrangements of states now subordinate the three services to a single Ministry of Defence; and current strategy emphasizes the need for versatility and flexibility of weapons, for force that can be used in multiple ways. Missiles in remote continental spots in hardened bases, which can only be destroyed by direct hit, and missiles carried on nuclear submarines, which are virtually invulnerable, and can cruise submerged for two years without surfacing: these illustrate the mutual deadlock of land and sea power. These have the functions of artillery, magnified to the highest degree: they are not conceived of as commanding a realm of space, but as delivering a destructive force.

One negative thing can be said. The belief that the air could become the decisive theatre has been discredited. The advantage of air transport over land or sea, in peace and war, is speed combined with range. Its corresponding defects are limited carrying power, for bulk cargoes cannot be moved by air; and the need for refuelling with a frequency in proportion to its greater speed than sea power. It would not be surprising if the strategic use of aircraft died away, and their future was confined to tactical purposes in limited war, and they were replaced by missiles in general war.[26]

25. Admiral Sir W. M. James, *The Influence of Seapower on the History of the British People*, C.U.P., Cambridge, 1948, p. 61.
26. This draft was apparently written in the 1960s. Eds.

7 : International Revolutions

It is not possible to understand international politics simply in terms of mechanics. Powers have qualitative differences as well as quantitative, and their attraction and influence is not exactly correlated to mass and weight. For men possess not only territories, raw materials and weapons, but also beliefs and opinions. It is true that beliefs do not prevail in international politics unless they are associated with power (though all beliefs, whether Christianity or Communism or National Socialism, have gone through an important period before they captured state power). But it is equally true that power varies very much in effectiveness according to the strength of the beliefs that inspire its use.

What we usually mean by the word 'revolution' is a violent change of regime within a single state, of which the French Revolution is the classic European example. But we must remember that such revolutions have their international aspect. The Revolt of the Netherlands began one general war; the French Revolution led to another; the Russian Revolution was the result of another. The English Revolution (to give the Civil War of the mid seventeenth century a more accurate name) ended with Cromwell's intervening in the Franco-Spanish War of 1635–59; and the Glorious Revolution of 1688 was the first move in committing England to the general war against Louis XIV. The American Revolution was a war of national independence, that is to say an international event, and the shot the embattled farmers fired reverberated diplomatically in Paris, Madrid and St Petersburg, and militarily as far as the Carnatic.

The international repercussions of these national revolutions have not been accidental. They illustrate, first, that there is a degree of unity in international society making the internal events of one power of concern to other powers. But they are also connected with a series of organized movements for revolutionizing, not simply a single state, but international society as a whole. If we look at international history, not for the sequence of dominant powers and the fluctuations of the balance, but for the recurrent blaze of conviction and fanaticism, we shall find three such doctrinal conflagrations. The first began with the Reformation; the second with the French Revolution; the third with the Russian Revolution.

The wars of the Habsburg ascendancy between the mid sixteenth and mid seventeenth centuries were also the Wars of Religion. Spain and Austria were the champions of Counter-Reformation Catholicism; though it may be noted that the relations between them and the papacy were often bad, and the Popes wanted to be rescued from their supporters. The political leadership of the Reformation cause lay with no single power. It passed from the German princes, to the city-state of Geneva under Calvin, to Elizabethan England, to the Holland of Maurice of Nassau, to the Sweden of Gustavus Adolphus, and finally to Cromwellian England. They were like a pack of hounds who through a hundred years wore down the strength of the House of Habsburg. The aim of the Habsburgs, at its highest, was to restore the Christian Roman Empire, which was ordained to rule the world politically as the Church ruled it spiritually, and which had almost reappeared again under Charles V. The aim of the Reforming powers had to be less grandiose. It was expressed in the idea of a Protestant League, which should wrest from the conservative powers a religious and political equality of rights. This aim bore fruit in the compromise expressed in the famous formula, *Cuius regio eius religio*, agreed upon in Germany at the Peace of Augsburg in 1555, which allowed Lutheran princes the same right to determine the religion of their subjects as Catholics. But the compromise went against the deepest convictions of Catholics and Protestants alike, and especially of the Calvinists, who were excluded from it. The Calvinists aimed at remodelling international society according to their own principles, and saw themselves as Israelites, and papists as Midianites to be smitten with the sword of the Lord and of Gideon. It was not until the Peace of Westphalia in 1648, or more truly till the death of Cromwell in 1658, that religious passions went out of international politics.

From the time of Louis XIV down to the French Revolution the fundamentals of international society were not challenged. This is the classic age of power politics without doctrinal overtones. Diplomacy was no longer the servant of religion, and wars were restricted in their objects. This was partly because the art of fortification had for the time being outstripped the powers of the offensive, so that, as Hamilton wrote of eighteenth-century Europe, 'The history of war in that quarter of the globe is no longer a history of nations subdued and empires overturned; but of towns taken and retaken; of battles that decide nothing; of retreats more beneficial than victories; of much effort and little acquisition'.[1] It was partly, too, because there was a temporary balance of power in Europe, and expansionist tendencies were diverted overseas. In Europe towns were taken and retaken, Prussia and Austria struggled for Silesia, and the greatest success of French arms and diplomacy was the acquisition of Lorraine; but overseas vast territories like Canada and Louisiana changed hands, the Empire of the Moguls passed under British ascendancy, great provinces of the Ottoman Empire were given by the Turk to Austria and to Russia, and Russian power expanded the length of Asia and down the Pacific coast of North America.

It was the French Revolution that reintroduced fanaticism into international relations. The revolutionaries remodelled the French state according to ideals that had no national limitation, and wanted to spread these ideals throughout Europe. The powers that opposed them repudiated these ideals, though negatively rather than with any positive counter-ideal, and thus the conflict became ideological. (It was at this time that the word 'ideology' came into use to describe the new political creeds that had replaced the old religious creeds.) It was not till after the defeat of Napoleon that the anti-French powers produced a counter-revolutionary ideal in the shape of the Holy Alliance, which preached an international Christian conservative monarchism. 'The Holy Alliance was the Cominform of Kings.'[2] The conflict

1. *The Federalist*, Random House, New York, 1937, p. 42.
2. A. J. P. Taylor, *Rumours of War*, Hamish Hamilton, London, 1952, p. 32.

of French revolutionary ideals with Holy Alliance ideals continued until the Holy Alliance disappeared in the Crimean War, and nationalism shattered the Vienna Settlement finally with the unification of Italy and Germany in 1870–71. Germany, emerging as dominant power, was the gainer from the ideological struggle between France and Russia, as France had been the gainer from the religious struggle between the Habsburgs and Sweden.

Thus the century between 1815 and 1914 was not so evidently a period of international stability as the eighteenth century. The foundations of international society were under attack again. More members of international society disappeared by revolution or conquest between 1859 and 1871 than during the whole century and a half between 1648 and 1795. Mazzini preached that the Vienna Settlement of 1815 had no moral validity and that it was necessary to reconstruct the map of Europe 'in accordance with the special mission assigned to each people'.[3]

The Treaties of Vienna were not to the Revolution, what the Peace of Westphalia was to the Reformation [wrote Morley in 1867] . . . The history of Europe since the Treaties of Vienna has been little else than the history of their abrogation; in other words, of the revival and spread of that Revolution which they were believed to have finally quelled. Old dynasties, old divisions of classes, old forms of privileged government survive, but little political foresight is needed to disclose that they are all doomed, and that they are only endured as temporary resting-places on an onward road. The conception of finality and equilibrium might seem to have vanished from the midst of every nation in Europe. Every statesman recognizes more or less frankly the transitory character of the system which he for the hour administers and upholds. Everywhere we discern the hand and hearken to the tread of the Revolution.[4]

If the nineteenth century seems in retrospect an age of international stability, it is perhaps for two reasons. The revolutionary turmoil did not, despite the fears of contemporaries, occasion a general war, and it was followed, between 1871 and 1914, by the longest period of peace that Europe had known since the Roman

3. G. Mazzini, *Life and Writings*, Vol. I, Smith Elder, London, 1890, p. 176.
4. John Morley, *Edmund Burke*, Macmillan, London, 1867, pp. 227–8.

Empire. The balance of power, the Concert of Europe, the Monroe Doctrine and the opening up of the world by Western capitalism seemed together to form a system of international relations that combined stability with elasticity, security with progress. Moreover, the aim of the revolutionary turmoil was to reconstitute international society in accordance with principles that were everywhere becoming accepted. A new doctrine of international legitimacy was modifying the foundations of international society, replacing tradition by consent, prescription by national self-determination. The theoretical attack on the foundations of international society was becoming the new orthodoxy. The doctrine that there are no valid members of international society save those born of national self-determination triumphed when in the shock of the First World War, the military multi-national empires of Eastern Europe – German, Habsburg, Russian and Ottoman – collapsed. The Versailles Settlement was the final victory in Europe of the French Revolution over the Holy Alliance.

But since this second international revolution had been contained and long drawn out, it had not been so destructive as the first. It had also overlapped with a third international revolution. The First World War was the grave of one and the birth of the other. From then on the principles of democracy and national self-determination seemed to go into reverse, and to produce consequences the opposite of what their champions had wanted. The capture of the broken Russian state by a band of determined revolutionaries, led by a commanding genius, was the most striking example of how personal force and doctrinal fanaticism can cut across the regularities of power politics since Calvin, from the petty state of Geneva, perpetually threatened with conquest by Savoy, had poured out a stream of preachers, fanatical, intolerant and heroic, to subvert the kingdoms of Europe from Edinburgh to Budapest. With the Russian Revolution there was once more a state, potentially a great power, that repudiated the foundations of international society. 'It is permissible to suggest', Professor H. A. Smith has written, 'that the deepest significance of the Bolshevik revolution will in future be found, not in the changes which it introduced in Russia and elsewhere, but in its successful repudiation of the rule of law among the nations.'[5] For years the Soviet state was an outlaw, unrecognized by other powers for the good reason that they could not trust its acceptance of the rules of the society to which they belonged. It maintained an international revolutionary organization, the Third International, for undermining them.

But Communism evoked Fascism, so that once again in international society there was revolution and counter-revolution, each deriving strength from the hostility of the other. These other revolutionaries resembled gangsters rather than missionaries. One group, led by a bombastic journalist of mediocre political ability, seized the Italian state in 1922. Fascist Italy had a policy of aimless restlessness, pursued by illegal gun-running, subsidizing of terrorists in other countries and discreet countenancing of political assassination. It was Fascist Italy that lowered the standards of international intercourse after 1919, as Napoleon III had done after 1815. A more formidable group of gangsters seized the German state, and used these subversive methods more powerfully, in the service of a creed of racial hierarchy. 'Instead of a horizontal classification of European races, there must be a vertical one. This meant that a German élite was destined to be the *Herren*-class of Europe, and ultimately of the world.'[6] The ideological conflict that followed had some resemblances to the Wars of Religion. As Catholics, Lutherans and Calvinists fought a three-cornered struggle, so did the democracies, the Fascists and the Communists, with each party sometimes drawing nearer one of its rivals than the other. And when a temporary coalition of democracies and Communists had eliminated the Fascists in war, the conflict was simplified into a direct antagonism of the democracies and the Communists, each of them believing the other to be closer to the defeated Fascists than to itself.

These recurrent waves of international revolution, that is to say, of organized attempts to transform international society by force, by war or revolution or both, offer a different picture of

5. H. A. Smith, 'The Anarchy of Power', in *The Cambridge Journal*, Vol. I, No. 4, January 1948, p. 215.

6. W. Darré (later Reich Minister of Food and Agriculture), quoted in H. Rauschning, *Hitler Speaks*, Thornton Butterworth, London, 1939, pp. 43-4.

international society from that which we have been analysing so far. Instead of a loose company of sovereign states, it seems more of an organic unity; individuals feel international loyalties, which override national allegiance. But this more organic unity is only apparent, by a paradox, because the unity is sharply broken by a horizontal fracture. The unity of international society is thrown into sharpest relief when it is riven by an international civil war. Catholics hate Protestants, ultras hate Jacobins, Communists hate the bourgeoisie, with a fiercer passion than Frenchmen hate Germans or Americans hate Japanese. In 1565, when France and Spain were beginning to concert their policy against the forces of the Reformation, an Italian diplomat wrote:

Today Catholic sovereigns must not follow the same policy as before. Formerly friends and enemies have been distinguished according to frontiers and states, and have been called Italians, Germans, French, Spaniards, English and so on. Now we must say Catholics and heretics; and the Catholic prince has to have as his allies all Catholics in all countries, just as the heretics have for their allies and subjects all heretics, whether at home or abroad.[7]

Burke was struck by the corresponding stratification of loyalties throughout international society produced by the French Revolution. In 1832 the British ambassador in Vienna wrote, 'The principle of *mouvement* and that of repose are at war openly or underhand throughout Europe, and people are much more Liberal or the reverse than they are Frenchmen or Germans or Italians.'[8] The National Socialist Revolution was a marginal case. It generated a monstrous force because it raised to revolutionary intensity an ancient national feeling, the Germans' sense of superiority over other European peoples and especially over the Slavs. But its international appeal was correspondingly limited to the German minorities abroad, such ruling groups in Eastern Europe as had an interest in persecuting the Jews, and the embittered dregs of upper classes; Hitler's world-wide network of

7. Erich Marcks: *Die Zusammenkunft von Bayonne*, Trübner, Strasbourg, 1889, p. 14n. Author's translation from the Italian.
8. C. K. Webster, *The Foreign Policy of Palmerston*, Vol. 1, G. Bell, London, 1951, p. 177. The ambassador was Sir Frederick Lamb.

revolutionary unrest proved a flop. Communism has been much more truly an international movement, and if since 1945 the liberals of the West have been less easily seduced than formerly by the Soviet myth, Communism has gained more believers than it ever lost among the intelligentsia of Asia and Africa.

These international revolutionary doctrines transpose the melody of power politics into a new key. They introduce passion and fanaticism into calculations of political utility, and doctrine sometimes overrides or reinterprets interest. They blur the distinction between domestic and foreign policy; they transform diplomacy; and they transform war.

International relations are normally conducted between governments, which are supposed to represent their peoples, by diplomacy, which is the attempt to adjust conflicting interests by negotiation and mutual compromise. But international revolution, by making a stratification throughout international society, makes a potential stratification within every nation. A revolutionary power, in the sense of one that wishes to alter the foundations of international society, will assume that other governments do not represent their peoples, and will try to manipulate or take advantage of the potential stratification of loyalties within other countries.

Russia is in a strong position . . . because she can appeal in Asia to both governments and peoples. As a great power, she offers governments (who may fear their subjects) certain inducements to be her ally: as the champion of Communism, she offers to the mass of the people (who may dislike their governments) a transformation of their lives. The impunity with which it can play a double game is shown by the present propaganda of Messrs Bulganin and Khrushchev. They are representing themselves as venerators of Gandhi. Yet at home the authoritative Soviet writings still portray Gandhi as the great trickster, who betrayed the people to the capitalists.[9]

If the revolutionary power has small hope of winning the government, it can try to drive a wedge between the government and its people. Like the Assyrian general Rabshakeh, when he came to frighten Hezekiah of Judah into submission,[10] it will appeal over

9. *The Manchester Guardian*, 28 November 1955, p. 6.
10. The Old Testament, II Kings, Chapter 18, verses 26–36.

the heads of the government to the people. There were dramatic examples at the end of the First World War, first by Trotsky, when he made the Brest-Litovsk Conference between Soviet Russia and the central powers a platform to subvert the morale of the German and Austro-Hungarian armies, and secondly by Wilson, when in Rome in December 1918 he angered the Italian government whom he had failed to talk round by speaking directly to the Italian people.

Revolutionary politics tend to break down the important distinction between diplomacy and espionage. The effectiveness of diplomatic representation used in this way obviously increases with the weakness of the state where it operates: huge Soviet missions are more likely to bear fruit in Jakarta or Addis Ababa than in Berne or Brussels. And since men are prone to attribute to others their own political motives, revolutionary powers are likely to see the embassies of other powers as nests of spies, and to impose restrictions on diplomatic freedom. The French Directory violated international practice by dismissing envoys of foreign powers without reason given or because of their ideological distaste;[11] Soviet Russia imposes restrictions that make them virtual prisoners.

And if diplomacy is subordinated to subversive intrigue, it is subordinated also to propaganda. Diplomacy is the attempt to adjust conflicting interests by negotiation and compromise; propaganda is the attempt to sway the opinion that underlies and sustains the interests. Conversion therefore undercuts the task of compromise. Conferences with revolutionary powers tend to be, not meetings where statesmen strike bargains, but forums where positions are asserted, either simply 'for the record', or in a direct appeal to public opinion on the other side. It must be noted that Wilson's creed of 'open diplomacy' was revolutionary, which was why it aroused suspicion among diplomatists of the old school in Europe. Open diplomacy, if it means that all negotiation is to be conducted in public, tends inevitably to slip away from negotiation into propaganda, as the history of the United Nations has repeatedly shown.

International revolution also transforms the character of war.

11. *Diaries and Correspondence of the Earl of Malmesbury*, Vol. III, p. 347.

It blurs the distinctions between war and peace, international war and civil war, war and revolution.

A revolutionary power is morally and psychologically at war with its neighbours all the time, even if legally peace prevails, because it believes it has a mission to transform international society by conversion or coercion, and cannot admit that its neighbours have the same right to continued existence which it assumes for itself. Hence in revolutionary periods we find long tracts of time in which it is difficult to say whether there is peace or war: there is a diplomatic twilight of mutual suspicion and alarms, of hostile acts which do not amount to war, and of war which is prosecuted without observance of the due formalities. There are not frontal clashes but penetration and undermining, and under-hand war merges into full war without its having been declared. For a writer born in the year of the Spanish Armada and living through the Thirty Years War and the English Civil War, it seemed that this was the essential nature of war: '. . . as the nature of foul weather, lieth not in a shower or two of rain, but in an inclination thereto of many days together, so the nature of war, consisteth not in actual fighting, but in the known disposition thereto, during all the time there is no assurance to the contrary.'[12] This describes what, since 1945, we have called cold war. But there are many earlier examples. Europe was in a state of cold war for years before the Second World War broke out, at least since the Nazis succeeded in assassinating Dollfuss, the head of the government of a neighbouring friendly state, in 1934. Trotsky in 1918 tried to end the first international conference that Soviet Russia took part in by the famous declaration, 'No war! No peace!'[13] and though Russia was compelled to sign a peace, the slogan has continued to describe the general aim of Soviet diplomacy. And the England of Elizabeth I was in a state of cold war with Spain for nearly twenty years before Elizabeth expelled the Spanish ambassador in 1584 and Philip decided to launch an armada for the invasion of England.

12. T. Hobbes, *Leviathan*, J. M. Dent, London, 1943, p. 64.
13. 'We are going out of the war, but we feel ourselves compelled to refuse to sign the peace treaty', quoted in J. W. Wheeler-Bennett, *Brest-Litovsk: The Forgotten Peace*, Macmillan, London, 1938, p. 227.

One aspect of cold war is likely to be civil war. Many countries are fractured horizontally by the international revolution; these internal cleavages are likely to flare into war. An English states-man, looking back on what we call the Wars of Religion, naturally described them as 'The long Civil-Wars, at first of France, then of Germany, and lastly of England'.[14] The French Revolutionary Wars were accompanied by civil strife in all the states and cantons of Germany, Switzerland and Italy, as well as a civil war – the war of the Vendée – in France itself. The Second World War was likewise preceded, accompanied and followed by civil wars be-tween Fascists and anti-Fascists (among whom the Communists often gained the ascendancy) in Spain, Yugoslavia, Greece and elsewhere, and the resistance movement and liberation in France had something of the character of a civil war. And such civil wars will be fomented and encouraged (or will seem to be, for in an atmosphere of doctrinal passion the distinction between fact and surmise, fact and possibility, are other distinctions that become obliterated) from abroad. During the Spanish Civil War a Nationalist general said that the four columns marching on Republican Madrid would be aided by a 'fifth column' within,[15] and the phrase is useful to describe any body of men within a country whose loyalty is to the enemies of that country. In other language, Cromwell told Parliament in 1656 that Spain 'hath an interest in your bowels; he hath so. The Papists in England, – they have been accounted, ever since I was born, Spaniolised'.[16] Such an overriding international loyalty is, from the national point of view, nothing but treason; and treason and fear of treason are great marks of a period of international revolution.

International revolutions generate revolutionary wars, in the sense that their wars are tinged with doctrinal ferocity, and have unlimited aims. They tend to be not wars for defined objectives,

14. Sir William Temple, *Observations upon the United Provinces of the Netherlands*, first published 1673, G. N. Clark (ed.), Cambridge, 1932, p. 132.
15. *Survey of International Affairs*, 1937, Vol. II, O.U.P. London, 1938, p. 59.
16. Speech to Parliament, 17 September 1656, in W. C. Abbott (ed.), *The Writings and Speeches of Oliver Cromwell*, Vol. IV, Harvard University Press, Cambridge, 1947, p. 264.

but crusades or wars for righteousness. They aim, not at a negotiated settlement, but at a 'Carthaginian peace' or 'unconditional
surrender' – the two kinds of peace the Western powers have
imposed after the general wars of the twentieth century which
they happen to have won, and which for all their faults were
considerably less ferocious than Germany would have imposed if
she had won. And the wars of international revolution usually lead
to domestic revolution, on the side of the defeated party. In the
Wars of Religion, when revolution meant a violent change of
ruler and creed, defeated rulers could expect to lose their thrones
or their heads, like Mary Queen of Scots and Frederick Elector
Palatine and Charles I, and undefeated rulers lived under the
shadow of assassination like Coligny and William the Silent and
Henry IV and Wallenstein. Since Bismarck's time, every war
between great powers has ended with a revolution on the losing
side, whether erupting from forces within the defeated state or
imposed by the victors, and ranging in violence and intensity
from the establishment of the dual monarchy in defeated Austria
after 1866 and the controlled democratization of Japan after 1945
to the Bolshevik Revolution in defeated Russia in 1917 and the
annihilation of the Nazi regime in Germany in 1945. We cannot
now imagine a great war which would not aim at overthrowing the
regime of our adversary.

We have contrasted international revolution with normal international relations: the states-system before 1789 seemed normal
in retrospect to Burke, and the years between 1870 and 1914 seem
normal to us, periods of law and custom and calculable power
politics. It might well be asked why unrevolutionary international
politics should be regarded as more normal than revolutionary,
since the history of international society has been fairly equally
divided between the two.[17] It is worth remarking that international revolution has never for long maintained itself against

17. If, taking conventional dates, we regard 1492–1517, 1648–1792 and
1871–1914 as unrevolutionary, and 1517–1648, 1792–1871 and 1914–60 as
revolutionary, there are 256 years of international revolution to 212 unrevolutionary. If it be argued that religion was not the dominant influence on
international politics until after 1559, the numerical balance is almost
exactly reversed.

national interest. Doctrinal considerations have always within two generations been overridden by *raison d'état*.

No power has ever been able to limit its alliances by doctrinal considerations. The infidel Turk became a weight in the Western balance of power even before he captured Constantinople, and Francis I of France and Elizabeth I of England made notorious alliances with him in the course of their conflicts with the Habsburg power. Catholic France consistently supported the Protestant powers in Germany against the Emperor, and Richelieu encouraged and financed the intervention of Sweden in the Thirty Years War. Napoleon, the child of the Revolution, ended by making a dynastic marriage with the daughter of the Habsburgs. Republican France allied with Tsarist Russia in 1892; bourgeois France allied with Soviet Russia in 1935. A proverb was current in seventeenth-century France, that in defence of one's interests it is permissible to enter an alliance not only with heretics and Turks, but with the Devil himself; Hitler once said that he would accept the same ally against France; and Churchill said: 'If Hitler invaded Hell I would at least make a favourable reference to the Devil in the House of Commons.'[18] In the last two cases the Devil proved to be Soviet Russia. The Nazi-Soviet Pact of 1939 which inaugurated the Second World War was perhaps the most startling example in international history of the flouting of boasted ideological principles for the sake of immediate national interest.

It has been a chief effect of international revolution to give a new drive to the imperialism of a great power. The Counter-Reformation became confounded with the politics of Habsburg aggrandizement. The cause of the Reformation, having ministered in turn to the territorial appetites of the German princes and Sweden, and to the commercial interests of the Dutch and the English, was represented at last by the very cynical 'Protestant hero' Frederick the Great. The cosmopolitan idealism of the French Revolution became quickly transformed into Napoleonic imperialism; the revolutionary element in the Nazi movement was inseparable from German imperialism. The Communist

18. W. S. Churchill, *The Second World War*, Vol. III, Cassell, London, 1950, p. 331.

8 : Vital Interests and Prestige

In a system of power politics the chief duty of each government is regarded as being to preserve the interests of the people it rules and represents against the competing interests of other peoples. There are certain things that a power deems essential to its continued independence; these are its vital interests, which it will go to war to defend. When powers agree to submit their disputes to arbitration (i.e. settlement by a third party) or to judicial settlement (i.e. settlement by the Permanent Court of International Justice created in 1921), they nearly always expressly exclude disputes affecting their vital interests. Every power is confident that its interests are compatible in a general way with the interests of the community of powers, but its own interests are its first concern. A Foreign Minister is chosen and paid to look after the interests of his country, and not to be a delegate for the human race.

The vital interests of a state, furthermore, are what it thinks them to be and not what another power says them to be. It is no good a satisfied power (let us say, Philip II's Spain) telling a dissatisfied power (let us say, Elizabethan England) that its legitimate interests can be fully secured within the existing arrangement of power, for there will be no possibility of agreement between what Spain calls 'legitimate' and what England calls 'vital'. Or to take a different example, Ribbentrop's attempt to teach Britain what its vital interests were in the nineteen-thirties might be contrasted, both as to the purpose in view and the degree of success achieved, with Churchill's refusal to teach America what its vital interests were in the days of 1940–41 before Pearl Harbor.

It follows that vital interests are sometimes uncertain and apt to change. In the nineteenth century it was a British vital interest that Russia should not have Constantinople; but in 1915, under the stress of a common war against Germany, Britain consented to Russia's obtaining Constantinople, and it was only the overthrow of the Tsarist regime by the Revolution that invalidated the agreement. Imperial Germany regarded maritime expansion as a vital interest; Nazi Germany regarded this as an illusion and pursued expansion in Eastern Europe instead. In 1934 Mussolini regarded it as a vital interest to prevent the union of Austria with Germany and moved four divisions to the Brenner when Dollfuss was murdered; in 1938 he acquiesced in it, and received in acknowledgement the telegram from Dollfuss's murderer, 'Mussolini, I shall never forget this.' But a settled and mature power generally has settled and agreed notions about its vital interests. There was long substantial agreement among all parties in Britain about the necessity of defending Belgium, Gibraltar, the Suez Canal and Singapore. Moreover, whatever their personal cranks, statesmen usually end up as the agents of national interest. Gladstone was bitterly assailed in his day as the betrayer of the Empire's interests, but it was his government that in 1882 occupied Egypt. Lloyd George was regarded as the most pacifist minister in the Asquith government, but it was he who broke the peace party in the Cabinet in 1914 by coming round to the necessity of supporting France, and who organized the first victory over Germany. Neville Chamberlain was thought by his opponents to have endangered British interests in a manner unique in history, in order to appease the dictators, but it was he who declared war on Hitler. As Lord Grey of Fallodon wrote, in great affairs there is much more 'in the minds of the events (if such an expression may be used) than in the minds of the chief actors'.

'Vital interests' is a phrase that did not become usual until the latter part of the nineteenth century. The older expression used to be 'the dignity, honour, and interests of such-and-such a crown'. The notion of a state, a power, having dignity and honour belonged to the politics of the dynastic age, when the state was legally indistinguishable from the King, and foreign affairs were his personal relations with his fellows. In these circumstances there was reality in saying that if Louis XIV made a treaty with James II, his honour was involved in its fulfilment. But honour is an ambiguous word. It can mean allegiance to accepted standards of conduct (as it usually has in the English tradition), or it can mean pride and consciousness of status (as it usually has meant in the German tradition). The honour of powers in international relations tends to be the latter kind, and has perhaps become increasingly so since the monarchical state was replaced by the democratic or mass state, where the obligation of honour is diffused and lost among an anonymous electorate. The phrase 'national honour' is coming to have an old-fashioned and rhetorical flavour, and 'national interest' describes more truly what the motive of powers really is.

Closely bound up with the idea of 'honour' is the idea of 'prestige'. Honour is the halo round interests; prestige is the halo round power.

What prestige is, it would be hard to describe precisely. It may be nothing more substantial than an effect produced upon the international imagination – in other words, an illusion. It is, however, far from being a mere bubble of vanity; for the nation that possesses great prestige is thereby enabled to have its way, and to bring things to pass which it could never hope to achieve by its own forces. Prestige draws material benefits mysteriously in its train. Political wisdom will never despise it. Usually it is gained slowly and lost quickly. The unexpected happens. Some upstart minor power commits the sin of impudence without being crushed forthwith by the falling skies. Or a single battle is lost, as at Tours, or Granson, or Valmy. Thereupon the nation that has been predominant becomes suddenly aware that its counsels, admonitions and threats are no longer heeded, and that the awe in which it was so lately held, is being transferred rapidly to another.[1]

Prestige is one of the imponderables of international politics, but it is too closely connected with power to be considered as belonging to the moral order. It is the influence derived from power. And unless the power is *present* power there can be little prestige. Deference to historical importance and gratitude for past achievement are even less apparent in international politics than in other kinds of politics. In 1953 Monsieur Mendès-France warned the French National Assembly that no country, however glorious,

1. F. S. Oliver, *The Endless Adventure*, Vol. II, Macmillan, London, 1931, pp. 123-4.

could found authority on the respect inspired by its past. 'Sacrifices accepted or battles won in the past can stand as examples but they cannot form barter-money for our diplomacy.'[2] And Lord Keynes gave the same warning to the House of Lords when describing his visit to the United States to negotiate the American loan in 1945:

Men's sympathies and less calculated impulses are drawn from their memories of comradeship, but their contemporary acts are generally directed towards influencing the future and not towards pensioning the past ... We soon discovered, therefore, that it was not our past performance or our present weakness but our future prospects of recovery and our intention to face the world boldly that we had to demonstrate. Our American friends were interested not in our wounds, though incurred in the common cause, but in our convalescence.[3]

'Prestige', says E. H. Carr, 'means the recognition by other people of your strength. Prestige (which some people scoff at) is enormously important; for if your strength is recognized, you can generally achieve your aims without having to use it.'[4] The matter does not quite end here, because prestige is not only something that other people recognize, it is also something that you assert; and it can be asserted wisely or unwisely, necessarily or unnecessarily. The wise enjoyment of prestige may be shown when a power refrains from using a military victory to aggrandize itself. In the Napoleonic War Britain captured all the French colonies; at the Vienna Settlement it returned most of them to France. 'I am sure,' said Castlereagh, 'our reputation on the Continent, as a feature of strength, power, and confidence, is of more real moment to us than an acquisition thus made'[5] – a classic statement of the value of prestige. Bismarck followed the same policy by refusing

2. Speech as Prime Minister-designate to the National Assembly, 3 June 1953, in *Le Monde*, 4 June 1953, p. 3.

3. Speech in the House of Lords, 18 December 1945, *Parliamentary Debates*, Fifth Series, Vol. 88, cols. 781–2.

4. E. H. Carr, *Great Britain as a Mediterranean Power*, Cust Foundation Lecture, University College, Nottingham, 1937, p. 10.

5. C. K. Webster, *The Foreign Policy of Castlereagh 1812–1815*, G. Bell, London, 1931, p. 273.

to annex Bohemia after the defeat of Austria in 1866, with the result that he bound the Habsburg Empire to Germany for the rest of its time. But prestige is often most asserted where it is least needed, for example when success has unbalanced the judgement of a country or its rulers. The assertive and aggressive policy of the Kaiser's Germany after Bismarck's fall wove itself round questions of prestige; the building of the German navy was largely a prestige matter; Germany's predominance was recognized by everybody, but Germany could not refrain from exploiting it. Similarly, after the victory at Stalingrad in 1942 gave Russia confidence that it would in the end crush Germany, Soviet policy has been guided on many issues by considerations of the external, and perhaps even more of the internal, prestige of the regime. And it seemed that the Chinese renewed heavy fighting in Korea just before the armistice in 1953 for reasons of prestige, in order that the armistice should be signed when they were taking the military initiative, and thus should not appear to have been forced upon them.

Thus prestige, like honour, is an ambiguous term. It may mean deliberately refraining from exploiting your power because you prefer the advantages of not having done so; and in this sense it comes very near to being magnanimity, which as Burke said is not seldom the truest wisdom in politics. Or it may mean forcing other people to admit your power on every occasion; and in this sense it is simply an extreme policy of asserting your 'honour' and interests. Sir Harold Nicolson has very well summed up the two by saying that one is 'power based upon reputation', and the other is 'reputation based upon power'.[6]

6. H. Nicolson, *The Meaning of Prestige*, C.U.P., Cambridge, 1937, p. 9. This draft is basically the corresponding chapter of the original *Power Politics*, with a number of additional quotations and illustrations. Eds.

9 : International Anarchy

We have seen how international history is punctuated by wars. The great dividing lines are the general wars, which may be defined as those that involve all the existing great powers. Every general war begins as a local war, and widens its scope as each great power in turn finds that its interests would be endangered if it stayed out. Sometimes it wants to further its aggressive interests, as in the case of Italy in 1915 and of Japan in 1941; sometimes it wants to defend its existing interests, as in the case of the United States in 1917 or of Britain and France in 1939. But between the general wars are many minor wars that mark the changing pattern of power. The Crimean War (1854–6) is the classic example of a war involving more than two great powers which nevertheless stopped short of becoming a general war. The Franco-Prussian War (1870–71) is the classic example of a war between two great powers which decisively changed the balance of power without other powers having been directly involved. The Italo-Abyssinian War (1935–6) is a classic example of a war between a great power and a small power which decisively altered international relations. The quarrels between small powers seldom harm anybody except themselves, and they have never in history occasioned a general war. It is the great powers that create international upheavals. In 1912–13 the Balkan powers fought two bitter wars among themselves, while the great powers held the ring. It was when Austria-Hungary quarrelled with Serbia, and Russia came to Serbia's aid, that the First World War began.

Until the creation of the League of Nations, international law had no alternative but to accept war as a legitimate relationship between states irrespective of the justice or injustice of its cause. The League rigidly restricted the conditions under which war might legally be resorted to, but did not outlaw it. The Kellogg

Pact of 1928, midway between the First and Second World Wars, by which war was renounced as an instrument of national policy, is perhaps the most extraordinary example in history of the contrast between the way powers talk under the pressure of enlightened public opinion and the way they act under the pressure of conflicting national interests.

Thus the international scene is properly described as an anarchy – a multiplicity of powers without a government. In the years after the First World War there was anxious inquiry among enlightened men concerning the causes of war, 'as though war' (A. J. P. Taylor has caustically observed) 'were the most unusual, instead of the most regular, of human activities'.[1] The fundamental cause of war is not historic rivalries, nor unjust peace settlements, nor nationalist grievances, nor competitions in armaments, nor imperialism, nor poverty, nor the economic struggle for markets and raw materials, nor the contradictions of capitalism nor the aggressiveness of Fascism or Communism; though some of these may have occasioned particular wars. The fundamental cause is the absence of international government; in other words, the anarchy of sovereign states. This was the example brought forward by the seventeenth-century philosopher Thomas Hobbes to support his argument that the natural condition of mankind (that is to say, their condition before society was established) was one of 'war of every man against every man'. Even if there is no historical evidence that *individuals* have ever been generally in such a condition of war one against another, he said,

yet in all times kings, and persons of sovereign authority, because of their independency, are in continual jealousies, and in the state and posture of gladiators; having their weapons pointing, and their eyes fixed on one another; that is, their forts, garrisons, and guns, upon the frontiers of their kingdoms; and continual spies upon their neighbours; which is a posture of war.[2]

In such a situation, mutual mistrust is fundamental, and one power can never have an assurance that another power is not malevolent. Consequently, with the best will in the world no

1. A. J. P. Taylor, *Rumours of War*, p. 256.
2. T. Hobbes, *Leviathan*, p. 65.

power can surrender any part of its security and liberty to another power. This is the situation of 'Hobbesian fear' which Herbert Butterfield has called 'the absolute predicament and the irreducible dilemma' of international politics.[3] Wars are fought for many different causes; some are blundered into through a maze of mixed policies, as historians have usually seen the Crimean War; some are coldly willed and planned by a single power, as Hitler undoubtedly willed the Second World War. But all particular causes of war operate within the context of international anarchy and the Hobbesian fear. When Thucydides reflected on the causes of the Peloponnesian War, he said he would describe the dispute which led to the outbreak of hostilities, but added: 'The real though unavowed cause I believe to have been the growth of the Athenian power, which terrified the Lacedaemonians and forced them to war . . .'[4]

Anarchy is the characteristic that distinguishes international politics from ordinary politics. The study of international politics presupposes absence of a system of government, as the study of domestic politics presupposes the existence of one. Qualifications are necessary: there is a system of international law and there are international institutions to modify or complicate the workings of power politics. But it is roughly the case that, while in domestic politics the struggle for power is governed and circumscribed by the framework of law and institutions, in international politics law and institutions are governed and circumscribed by the struggle for power. This indeed is the justification for calling international politics 'power politics' *par excellence*.

In the past two or three generations much emphasis has been laid on the economic factor in history and politics. This has provided a new dimension of historical interpretation, but it has led to the neglect, perhaps, of the power-political factor – of the influence exerted by the existence of international anarchy itself. We do not have to subscribe to the follies of militarism, asserting the goodness or beauty of war, or that 'the struggle for existence' is the mechanism of progress, if we recognize that war has been no

3. H. Butterfield, *History and Human Relations*, Collins, London, 1951, p. 19; also *Christianity and History*, G. Bell, London, 1949, pp. 89–90.
4. *The Peloponnesian War*, Book I, 23, p. 16.

less important in historical causation than economic needs. Conflict has been an essential factor in the development of national consciousness and statehood: we need only remember how Scotland was hammered into a nation by English aggression, how France and England were hammered into nations by their mutual warfare, how Germany was hammered into a national state by French aggression, how the American nation had its birth of freedom in one great war and a new birth of freedom in another. And international pressures short of war (the threat of war or the indirect effects of other people's wars) have been a normal condition of political growth. The British conquest of Canada in 1761 removed the only military threat to the American colonies and so made their independence a practical possibility; and conversely a hundred years later the American Civil War produced a concentration of military force in the United States which alarmed the Canadian provinces into federation. The Swiss federal constitutions of 1848 and 1874 were largely a reaction against the German march towards unity at the expense of freedom from the Revolution of 1848 through the wars of 1866 and 1870. The federation of the Australian colonies in 1900 was largely a response to German territorial acquisitiveness in the western Pacific. And the establishment of the North Atlantic Treaty Organization in 1949 was entirely due to the external pressure of Soviet Russia.

It is not only governments that are in a state of potential enmity. The patriotism of ordinary people can have its ugly side, if it is joined to suspicion and ignorance of other countries. The growth of democracy and socialism has probably tended to accentuate this, by spreading among the middle classes and the masses the sentiments of national pride that used to be confined to kings and courts; and in most countries there is a powerful section of journalism that thrives by promoting distrust of foreigners and the illusion of self-sufficiency. But it is important to realize that the problem of international goodwill goes deeper than the mere dispelling of ignorance, vitally important as this is. Knowledge alone does not engender benevolence. During the inter-War period great hopes were founded on foreign travel and inter-national intercourse between ordinary persons as a means of promoting international goodwill; but it was not shown why it should not lead just as much to international dislike, and the German tourists of the nineteen-thirties were in fact primarily spies and fifth columnists.

In a world of independent sovereign powers, war is the only means by which each of them can in the last resort defend its vital interests. This is equally true whether it considers its interests to require pacification or aggression; the distinction indeed is usually a matter of centuries and not of morals, for the dissatisfied power is often seeking to take what the satisfied power took by aggression previously; and defence as well as attack is a mode of war. Hence the grain of truth in the famous dictum of the Prussian military writer Clausewitz, that 'War is the continuation of political relations by other means',[5] and the complementary saying of a modern English writer, that 'diplomacy is potential war'.[6] Consequently it appears that while wars are occasioned by particular circumstances, it is impossible to say that without those particular circumstances the wars would not have occurred. The causes of war are inherent in power politics. Alexander Hamilton stated this very clearly when he was urging that the original Thirteen United States would only avoid wars among themselves if they agreed to federate: 'To presume a want of motives for such contests as an argument against their existence, would be to forget that men are ambitious, vindictive, and rapacious. To look for a continuation of harmony between a number of independent, unconnected sovereignties in the same neighbourhood, would be to disregard the uniform course of human events, and to set at defiance the accumulated experience of ages.'[7]

5. J. J. Graham (trans.), *On War*, Vol. I, Routledge, London, 1949, Book I, 24, p. 23.
6. R. G. Hawtrey, *Economic Aspects of Sovereignty*, Longmans, London, 1952, p. 72.
7. *The Federalist*, No. 6, p. 27. This draft is a slight expansion of the corresponding chapter of the original *Power Politics*. Eds.

10 : International Society

Hitherto we have been discussing the various classes and kinds of power. We must now consider the society they compose. It has been variously called the family of nations, the states-system, the society of states, the international community.

There are those who hold that international society is so lacking in the requirements of what we normally understand by society that it is not a society at all. They declare that the condition of international relations, because of the prevalence of war and conflict, is best described as 'international anarchy'. If anarchy is understood to mean the absence of common government, then this is indeed precisely the feature in which international politics differ from domestic politics. But if anarchy means complete disorder, it is not a true description of international relations. There is cooperation in international affairs as well as conflict; there are a diplomatic system and international law and international institutions which complicate or modify the workings of power politics; and there are even rules to limit the wars, which have not been entirely without influence. It can scarcely be denied that there is a system of states, and to admit that there is a system comes halfway to admitting that there is a society; for a society is a number of individuals joined in a system of relationships for certain common purposes. It is interesting to note the eagerness with which newly independent states seek admission to the international system in the belief that it is a society, by exchanging diplomatic representatives and gaining admission to the United Nations; and conversely, how the Afrikaners of South Africa, who throughout their history have sought isolation and freedom from the shackles of international obligation, have found it impossible to obtain.

There are others who not only accept the existence of

international society, but believe that it is evolving steadily towards the more familiar kind of society that we find in the nation-state. The first of the two positions, the denial of international society, leads to an argument about words. The second leads to an argument about facts, and is therefore more dangerous.

International society is a society unlike any other, for it is the most comprehensive form of society on earth. It has four peculiarities: 1. It is a unique society composed of the other, more fully organized societies which we call states. States are its prime and immediate members, even if there is a sense in which its ultimate members are men.

2. The number of its members is consequently always small. Almost all national societies count their members in millions; international society has not exceeded two hundred. After the Peace of Westphalia in 1648 it perhaps reached its highest, with some 200. In the nineteenth century the number dropped rapidly. The reorganization of Europe along national lines reduced Italy and Germany to single states, before its opposite effect on the Ottoman Empire, Austria-Hungary, Russia and the United Kingdom had run its course, and before the admission of non-European states had truly begun. Between the establishment of the German Empire in 1871 and the First Hague Conference in 1899 international society had less than fifty members, a European core of twenty, another twenty in the separate American system, and a doubtful fringe of two or three Asian states, with whom some powers had exchanged legations, but who were not yet generally regarded as belonging to the family of nations. Since the Hague Conference the number has steadily swelled again.[1]

3. The members of international society are more heterogeneous than individuals, and the heterogeneity is accentuated by their fewness. There is great disparity between them in territorial size, geographical position and resources, population, cultural ideals and social arrangements. 'When one has said that all states possess territory, and that they all claim to exercise sovereignty over societies of persons attached to them by the legal bond of

1. For the latest figures, see above, Ch. 5, p. 61.

nationality, it is not easy to think of other features common to them all.'[2] There is no average state.

4. The members of international society are, on the whole, immortals. States do die or disappear, from time to time, but for the most part they far outlive the span of human life. They are partnerships of the living with the dead and with posterity. Their policies are based on the expectation of survival, and they see it as their duty to protect their vital interests. Our common mortality makes us more interdependent than we might otherwise be. As Homer's description of Olympus shows, a society of immortals will be looser than one of mortals. Such a society cannot easily coerce a recalcitrant member if consensus breaks down, and it cannot ask of its members the self-sacrifice which states in certain circumstances ask of individuals. Nor can it attribute moral responsibility to its members in the same way as it can to individuals. There are moral difficulties about indicting a whole nation, because it makes the passive majority suffer for the acts of the criminal minority, and future generations for the sins of their fathers.

The most essential evidence for the existence of an international society is the existence of international law. Every society has law, which is the system of rules laying down the rights and duties of its members. Consequently, those who deny the existence of international society begin by denying the reality of international law. They say that international law is not 'true' law (because they define 'law' in a way which excludes international law), or they argue that it is abstract stuff consistently ignored by states in practice. And on the other side, those who imagine international society is steadily turning into something like domestic society see international law as a kind of 'primitive' law steadily becoming like law within the state.[3] But here again, the first ignore the evidence and the second exaggerate it to suit their wishful preconceptions. International law is a law of a peculiar kind, the law

2. J. L. Brierly, *The Outlook for International Law*, Clarendon Press, Oxford, 1944, p. 41.

3. Lawyers call this 'municipal' law, to distinguish it from international law.

of a society divided politically into a multiplicity of sovereign states. It may be that the historic logic of international law is to become backed by international government, like municipal law. But many writers who verge towards this conclusion wistfully hasten to add that international government is out of the question and that international law must always be the law between sovereign states.

1. The subjects of international law are states, not individuals. It is states alone that are 'international persons'. International society is the sum-total of those who possess international personality.

2. The purpose of international law is to define the rights and duties of one state, acting on behalf of its nationals, towards other states. In other words, it is not to regulate all international intercourse between private individuals, but to delimit the respective spheres within which each state is entitled to exercise its own authority. This means to say that it can never cover the most important matters relating to the maintenance of political power. These are reserved within the domestic jurisdiction of states.[4]

3. International law is a system of customary law. It is the sum of the rights and obligations established between states by treaties, tacit convention and custom; and even a treaty depends ultimately upon the customary rule that its terms are binding upon the parties who have made it.

4. The bulk of international law consists of treaties. But these are contracts between those who sign them. If legislation is the making of laws by a person or assembly entitled to make laws binding the whole community, there is no such thing as international legislation. For treaties bind only those who have made them. International society has developed something comparable to legislation in the form of multilateral treaties, either dealing with matters of general interest or creating international organs. Such are the Hague and Geneva Conventions dealing with the laws of warfare; but these engagements are binding only on those who have accepted them, and are often indeed not ratified by the very states whose representatives have signed them in the first place.

4. League of Nations Covenant Article 15; United Nations Charter Article 2(7).

5. International law has no agents for its enforcement, except the states themselves. It lacks an executive. This means to say, that cooperative self-help is as far as it can get in making itself effective. The members of international society never reach the point where, like good men in frontier society waiting for the sheriff to appear, they must 'take the law into their own hands'; because there is no sheriff and the law is never in anybody else's hands but their own. This is the point of the famous joke in *Punch* in the crisis of 1914, when the old lady who was told that war seemed imminent said, 'Oh no, the powers will intervene.'

6. International law has no judiciary with compulsory juris-diction. The Hague Conference of 1907 established the Perma-nent Court of Arbitration, which became the Permanent Court of International Justice under the League and (by a tiresome and unnecessary change of name) the International Court of Justice under the UN. But its jurisdiction extends only to cases which the parties have agreed to refer to it. It is true that they have provided for states recognizing its jurisdiction as compulsory *ipso facto* in certain kinds of legal dispute, but these kinds are of minor importance, and most states which have made such recognition have hedged it about with reservations to weaken it. In fact, the number of cases brought before the International Court has steadily dwindled.

The moral and aspiring aspect of international law is best seen in the law of war. Sometimes it has set up a standard to which international anarchy should conform, sometimes it has fallen back abreast of it in acquiescence. Until the middle of the seven-teenth century, international politics were haunted by the tradi-tional Christian distinction between just and unjust war. It is a distinction very difficult to apply in practice, because in almost all wars each combatant is convinced of the justice of his own cause, and in few wars does even the neutral observer see all the justice concentrated on one side. In the eighteenth century it came to be accepted, therefore, that every war must be treated as if it were just on both sides; and international law came to accept war as a legitimate relationship between states, irrespective of the justice of its origin.

With the Covenant of the League of Nations, the pendulum

swung back again. It modified the law of war in two ways. 1. It declared that 'Any war or threat of war, whether immediately affecting any of the Members of the League or not, is hereby declared a matter of concern to the whole League' (Article 11). This implied that all states alike were endangered by any disturbance to the peace of the world, and that the League collectively or any power individually might intervene to stop it. The principle was put in a popular form in Litvinov's famous dictum, 'Peace is indivisible'. If this meant that henceforward there could be no local wars, because any local war would at once become general, it is obviously untrue: only the Sino-Japanese War and the German-Polish War have since become general, and there have been at least twice as many which have been localized, including one, the Chaco War between Paraguay and Bolivia (1933–5), which never endangered other powers at all. If it meant that any local war was likely to set up a chain-reaction which might culminate in a general war, it was saying what had been no less the case in previous centuries.

2. The Covenant laid down that members of the League must seek to settle disputes by certain peaceful procedures; and that if a member of the League went to war in disregard of these procedures, 'it shall *ipso facto* be deemed to have committed an act of war against all other members of the League' (Article 16). This resumed the old distinction between just and unjust wars by making a simple procedural test the basis for a distinction between legitimate and illegitimate wars. But the distinction was ineffectual unless the other members of the League did in practice treat a state resorting to war in disregard of its covenants as if it had gone to war with them all; and this they lacked the moral solidarity to do.

The Kellogg Pact of 1928 (whose proper name was the General Treaty for the Renunciation of War) carried the law of war still higher. It was signed by a majority of the powers of the world and all the great powers, and they renounced war as an instrument of national policy. Yet this did not, as is sometimes said, 'outlaw' war by making all war illegal. War remains legitimate between signatories of the Paris Pact and non-signatories, as when Paraguay in 1933 declared war on Bolivia which had not signed the pact, or between signatories and any signatory who had violated the pact, as when Britain and France declared war in 1939 on Germany. War remains legitimate as an act of *international* policy, as in collective action under the Covenant or the United Nations Charter. Above all, war remains legitimate in self-defence. This was a generous loophole for legitimate war. 'Every nation alone is competent to decide whether circumstances require recourse to war in self-defence,' declared the American Secretary of State at the time.[5] The United States declared that self-defence covered the Monroe Doctrine; Britain, that it covered the Suez Canal. Japan later declared that she undertook the conquest of Manchuria in self-defence, and the Germans who were tried for violation of the Kellogg Pact by the War Crimes Tribunal at Nuremberg made the same plea. The plea was rejected, because it was decided that they had been guilty of waging aggressive war.

This was the first example in the history of international society of the leaders of a sovereign power being tried for planning and waging aggressive war defined as a crime. It was not a case of condemning them according to law made after the event, for it was enforcement of the law laid down in the Kellogg Pact. Nor was the moral significance of the Nuremberg verdicts invalidated by their having been imposed by the victors upon the vanquished, by interested parties. Such a judgement ignores the part played by political power in the development of law and freedom: Magna Carta was imposed by a rebellious baronage to codify their own interests, and the emancipation of the slaves in the United States was imposed upon the slave-owning states as an act of war by the free states. The paradox of the Kellogg Pact is simpler and more obvious. It was necessary, to decide authoritatively that the General Treaty for the Renunciation of War had been violated, to fight and win the greatest war in history. There could be no more striking evidence of the place of war as an institution of international society.

The institutions of international society are according to its nature. We may enumerate them as diplomacy, alliances, guarantees, war and neutrality.

5. Note of 23 June 1928, quoted in F. P. Walters, *A History of the League of Nations*, Vol. I, O.U.P., London, 1952, p. 385.

11 : Diplomacy

Diplomacy is the system and the art of communication between powers. The diplomatic system is the master-institution of international relations. It may be conveniently divided under two heads, resident embassies and conferences.

Probably all civilizations have known the use of ambassadors between independent powers. But the practice of establishing permanent, that is, resident embassies in one another's capitals is a Western European invention. It grew up in Italy in the fifteenth century, where it quickly proved itself an incomparable method of communication in a close-knit political world of shifting alliances. In contrast with the old method of sending a special envoy at a particular crisis, the network of resident agents had the advantage of what is now called a 'hot line' between the capitals of every power. The utility and efficiency of the system made it spread generally among the powers beyond the Alps in the sixteenth century. It is one of the ways of marking the development of the modern states-system out of medieval Christendom. Thus the right of legation was established, which is the principle that every power is entitled to send diplomatic agents to represent its interests in other states, and reciprocally to *receive* such agents. It has never been agreed in international law that there is a corresponding duty on independent states to receive embassies from other powers, but in the nineteenth century the great powers none the less forcibly imposed the system on reluctant states in Asia, and thus extended the states-system from Europe to the world at large.

A diplomatic minister has privileges in the country he is sent to, of a kind to assure his dignity and comfort and make possible the free exercise of his functions. He is broadly immune from local jurisdiction. His person is inviolable as long as his conduct is correct: he may not suffer arrest, or be compelled to appear in court without his own consent. He is exempt from taxation. His archives and official correspondence are inviolable when carried by his own couriers (the 'diplomatic bag'). These immunities are extended, by courtesy if not by right, to his family and in diminishing degrees to his staff. Moreover, his official residence is itself inviolable. It is not correct to say that an embassy possesses extra-territoriality in the sense of being an enclave of foreign territory, for it seems to be agreed that in exceptional circumstances the authorities of the state where the embassy is situated may force an entry. It became established doctrine in Europe that embassies do not have the right of granting asylum to political refugees; but the contrary practice continued in less settled parts of the world, especially in Latin America, where political refugees are numerous.

To establish these and similar rules has taken centuries, and the history of diplomacy has many entertaining cases of diplomatic agents seeking to cloak scandalous behaviour under their immunity. The most recent international agreement about them is the Vienna Convention on Diplomatic Relations of 1961, negotiated by some eighty governments. There will be uncertainty and disputed interpretations as long as independent powers remain. But these immunities have arisen because they are mutually useful, and their reciprocity creates the guarantee that they will be respected. A power that violates the privileges of foreign diplomatists invites reprisals against its own diplomatists abroad. On the other hand, the ability to exact reciprocity varies with the circumstances and especially with the relative strength of the powers concerned. When Chinese troops and the Boxer rebels attacked the foreign embassies in Peking in 1900, China received brutal retribution from the great powers. When the Chinese Red Guards attacked the Soviet Embassy in Peking in 1967, the reaction of the Soviet Union was confined to verbal protests. During the Soviet repression of the Hungarian Revolution of 1956, Imre Nagy found asylum in the Yugoslav Embassy: he came out under a safe conduct guaranteed by the Hungarian government to the Yugoslav government, was arrested by the Soviet Military Command, and taken off to his death.

Cardinal Mindszenty at the same time took asylum in the US legation, where he remained until September 1971.

The Congress of Vienna arrived at agreement on four classes of diplomatic agent: ambassadors, envoys extraordinary and ministers plenipotentiary, ministers resident, and chargés d'affaires. The word 'legation' subsequently became specialized to denote the official mission and residence of a diplomatic agent lower than ambassador. The status of diplomatic agent originally corresponded in rough measure with the classes of power, so that great powers would exchange ambassadors, and small powers be content with ministers. The United States for its part, disapproving on the whole of foreign relations, made it a rule until 1893 not to appoint agents of higher rank than minister. But in the twentieth century there has been a universal levelling-up, in the interests of national self-esteem everywhere. Now the majority of powers, including the United States, exchange ambassadors, though the Chinese People's Republic has kept her diplomatic missions in the West at a lower status as a mark of doctrinal disapproval. Thus the impulses of international egalitarianism have eroded an external mark of great power rank at a time when the real preponderance of the Great Powers has been increasing.

There has been a parallel inflation in the size of diplomatic missions, owing to the increasing number of fields in which international intercourse is conducted. The embassy of a great power in the capital of another great power today has a staff of many hundreds, and an organization reflecting the governmental machine at home, and with military, naval, air, commercial, financial, cultural, press and other attachés.

The diplomatic agent has a threefold function: communication, negotiation, information. He is the representative of his own government, who transmits and expounds its messages to the government to which he is accredited and he transmits messages from the foreign government back to his own government, with his comments. According as he may be instructed, he negotiates with the foreign government. And he sends back to his own government all the information he can obtain about the country where he is stationed that may be relevant to the making of policy.

The sending back of information is the one of the three

functions which does not involve a relationship with the foreign government. It is a function that the ambassador shares with the spy, who is a clandestine agent in search of secret information, authorized by his government but disavowed if captured. A Dutch diplomatist of the seventeenth century described the overlapping in a famous sentence: 'On the one hand, the ambassador is a *messenger of peace*; on the other hand, *he is an honourable spy*.'[1] Serving as an honourable spy, he explained, meant not only penetrating secrets, but also being able to give affairs a turn that suited the interests of one's own government by bribing or corrupting the ministers of the government one is sent to; though he condemned the promoting of treason or assassination and the fomenting of rebellion or undeclared hostilities.[2] But the lines are hard to draw, and subversive intrigue is the flower of espionage, as negotiation is of diplomacy. Diplomacy and espionage were always distinct in principle. But they have enough in common to be long confused with one another, and the institution of the resident envoy had to establish itself against the fears of those who with good reason expected him to be a centre for hostile intrigue in one's own capital. The multiple secret diplomacy of the eighteenth century prolonged the connection with espionage, bribery and subversion. It was not until the nineteenth century that the two professions were fully disentangled. And even now it was partly due to the increase in diplomatic staffs, allowing for a discreet division of functions. Ambassadors need not now engage in undercover activities. A military attaché has different duties, different contacts and different possibilities from the head of his mission.

At the same time, secret services swelled for the same reasons as diplomatic services: the expansion of the states-system and the growth of international intercourse. It will probably never be possible to write the history of espionage as an international institution; so much of the evidence in the nature of the case will not exist. We cannot know in general how often the information obtained through intelligence sources is valuable; nor how often, when valuable, it has been acted upon. But the secret agent,

1. A. de Wicquefort, *L'Ambassadeur et ses fonctions*, Vol. II, p. 10.
2. ibid., pp. 200–201.

disreputable and disavowed, has remained the inescapable shadow of the honourable and honoured diplomatist. The Congress of Vienna was accompanied by intense activity on the part of the Austrian secret police in opening the correspondence and ransacking the wastepaper-baskets of the diplomatic missions. Churchill, as Home Secretary and then First Lord of the Admiralty before 1914, was concerned to keep watch on the network of agents in German pay in British naval ports through whom the German Naval Attaché was so well informed of British dispositions. The visit of Bulganin and Khrushchev to England in April 1956 was marked by the mysterious death of the naval frogman, Commander Crabb, who disappeared swimming near the Soviet guests' warships in Portsmouth Harbour. The world of international relations contains Alec Leamas as well as M. de Norpois.

The difference between diplomacy and espionage is the difference between the arts of peace and the arts of war; it is also in part the difference between the arts of constitutional government and the arts of despotism. When peace approximates to war, diplomacy and espionage tend once more to become confused. Or we might rather say that normal diplomacy is replaced by revolutionary diplomacy. Revolutionary diplomacy has its perversions of the threefold function of diplomacy: espionage in place of information, subversion in place of negotiation, propaganda in place of communication. An evolution of emphasis from the first to the third may be traced in the history of Soviet diplomacy.

The first impulse of a revolutionary power is to abolish diplomacy altogether, even to abolish foreign policy. Dumouriez, who was French Foreign Minister at the outbreak of the Revolutionary Wars in 1792, declared that 'the Foreign Ministry is less complicated than any other department, and requires less mystery. A great people, a people free and just, is the natural ally of all peoples, and need have no special alliances to bind it to the destiny, interests and passions of this nation or that'.[3] It was in the same spirit that Mazzini, the conspirator and propagandist of

3. Mémoire sur le ministère des affaires étrangères, 1791. See F. Masson, *Le Département des Affaires Etrangères pendant la Révolution*, Plon, Paris, 1877, p. 151. Author's translation.

the Italian Risorgimento, argued against Cavour the politician that an honest faith in ideals and principles was worth more than the calculations, indecisions and dishonesties of diplomacy. Thus Cobden, the greatest of English international idealists, told the House of Commons that he 'felt the most sovereign contempt for diplomacy',[4] and his colleague John Bright declared that 'the foreign policy of this country for the last 170 years has been a system of gigantic out-door relief to the English aristocracy . . .'[5] When Trotsky became first People's Commissar of the Soviet Republic he announced that the Revolution had no need for diplomacy: 'I shall publish a few revolutionary proclamations and then close shop.'[6] President Eisenhower expressed the same vein in the American tradition: '. . . people want peace so much', he said unguardedly in 1959, 'that . . . governments had better get out of their way and let them have it'.[7]

The Fascist powers have had most success in subordinating diplomacy to propaganda. Mussolini, who never ceased to be a journalist in power, preferred reading stolen documents and intercepted letters to his ambassadors' reports, and it was symbolic that his Minister of Propaganda, Ciano, took over the Foreign Ministry. Hitler reduced foreign policy to propaganda, threats and subversion. He was contemptuous of the German Foreign Ministry, and 'as crises approached, ambassadors were generally withdrawn from the capitals of the intended victim and its potential allies, and interest was seldom displayed in any reports they might wish to deliver on their return'.[8] The Foreign Ministry has never ranked high in the Soviet system, and Soviet diplomatists have not been allowed freedom to negotiate. Litvinov, the best known in the West before 1939, once said bitterly, 'You

4. Speech on 28 June 1850, in the Don Pacifico debate, in J. Bright and T. Rogers (eds.), *Speeches by Richard Cobden MP*, Vol. II, p. 219.

5. Speech in Birmingham, 18 January 1865, in T. Rogers (ed.), *Speeches by John Bright MP*, Vol. II, Macmillan, 1868, p. 105. He had already used the phrase in 1858, ibid., p. 382.

6. I. Deutscher, *The Prophet Armed*, O.U.P., London, 1954, p. 327.

7. Television broadcast with Harold Macmillan in London on 31 August 1959, *The Times*, 1 September 1959, p. 8.

8. C. Thorne, *The Approach of War 1938–1939*, Macmillan, London, 1967, p. 27.

know what I am. I merely hand on diplomatic documents.'[9]

The second impulse of a revolutionary power is not to discard diplomacy but to use it for propaganda and subversion. Envoys of revolutionary powers address themselves not only to the governments to which they are accredited but also to the faction of which their country is the moral leader. In Elizabethan England the Spanish ambassador was at the centre of Catholic intrigue against the English government. Genest, the first minister of the French Republic to the United States, having already been expelled from the court of Catherine the Great, behaved in America as a missionary to the people, enlisted volunteers to serve under the French flag, and tried to organize a Franco-American conquest of Spanish Louisiana. Soviet Russia had a highly disciplined organization for this purpose, on a wider scale than ever before, in the Third International, and the limited success of the Third International is the classic evidence for the limits of effectiveness of such aims. Chinese Communist diplomacy is in a similar phase, though the split in the world Communist party has deprived China of an international network as effective as Russia used to have, and perhaps enhanced her dependence on her own diplomatic missions. It is through these that China has organized her subversion, especially in Africa, with grants, interest-free loans, arms and guerrilla training.

Stalin abolished the Comintern in 1943, as a small gesture of reassurance to his wartime allies, when he no longer needed this link with Communist parties in other countries. After the war Soviet Russia found herself for the first time playing a world-wide role as one of the dominant powers. Her diplomacy now became marked by two characteristics: the use of international conferences for propaganda, and the use of the regular diplomatic system for espionage. Propaganda by conference was pursued in the World Peace Congresses of 1948–52 and in the United Nations. We have become so accustomed to the connection between Soviet diplomacy and espionage that the discovery of a new spy-network and the expulsion of the Russian diplomatists connected with it have ceased to seem extraordinary. Ulbricht explained in 1960

9. Quoted in G. A. Craig and F. Gilbert, (eds.), *The Diplomats 1919–1939*, Princeton University Press, New Jersey, 1953, p. 371.

that while such an activity as the dispatch of a U-2 reconnaissance plane by an imperialist power was spying, the collection of military information by peace-lovers was not spying but a humane duty. In 1964 the Soviet government gave public recognition to the role of the spy by posthumously designating the greatest Soviet secret agent of the Second World War a Hero of the Soviet Union. 'A spy is above all a man of politics, who must be able to grasp, analyse and connect in his mind events which seemingly have no connection. He must have the breadth of thought of a strategist, and meticulous powers of observation. Espionage is a continuous and demanding labour which never ceases.'[10]

It is interesting to observe how, since men are prone to attribute their own political motives to others, revolutionary powers are likely to see the embassies of other powers as nests of spies, and to violate diplomatic immunities accordingly. The French Directory violated international practice by abusing envoys of foreign powers as agents of intrigue against the French Republic and dismissing them on grounds of ideological distaste. Soviet Russia has imposed restrictions on movement of foreign diplomatists that make them virtual prisoners. She bugs embassy buildings and the flats of foreign diplomatists. And the Soviet objection against all proposals for international inspection, especially in relation to a limitation of nuclear weapons, is that this would amount to 'espionage'. This is the only category under which a revolutionary power can conceive of an impartial international authority.

Traditional diplomatic standards probably reached their highest level during the century before 1914. Since then they have steadily declined. The Communist powers implicitly repudiate these standards except when it suits them to claim observance of them; the Afro-Asian states do not yet understand or value them. In October 1966 the foreign minister of Guinea took a plane with his delegation to a meeting of the Organization of African Unity in Addis Ababa. The plane stopped in Accra, where the Guinea delegation were arrested by the Ghana military regime, and held as hostages for Ghanaian citizens said to be wrongfully detained in Guinea. Since the plane had been Pan American, the government

10. F. W. Deakin and G. R. Storry, *The Case of Richard Sorge*, Chatto, London, 1966, p. 351, quoting apparently from *Izvestia*, 4 September 1964.

of Guinea retaliated by placing the United States ambassador to Guinea under house arrest, and denouncing Ghana as a satellite of American imperialism. An incident of this kind is as diverting as some of the disreputable cases from earlier centuries illustrating diplomatic precedence or immunity which adorn the histories of international law. But in July 1966 there had been a more sombre scandal in The Hague, which was perhaps more characteristic of diplomacy since 1945. A Chinese engineer who had been working in the Netherlands was found mysteriously injured on the pavement and taken to hospital. There he was kidnapped by other Chinese, thrust helpless into a diplomatic car, and driven to the Chinese legation. The Chinese chargé d'affaires refused to surrender him to the Dutch authorities, later informed them that the man was dead, and tried to dispose of his body surreptitiously. The shadowy right of granting asylum on diplomatic premises has been turned inside out. They have acquired a new role as a dungeon in which would-be defectors are imprisoned, or escaping from which they meet their death.

It is indeed a question whether traditional diplomatic practices have become obsolete, and may be succumbing to revolutionary practices, as bad money drives out good. The Western powers are at a double disadvantage: their political and military affairs are largely public and open to observation, and they have difficulties in retaliating vigorously in kind against violations of diplomatic immunity. The U-2 flights were explained as made necessary by the secrecy of Soviet military preparations.[11]

11. This draft was apparently written in the late 1960s. Since the author begins by dividing diplomacy into resident embassies and conferences but deals only with the former, this is no more than half a chapter. However, the author deals with conferences in *Systems of States*, especially Chapters 1 and 5. Eds.

12 : Alliances

Alliances are not the friendships of international politics – unless, as Aristotle observed, we apply the word friendship to relationships based on utility.[1] Alliances cannot be disinterested. The range of friendship extends to where a man lays down his life for his friends; but the height of self-sacrifice is not permissible to governments whose duty is to protect the interests of their peoples. Even if a people itself were able by some means to make a valid collective decision, that combined the will of all its members of every age, it is by no means clear that it would have the right to extinguish its collective life, which spans the past and the future, for a particular and temporary cause.

But alliances are as various as friendships, in their character, their purpose, their occasion, their duration, the relative position of those who make them. The oldest classification is into equal and unequal, according to the relative status and power of the allies.[2] They can also be wartime or peacetime, offensive or defensive, political or economic or cultural, permanent or temporary, bilateral or multilateral.

Alliances for economic or cultural purposes may be formed simply for reasons internal to the partners and for their mutual benefit. Political alliances are always contracted with third parties in view; unlike friendships, they are necessarily, so to speak, self-conscious; their purpose is to enhance the security of the allies or to advance their interests, against the outer world.

1. P. Wheelwright (trans.), 'Nicomachean Ethics', in *Aristotle*, Odyssey Press, New York, 1951, Chapter 8, iv, p. 241.
2. For example, G. Botero, *The Reason of State*, Book VIII, 9, pp. 162–4, and H. Grotius, *De jure belli ac pacis libri tres*, F. W. Kelsey (trans.), Oceana Publications, New York, 1964, Book I, Chapter 3, 21, pp. 130–36; Book II, Chapter 15, 6–7, pp. 394–7.

'There is no state so powerful that it may not some time need the help of others outside itself, either for purposes of trade, or even to ward off the forces of many foreign nations against it,' said Grotius. 'In consequence, we see that even the most powerful peoples and sovereigns seek alliances.'[3] He was arguing that the essential sociability of human nature shows itself in the connections formed even by states and princes, and moreover that all these connections are governed by universal law.

The perfect alliance would show equality of interest and commitment between the two parties, with a reciprocity of advantage. The vision of this appears in wartime. In 1942 Britain and Russia arrived, after some acrimonious discussion, at the text of a treaty of alliance, which pledged the two parties to give each other all possible aid and left out the difficult issue of Soviet frontiers. 'For the present the mutual pledge is enough,' wrote the diplomatic correspondent of *The Times*. 'A country giving a promise so far-reaching naturally desires to see its partner strong in all forms of defence, economic, military and territorial.'[4] Sometimes the language of complete union is used.

There are associations between powers that seem to be deeper than formal alliances, to be based on affinity and tradition as much as interest, to be not so much utilitarian as *natural*. And obversely, there are dislikes and ancient conflicts that seem like natural enmities. Thus the British imagine their relationship to be with the United States (rather more generally than Americans imagine their relationship with England), and de Gaulle spoke of 'the great Russian people whom the French people throughout history have regarded as an appointed friend'.[5] Thus Charles Fox wrote in 1783: 'Alliances with the Northern powers [meaning Russia first and Prussia next] ever have been, and ever will be, the system of every enlightened Englishman,'[6] and an earlier gener-

3. Grotius, ibid., 'Prolegomena', 22, p. 17.

4. *The Times*, 12 June 1942, p. 4.

5. Press conference held on 9 September 1968; *The Times*, 10 September 1968, p. 11.

6. Malmesbury, *Diaries and Correspondence*, Vol. II, p. 40; also D. B. Horn, *Great Britain and Europe in the Eighteenth Century*, Clarendon Press, Oxford, 1967, p. 212.

ation of Englishmen regarded Austria as their natural ally. It is interesting to note that an historian regards it as 'a twentieth-century generalization' to say what at the beginning of the seventeenth century was 'widely considered an obvious fact of life, one which was not only frequently stated but often treated as an axiom by the makers of foreign policy: that, regardless of the fluctuations in day-to-day relationships, England and the United Provinces were not only former allies but were natural allies, France and Spain not only former enemies but natural enemies'.[7]

The notion of natural allies and natural enemies seems to have become current before that of natural frontiers, and to have prevailed less long, since it was more clearly contradicted by the changing alignments of international politics. When Pitt made his Commercial Treaty with France in 1786, he was criticized in Parliament by Burke on the grounds that he had neglected, for purely economic considerations, the abiding national danger from the ancient enemy. Pitt answered in famous words: 'To suppose that any nation could be unalterably the enemy of another, was weak and childish. It had neither its foundation in the experience of nations nor in the history of man.'[8] This was possibly the first time such doctrine had been voiced. The characteristic doctrine of Britain's great commercial predecessor, the United Provinces, at the height of their power, had been one of diplomatic isolation and freedom from alliances; and this is perhaps, from the point of view of international society, a more primitive or undeveloped stage than a doctrine of flexibility in making alliances. Pitt's doctrine was amplified sixty years later by Palmerston, who guided Britain at the summit of her power:

I hold, with respect to alliances, that England is a power sufficiently strong, sufficiently powerful, to steer her own course, and not to tie herself as an unnecessary appendage to the policy of any other government . . .

7. C. H. Carter, *The Secret Diplomacy of the Habsburgs 1598–1625*, Columbia University Press, New York, 1964, pp. 28–9.
8. Speech in the House of Commons, 12 February 1787, in *The Parliamentary History*, Vol. 26, Hansard, London, 1816, col. 392; also J. Ehrman, *The Younger Pitt*, Constable, London, 1969, p. 493.

. . . my conviction is, that as long as England keeps herself in the right . . . and as long as she sympathizes with right and justice, she will never find herself altogether alone. She is sure to find some other state of sufficient power, influence, and weight, to support and aid her in the course she may think fit to pursue. Therefore, I say that it is a narrow policy to suppose that this country or that is to be marked out as the eternal ally or the perpetual enemy . . . Our interests are eternal and perpetual, and those interests it is our duty to follow.

When we find other countries marching in the same courses, and pursuing the same objects as ourselves, we consider them as our friends, and we think for the moment that we are on the most cordial footing; when we find other countries that take a different view, and thwart us in that object we pursue, it is our duty to make allowance for the different manner in which they may follow out the same objects.[9]

Let us examine the substance in the idea of natural alliances. It is perhaps threefold. There are alliances which embody a common interest in relation to the balance of power. There is a strange class of associations which is a residue of changes in the balance of power. And there are alliances which are thought to arise from community of doctrine or ideology.

The sagacious Vergennes once wrote, 'the King of Prussia, being from his situation the veritable natural enemy of the House of Austria'.[10] Here he put his finger on a truth: it was not nature, but circumstances, that made Prussia the adversary of Austria. And circumstances, unlike nature, are continually changing. A natural ally, then, is an ally in the nature of a transient balance of power. Britain, the United Provinces and the Empire were natural allies against the preponderance of Louis XIV, as England, the United Provinces and France had been natural allies against the preponderance of Philip II. This kind of natural ally is made by a great common danger that lasts a long time, preferably for several

9. Speech in the House of Commons, 1 March 1848, *Parliamentary Debates*, Third Series, Vol. 97, col. 122; also J. Joll (ed.), *Britain and Europe 1793–1940*, Black, London, 1950, pp. 110–11.

10. 'Mémoire au commencement du règne de Louis XVI', 1774, in *Politique de tous les cabinets de l'Europe pendant les règnes de Louis XV et de Louis XVI*, Vol. I, Buisson, Paris, 1793, p. 388.

generations. The classic example in British history was the 'Old System', which governed British and Austrian policy from 1688 until the Diplomatic Revolution in 1756.

The classic example in French history was the alliance with the Sublime Porte, from 1526 down to France's failure to give Turkey adequate support in her war with Russia of 1768–74: here the common danger was the Habsburg Monarchy. In German history the classic example is the alliance between the German great powers and Russia. This ran through the eighteenth and nineteenth centuries, from the Austro-Russian alliance of 1726, renewed in the famous alliance of 1780 between Joseph I and Catherine the Great, until it finally disappeared, along with the Austrian and Russian Empires themselves, in the First World War. When the alliance was first contracted, the two imperial powers were separated by wide territories of Poland and the Ottoman Empire, and cemented by a common policy towards these declining states. The Partition of Poland continued to unite them, but the emergence of the Balkan successor-states of the Ottoman Empire, and Russian patronage of these states in a way that threatened to encircle and disrupt the Austrian monarchy itself, brought them into conflict with each other.

An earlier example of an association between great powers that seemed natural was the Habsburg family alliance, the dynastic axis between Madrid and Vienna, which governed the policies of Spain and Austria from Charles V's decision that his brother Ferdinand should succeed him as Emperor and ruler of the German territories of the house, and his son Philip II in the Spanish, Burgundian and Italian dominions, until the last Habsburg died at Madrid in 1700. This depended on family agreements and inter-marriage in each generation, rather than on formal treaties. For Spain, the relationship might be 'summed up in the statement that it was unthinkable ever to make war on the Austrian branch of the family'.[11] The statement is probably coloured by the relationship between the United States and the British Commonwealth, two parts of another great empire which was divided, not like Charles V's, by peaceable family discussion, but by war. Yet this Habsburg family alliance owed its existence

11. Carter, op. cit., p. 43.

to fear of France. Mary of Burgundy espoused Maximilian of Austria as a defender against France; their son's marriage with the Princess of Castile (from whom Charles V sprang) was arranged as an answer to Charles VIII's conquest of Italy. And it was opposition to France that kept Spain and Austria in co-operation throughout the seventeenth century.

We may notice a curious tendency that has shown itself throughout international history: a former dominant power tends to sink into dependence upon its supplanter, when you might have expected an undying hatred. (It is only between comparable or equal powers that there can subsist such long-standing antagonisms as that between France and Britain from the Hundred Years War onwards.) Spain sank into dependence on France, took a French dynasty, and in the Family Compacts of the eighteenth century became the most reliable ally of France. France in the next century accepted collaboration with Britain, and the Entente Cordiale replaced the Family Compacts. Holland, which had been the greatest commercial and maritime power in the world, sank within a hundred years into what Frederick the Great described as a launch (*chaloupe*) towed by England's man-of-war.[12] Bismarck varied the metaphor when he said just before the Crimean War broke out, 'It would distress me if we should seek protection from a possible storm by tying our trim and seaworthy frigate to the worm-eaten and old-fashioned Austrian man-of-war.'[13] But Austria, defeated in the struggle for supremacy of Germany, sank into diplomatic dependence on the German Empire, and it was ironically the worm-eaten battleship of the Habsburgs that in the end dragged down the gleaming Hohenzollern dreadnought. In the second half of the twentieth century Britain in her turn has become cock-boat to the United States man-of-war, and it remains to be seen whether a reunited Germany will be taken in tow by the Soviet Union.

'International policy is a fluid element,' said Bismarck, 'which

12. *Histoire de mon temps*, *Publicationen aus den K. Preussischen Staatsarchiven*, Verlag von S. Hirzel, Leipzig, 1879, Chapter 1, p. 173.

13. Letter to Manteuffel (Prussian Prime Minister), 15 February 1854, quoted in E. Eyck, *Bismarck and the German Empire*, Allen & Unwin, London, 1958, p. 34; cf. Taylor, *The Struggle for Mastery in Europe*, p. 262.

under certain conditions will solidify, but on a change of atmosphere reverts to its original diffuse condition.'[14] To understand the unstable and intractable nature of international politics, you need only study the relations between the motives and consequences of a war, or between the purposes and history of an alliance. The more general the scope of the alliance, the less does it work as either party intended. New circumstances constantly arise which show each ally its obligations in an unexpected light. The Family Compact of 1761 between France and Spain, the two great branches of the House of Bourbon, had a good life as alliances go: it governed their relationships for a generation. But the American Revolution put it under unforeseeable strains, and in the French Revolution it foundered. The alliance was formed at France's darkest moment of defeat and humiliation in the Seven Years War; she hoped to repair her losses by bringing a new ally into the struggle, and the common interest binding the two powers was the need to offset the towering preponderance of Britain. The pact gave Spaniards and Frenchmen virtually a common citizenship in matters of commerce, and provided that the two powers would regard any power which became the enemy of either of them as their common enemy: 'le principe, qui est le fondement de ce traité: qui attaque une Couronne, attaque l'autre'.[15] By a secret convention Spain undertook to enter the war against Britain, which she did in 1762, with unhappy consequences to herself. Choiseul, the French Foreign Minister, regarded the Family Compact, and not the ill-starred alliance of 1756 with the Habsburgs, as the foundation of French foreign policy. So essential did he judge it, that to compensate Spain for her losses in the common cause, and to induce her to make a quick peace, he ceded Louisiana to her at the peace, in order to confirm the alliance. But the French resented having had to pay this price, in addition to their losses to Britain.

A divergent interest had been recognized in the compact itself.

14. *Bismarck, The Man and the Statesman, Being the Reflections and Reminiscences of Otto Prince von Bismarck*, Vol. II, A. J. Butler (trans.), London, 1898, p. 280.

15. G. F. Martens, *Recueil des principaux traités*, Vol. I, Dieterich, Gottingue, 1791, p. 2.

It did not cover wars in which France might become involved in Germany as a guarantor of the Westphalia Treaties, 'considering that the said wars cannot in any way concern the crown of Spain'. But it was the American Revolutionary War, fifteen years later, that put the compact to the test. France, which no longer had colonists in North America, was ready to recognize the independence of the rebel colonies, in order to break up the British Empire. Spain on the other hand offered too many hostages to fortune to wish to encourage colonial rebellion across the Atlantic. All the same, she desired a new and happier war with Britain, provided she made tangible gains. When the Americans won their first great military victory at Saratoga in 1777, Vergennes, the French Foreign Minister, hastened to conclude an alliance with them for fear that Britain might now offer them acceptable terms short of full independence. This famous alliance of 1778 pledged France to war until the independence of the United States was secured. It was made without Spain's approval having been obtained. Once committed to the Americans, military necessity compelled Vergennes to seek Spanish help at Spain's price. Spain had now decided upon the recovery of Gibraltar as her war aim. She entered the war under a secret treaty of 1779, nominally putting the Family Compact into execution, and pledging France to war until Gibraltar was recovered. This treaty was made without the Americans' approval, and marked their first entanglement in a European situation beyond their will. France had committed herself to allies with divided war aims, for the Spaniards were averse to American independence, and the Americans were uninterested in the fate of Gibraltar. But Vergennes gave Spain no support in her great attack upon Gibraltar, believing that if she acquired it she would become too independent of France; and the attack having failed, Spain had to be content at the peace with acquiring Minorca and Florida.

The French Revolution enabled the ancient enemy against whom the Family Compact was originally formed to destroy it. The Spaniards regarded the progress of the Revolution with intense disapproval. But when British and Spanish interests clashed at Nootka Sound on the Pacific coast, and Britain assumed a threatening demeanour, Spain appealed for the last time to the

Family Compact. The French National Assembly had just set up a diplomatic committee to examine the country's treaty obligations. It recommended that, if Spain were to be supported, the Pacte de Famille should be replaced by a Pacte National, in accordance with revolutionary foreign policy; and it was suggested informally to Spain that in order to cement the renewed alliance she might restore Louisiana to France. The Spaniards preferred to come to terms with Britain, and their treaty in 1790 was the end of the Family Compact.[16] Three years later, after Louis XVI had been executed, Spain declared war on France. Ten years later she retroceded Louisiana to France.

The idea of a Pacte National in 1790 was doctrinaire and unformed. Perhaps an equivalent can be seen in the Anglo-French Union which the British government proposed to the French in June 1940, a product of a defeat more disastrous than that which led to the Family Compact. Instead of the bond of kinship uniting two monarchs wishing 'to perpetuate in their posterity the sentiments of their common and august great-grandfather, Louis XIV of glorious memory', the union would have been based on the 'common defence of justice and freedom'. It originated apparently with Vansittart, the Permanent Head of the Foreign Office, and Monnet, the head of the Allied Economic Coordination Committee in London. Churchill accepted it with misgivings, and de Gaulle foresaw the difficulties there would be in the complex negotiations necessary to give effect to it.[17] The circumstances of France and Britain were so different that it is unlikely that the union, even if the French government had accepted it in the stress of war, would have survived for a generation.

Let us take the Little Entente as an example of an alliance that is eroded as divergent interests come to eclipse common interest. The Little Entente was the alliance formed in 1920 by the three leading successor-states of the Austro-Hungarian dual monarchy, Czechoslovakia, Yugoslavia and Rumania. Its purpose was to

16. A. Sorel, *L'Europe et la Révolution Française*, II, Plon, Paris, 1885, pp. 94–5.
17. W. S. Churchill, *The Second World War*, Vol. II, Cassell, London, 1949, pp. 180–81; C. de Gaulle, *Mémoire de Guerre, L'Appel*, Plon, Paris, 1954, p. 62.

guard against the twin dangers of Hungarian revisionism and a Habsburg restoration, and its name was first given in derision by a Hungarian journalist. It consisted of bilateral treaties. In 1929 the three powers agreed that the treaties should be automatically renewed at the end of each five-year period, and began regular military conferences to discuss war plans. In 1933 they renewed the treaties in perpetuity, and set up a permanent council of Foreign Ministers, with a secretariat, to unify their foreign policies. This Pact of Organization, signed two weeks after Hitler came to power in Germany, was the high point of their union. Thenceforward the states of the Little Entente encountered circumstances which tore them relentlessly apart.

The Little Entente came into being as a ring of states facing inwards against their defeated oppressor. But each of them had a hostile great power sitting upon its tail, in the shape of a disputed frontier or a minorities problem. Czechoslovakia had the Sudeten German minorities over against the Reich. For fifteen years she was able to follow a foreign policy that was not dominated by this danger; but they then became the engine for her destruction. Rumania had acquired the partly Ukrainian province of Bessarabia from Russia in 1918 after the Empire had collapsed, and her diplomacy was governed by the knowledge that the Soviet Union did not acquiesce in the loss. Yugoslavia enjoyed the hostility of Italy, her fellow-victor of the First World War, who coveted the Dalmatian coast, opposed the enlargement of Serbia into a Kingdom of the South Slavs, annexed Fiume in disregard of the recommendations of the Allied Supreme Council at the Paris Peace Conference, encouraged Croat separatism, and patronized the terrorists who murdered King Alexander in 1934.

Yugoslavia was the least reliable member of the Little Entente. She contained fewer minorities than Czechoslovakia or Rumania, but she alone was crippled by a national conflict between her two main component peoples. Serbs and Croats were more equally balanced, numerically, economically and culturally, and therefore more mutually antagonistic, than were Czechs and Slovaks in the sister state.[18] Because Yugoslavia had a smaller Hungarian

18. Minorities formed approximately the following percentages of the total population of each state in 1938: Czechoslovakia (viz. other than Czechs and

minority than Czechoslovakia and Rumania, Hungarian re-visionism was less of a threat to her. On the other hand, she had a unique relationship with her fellow-South Slav state Bulgaria. At times she was threatened by Bulgarian revisionism, which aimed to acquire Macedonia, the inchoate province that was a bridge between Bulgars and Serbs; at other times she seemed within reach of amalgamation with Bulgaria into a Great South Slav state; in either case, this was a concern of foreign policy remote from Czechoslovakia, and possibly alarming to Rumania. But what distinguished Yugoslavia most from her two allies was that she alone was threatened from the beginning of her existence by a hostile great power. Italy made herself the instigator of Croat separatism, the patron of Hungarian and Bulgarian discontent with the *status quo*, the protector of Albania, encircling Yugoslavia with active malignity. And the Italian threat to Yugoslavia was an obstacle, not an inducement, to a full interdependence between Yugoslavia and France. The great aim of French policy was to find potential allies against the threat of German revival, and for this Italy bulked greater in French eyes than Yugoslavia. So she regarded herself not as a protector of Yugoslavia against Italy but as a reconciler of the two, not seeing that this was as unsatisfactory for Yugoslavia's security as Britain's attempt to be a reconciler between France herself and Germany was unsatisfactory for French security. The treaties that France made with Czecho-slovakia and Rumania (and with Poland) included in each case a military convention; the Franco-Yugoslav Pact of 1927 alone did not.

The failure of France and Britain to impose effective sanctions on Italy when she attacked Abyssinia showed Yugoslavia that the League was useless and that great powers could not be relied upon to protect small powers. In 1936, after the remilitarization of the Rhineland, the Little Entente met in conference, and proposed consolidating their treaties with France into a single pact of mutual assistance. But Yugoslavia (now under Stojadinovic) was

Slovaks), 33; Rumania, 25; Yugoslavia (viz. other than Serbs, Croats and Slovenes), 12. In Czechoslovakia, there were roughly 7¼ million Czechs to 2 million Slovaks; in Yugoslavia, 5½ million Serbs to 4½ million Croats and Slovenes.

reluctant, having already accepted German protection in autumn 1936, and led the rejection of the French offer in April 1937, backed by Rumania. Yugoslavia had indeed begun to come to terms with Hungary herself. The last time the Little Entente met was at Bled, in northern Yugoslavia, in August 1938, while the German attack on Czechoslovakia was preparing: the Little Entente states gave undertakings to Hungary for the treatment of their minorities, and she argued that she was already satisfied with the position of her minorities in Yugoslavia, and towards Yugoslavia she would renounce force. In the Munich crisis, Czechoslovakia's two allies of the Little Entente were passive in the main drama of Germany's partition of Czechoslovakia; their part was in the sub-plot of Hungarian claims on Czechoslovakia. The last flicker of the original principle of the Little Entente was a declaration proposed by Rumania and agreed by Yugoslavia at the height of the crisis, that they would accept a revision of Hungary's frontier with Czechoslovakia provided it was limited to regions containing a majority of Magyar inhabitants, but that they could not remain unmoved by a Hungarian annexation of Slovakia. But Germany forbade the *démarche* being made.

There are some similarities between the Little Entente, or rather we should say the French system of alliances in Eastern Europe, and NATO after the Second World War. In each case a group of smaller powers formed security arrangements for preserving the *status quo*, which became associated with and stiffened by a great power. The Little Entente powers formed their own alliances in 1920–21, and subsequently contracted treaties of alliance with France in 1925–7. Poland made her alliance with France in 1921. The West European powers made the Brussels Treaty in March 1948, nominally against the danger of renewed aggression by Germany, actually against the danger of Russia, a year before the North Atlantic Treaty was concluded in April 1949. The whole defence system depends on the support of the great power. The smaller powers have inadequate forces and inadequate political unity to cooperate without its leadership. France, like Poland, suffering from delusions of grandeur and of a return to great-power status, pursued an independent policy which weakened the alliance. In each case the great power was geographically removed from the allies: the United States by the Atlantic, which might become a psychological equivalent of the Maginot Line.

The contrasts are also noticeable. The French system of Eastern alliances was made against the revisionist threat of two defeated powers, Germany and Hungary. The Brussels Organization and NATO were formed against the threat of a triumphant victorious ally-turned-enemy. Though the defensive great power is in each case geographically distant from its small allies, the potential aggressor does not lie physically between them, able to cut them off from one another, as Germany did when she re-militarized the Rhineland. Most important of all, the United States maintains forces on the soil of its dependent allies, as France never did in Eastern Europe. And the two potential antagonists, the United States and the Soviet Union, have far more common interests, which might be pursued at the expense of their smaller allies, than France and Germany had.

It has been said that generals prepare to fight the last war. It may be noted, as a melancholy law of coalitions, that they are designed to avert the last war. If in 1914 Britain had had the degree of public commitment to France which she had after 1936, the war of 1914 might have been avoided. If in 1938–9 Hitler had been confronted with the Brussels Organization of 1948, he would have been deterred. And in the same way, the ramshackle Atlantic alliance falls short of that creativeness which might control and shape circumstances instead of following them. Nothing less than a federal union of the Atlantic world can create either the preponderant counter-balance to the Soviet Union and her allies, or an attractive centre of global unification.

The members of the Little Entente were further united to one another by their several alliances with France, the one great power with a concern to protect the Versailles Settlement in Europe, but they had no common policy towards the other great powers. Czechoslovakia and Rumania established diplomatic relations with the Soviet Union when she adopted an anti-revisionist policy and entered the League of Nations in 1934; Yugoslavia oddly refused, because of the Tsarist loyalties of King Alexander and his successor the regent Prince Paul. Czechoslovakia made a defensive alliance with the Soviet Union in 1935, and one of the subsidiary themes of the Munich crisis was uncertainty whether Czechoslovakia's ally Rumania would allow Soviet forces to come to the aid of Czechoslovakia across her own territory that intervened. When the Nazi Revolution began to spread its ripples across Europe, the Little Entente powers did not unite more closely against a danger greater to each of them than the Hungarians. A group of small powers cannot have a common policy towards great powers.[19]

19. This draft, which is unfinished, was apparently written in the early 1970s. Lists of contents found with the manuscript suggest that the author intended to deal with guarantees as well as alliances in this chapter. Eds.

13 : War

All political experience knows the tension between freedom and necessity, between individual initiative and social determinism; international politics seem to have it in a heightened degree. When we consider the crises of peace and war we are assailed by contradictory impressions: the occasions of war seem so tractable, the causes so ineluctable. The surface of the stream glitters with contingency: the play of personalities, like Stratford de Redcliffe at Constantinople at the outbreak of the Crimean War, or Neville Chamberlain taking control of British foreign policy; actions in themselves trivial, the toning down of a dispatch by the Prince Consort, the toning up of a telegram by Bismarck; chances that might have been otherwise, the murder of an archduke, the absence of a great power from its seat in the Security Council. But all the time we are aware of the irresistible current underneath. Thus we easily fall into twin errors, exaggerating the freedom or exaggerating the necessity. If only Marie Antoinette (we ask ourselves) had not intrigued with the Austrian court with such obstinate and childish disloyalty, need there have been war between the French Revolution and Europe? If Sir Edward Grey had defined British policy clearly in 1914, is it not possible that Germany might have been restrained? But we recoil from these ill-judged speculations, to measure the blind growth of state power, the drives of economic imperialism, the pressures of population, and persuade ourselves that these catastrophes had causes so deep-seated as to have been virtually predestined.

Between the World Wars these two exaggerations flourished in unison. The most consistent attempt was then made to explain war in terms of social determinism, to press its causes back from human decisions towards such circumstances as capitalism or the balance of power. But at the same time there was a belief that this system of necessity could be so modified as to abolish war altogether. Freedom and necessity in international politics would be reconciled in the final freedom of an inability to go to war, a *beata necessitas non peccandi*. Since 1945 there has been less tendency to push either analysis or expectation to such lengths. Political thought in the post-war period was marked, not so much by a belief that the hydrogen bomb had created an unprecedented situation, as by a return to traditional views about the part of war in international politics. In 1955 President Eisenhower was asked to comment on a statement by Admiral Radford that war might start anywhere at any time. He replied, philosophically, 'There is always the possibility of war.'[1] It is probably true to say that thirty years earlier, twenty years earlier, no democratic statesman would have dared give such an answer; though before 1914 no statesman would have thought it anything but an acknowledgement of the obvious.

If we consider the course of international politics during the perhaps transient, perhaps expiring, period since the sixteenth century in which there has existed this peculiar society composed of sovereign states, and if we wish to formulate the tension between determinism and human initiative in the matter of war, we can only say that war is inevitable, but particular wars can be avoided. The first half of this paradox is a statement of moral certainty, a proposition of the statistical order. There have been widely expected wars which did not happen, for instance between Britain and Russia in the last quarter of the nineteenth century. But the failure of such wars to occur was not due to a decline in the incidence of war, but to the potential conflict being transcended by a greater conflict. The second half of the paradox is a proposition in the context of diplomacy. It is the task of diplomacy to circumvent the occasions of war, and to extend the series of circumvented occasions: to drive the automobile of state along a one-way track, against head-on traffic, past infinitely recurring precipices. The notion that diplomacy can eradicate the causes of war was part of the great illusion after 1919. Diplomacy can do a little, perhaps, to mitigate the social conditions of war; it can

1. Washington press conference, 16 March 1955, in *The Times*, 17 March 1955, p. 6.

circumvent the occasions of war; but the causes of war, like the need for diplomacy itself, will remain so long as a multiplicity of governments are not reduced to one government and international politics transformed into domestic politics. Nor does experience or reflection give any reason to suppose that this can come about except by war itself.

If we ask about the cause of a particular war, the answer we normally find satisfying, and the answer the historian normally gives us, is in terms of a motive inspired by relationships of power. The classic example is Thucydides' judgement that the real reason for the Peloponnesian War (though the reason the least often given) was the fear aroused in Sparta by the growth of Athenian power. This sentence has earned criticism from a generation of classical historians, who have reproved Thucydides for neglecting the social and economic causes. Nevertheless it endures for the student of politics as the prototypic statement of how we usually express the causes of war. When all our research on the framework of necessity is complete, we find the origins of wars in the decisions of governments, and sometimes the passions of peoples, prompted by relationships of power.

There are many kinds of wars: aggressive wars and preventive, prestige wars and wars of security, idealistic wars and perhaps even just wars. But it is convenient to classify them under three chief motives: wars of gain, wars of fear, and wars of doctrine. This grouping corresponds to the causes of war suggested by Hobbes, who was himself adapting the motives of Athenian imperialism described by Thucydides. We must remember that every war has at least two belligerents, and every belligerent has complex motives; but a predominant motive is generally not beyond the power of historians to arrive at agreement about.

The motive of gain is seen most unmixed in the wars by which the European powers extended the frontiers of international society to enclose the whole world, and in the subsequent wars for dividing the spoils of this imperialist expansion – those wars with a transparently economic motive, like the Anglo-Dutch wars in the seventeenth century and the Anglo-French in the eighteenth, which Adam Smith ascribed to 'the impertinent jealousy of merchants and manufacturers'.[2] If these colonial wars are put on one side, the motive of gain, of sheer aggrandizement, is less conspicuous in international politics than you may expect. The peoples of Asia and Africa might be right in supposing that Western society has kept its aggressive impulses for export. To counter such a view (and confining ourselves to the great powers) we could only cite the earlier wars of both Louis XIV and Frederick the Great, together with Hitler's war, which was so shocking to Europeans precisely because he adopted within Europe the most ruthless methods of colonial expansion and exploitation.

With wars of fear, on the other hand, the problem is rather one of exclusion. By fear we mean, not an unreasoning emotion, but a rational apprehension of future evil, and this is the prime motive of international politics. For all powers at all times are concerned primarily with their security, and most powers at most times find their security threatened. It is worth remembering that the motive of fear prompts preventive war as well as defensive war, and that in the majority of wars between great powers the aggressor's motive has been preventive. 'There is perhaps no factor', G. F. Hudson has said, 'which drives a state into war so inexorably as a steady loss of relative power. Sooner or later a desperate now-or-never mood overcomes the calculations of prudence, and the belief that a war may be won today, but cannot be won tomorrow, becomes the most convincing of all arguments for an appeal to the sword.'[3] This is a luminous statement of the Thucydidean fear. It is also, like all political truths, prophetic. It describes the Japanese attitude towards the United States, and was written five years before Pearl Harbor.

War of doctrine means missionary or crusading war, war to assert principles and advance a cause. If qualitative change is more important than quantitative, the striking development in war in the past two hundred years is not its growing destructiveness, but the way it has increasingly become the instrument of

2. *The Wealth of Nations*, Vol. 1, Methuen, London, 1930, Book IV, Chapter III, part 2, p. 457.
3. *The Far East in World Politics*, O.U.P., London, 1937, p. 198.

doctrinal conviction. For since the end of the eighteenth century, international society has been in a condition of stasis. It is convenient to use this Greek word for strife within communities as distinct from strife between them, since the English equivalents (civil discord or class-war) are both too narrow and too flaccid. Stasis appears in the international community when, in several states, bodies of men acquire loyalties which attach them more to bodies of men in other states than to their own fellow-citizens. The consequence, said Burke, who is our supreme commentator on the matter, 'is to introduce other interests into all countries than those which arise from their locality and natural circumstances'.[4] Or, to borrow Arthur Koestler's language, 'horizontal forces' shake and distort 'the vertical structure of competing national egotisms'.[5] The word horizontal is useful since it allows us to avoid the ambiguities of the word 'international'. The members of international society have never all been national states, and nationalism itself has been one of the most disruptive international doctrines, an inter-state revolutionary movement. Besides Marx's International there have been Mazzini's and Hitler's. The climax of international stasis is when a horizontal doctrine acquires a territorial foothold. The doctrine then becomes an armed doctrine, and the state where it is enthroned becomes, for its adherents abroad, an examplar, an asylum, and perhaps a saviour.

International stasis changes both the motive and character of war. On the one hand, it approximates war to revolution; on the other, it blurs the distinction between war and peace. The classic example of the doctrinal motive is the French Revolutionary War, when France 'attacked Europe in order to regenerate it'. Probably a purer example was the Soviet invasion of Poland in 1920, when the Red Army crossed the Curzon Line westwards in an enthusiastic confidence of European revolution. Nor is it beyond question whether this motive stirred in Stalin's mind when the second Soviet invasion of Europe began in 1944. But every war in Europe

4. Edmund Burke, *The Works of the Right Hon. Edmund Burke*, with a Biographical and Critical Introduction by Henry Rogers, Samuel Holdsworth, London, 1842; Vol. I, *Thoughts on French Affairs*, p. 564.
5. *The Yogi and the Commissar*, Jonathan Cape, London, 1945, p. 107.

since 1792 has had some doctrinal motive, asserting some horizontal right against some vertical legitimacy, offering some state as saviour and liberator of some group of foreigners. Of the Crimean War this is least true, but yet not wholly untrue. And the assimilation of war to revolution is seen in effects as well as motives. Since the American Declaration of Independence in 1776, every war between great powers, with three exceptions and those before 1860, has led to revolution on the losing side.

The distinction between war and peace is the foundation of civilized life, and its observance rests on common moral and political standards. The horizontal doctrine repudiates the old international morality and the old international law; in Burke's phrase, it makes 'a schism with the whole universe'.[6] Camus has penetratingly observed how the adherents of the universal doctrine set out to build the universal city, and how, by the logic of history and of the doctrine itself, the universal city becomes transformed into an empire, an empire proclaiming: 'Beyond the confines of the empire there is no salvation'.[7] Since 1918, more effort has been spent than ever before on delimiting the theoretical borderline between peace and war, and in defining those acts which transgress it; while in practice the borderline has become more smudged than at any time since the Wars of Religion. Today it requires a mental effort from us to regard as abnormal circumstances in which ships are sunk and aircraft shot down without warning, peaceable citizens are kidnapped and disappear, traitors flee from one side to the other bringing secrets and receiving moral acclaim, prisoners are tortured into apostasy, and diplomacy is replaced by propaganda.

This blending of war with revolution, this indistinctness of war from peace, gives a new social dimension to war, and produces a range of military activities which outstrip both international law and military science, the kind of irregular warfare whose heroes are Garibaldi and T. E. Lawrence and Marshal Tito, which played a large part in the Second World War and has been the

6. 'Letters on a Regicide Peace: I', in *The Works*, Vol. V, Nimmo, London, 1887, p. 320.
7. Albert Camus, *The Rebel*, Anthony Bower (trans.), Hamish Hamilton, London, 1953, p. 208.

prevalent warfare in the world since. Such revolutionary sub-war is characteristic of doctrinal conflict. We all know that Engels described insurrection as an art, and expounded its principles; it is less often remembered that Mazzini, the Gandhi of nineteenth-century liberalism, wrote a set of 'Rules for the Conduct of Guerrilla Bands'.[8]

Revolution involves counter-revolution; doctrinal war encourages war of counter-doctrine. Is doctrinal warfare to be met by containment, whose aim is security and whose motive fear, or by liberation – liberation from the ascendancy of the doctrine – whose aim is counter-revolutionary? The question is not answered by an appeal to the principle of collective security, for this itself can be inspired by either motive. In Korea, collective security meant a coalition whose predominant motive was fear: eleven of the seventeen powers that sent contingents experienced the direct threat of Communism. The collective security we dreamed of in the 'thirties, the war against Mussolini, inspired and purified by the moral censure and punitive purpose of the fifty sanctionist states, would have been much more a war of principle, a doctrinal war, logically evoking stasis in Italy and entailing the overthrow of the aggressor regime. The same motive prompted General MacArthur's desire to chastise Red China. In the earlier years of the cold war the West debated this issue of containment or liberation, of limited war or counter-revolutionary crusade, and decided clearly in favour of containment. If we were to put it in terms of the ancient doctrine which lays down that there can be no just war without a right intention, we might say that it is the consensus of the West today that there can be no right intention in going to war unless the motive is fear.

It has often been argued that the invention of nuclear weapons has transcended the Hobbesian predicament, by transferring our fear from the potential enemy to war itself. But a moment's reflection will show that every great power, both government and people, fears atomic warfare *less* than it fears the consequences of not using it in certain circumstances against the potential enemy. The motive of gain may indeed have been weakened, the motives of fear and doctrinal conviction continue to be part of our daily

8. *Life and Writings*, Vol. I Appendix, pp. 369.

experience. And as Smuts once pointed out, the more we suppose that nuclear weapons have reduced the likelihood of direct military encounter between great powers, the more we must suppose that international conflict will take the form of revolutionary sub-war, of infiltration, guerrilla strife, terrorism, and propaganda.[9] War is inevitable, but particular wars can be avoided. This means living with endless uncertainties and crises.[10]

9. Speech on becoming Vice-Chancellor of Cambridge University, 10 June 1948, in *The Times*, 11 June 1948, p. 4.

10. This chapter is a reprint with minor editorial changes, of a talk entitled 'War and International Politics' given by the author on the BBC Third Programme and published in *The Listener* on 13 October 1955 (Vol. LIV, No. 1389, pp. 584–5). It takes the place of a projected chapter on 'War and Neutrality', a fragment of which has been incorporated in Chapter 10 above. Eds.

14 : The Expansion of Powers

It is the nature of powers to expand. The energies of their members radiate culturally, economically and politically, and unless there are strong obstacles these tendencies will be summed up in territorial growth. Lord Acton described it as the governing impulse of modern history:

This law of the modern world, that power tends to expand indefinitely, and will transcend all barriers, abroad and at home, until met by superior forces, produces the rhythmic movement of history. Neither race, nor religion, nor political theory has been in the same degree an incentive to the perpetuation of universal enmity and national strife.[1]

The German philosopher Kant, in his ironic and penetrating essay *On Perpetual Peace*, pressed the tendency to its logical conclusion when he said, '. . . it is the desire of every state, or of its ruler, to attain to a condition of perpetual peace . . . by subjecting the whole world, as far as possible, to its sway'.[2] And much earlier Dante, reflecting on Italy in the fourteenth century, described how 'the human mind does not rest content with limited possession of territory, but always desires to acquire territory, as we see from experience', and argued that there would be no peace until there was a universal state.[3]

It is of course the great powers that display this expansionist tendency most successfully. Britain, the United States, Russia

1. Lord Acton, *Lectures on Modern History*, Macmillan, London, 1952, p. 51.
2. M. Campbell Smith (trans.), *On Perpetual Peace*, Sonnenschein, London, 1903, p. 156.
3. E. Moore and P. Toynbee (eds.), 'Il convivio' in *Le opere di Dante Alighieri*, O.U.P., Oxford, 1963, IV, 4, pp. 298–9.

and France, to take the most obvious examples, have each had histories of steady territorial growth. In 1811, when Napoleon had just seized the Duchy of Oldenburg, and was preparing his invasion of Russia, the Tsar Alexander happened to meet the American ambassador walking in St Petersburg, and questioned him about the United States' recent seizure of West Florida from Spain. Adams explained it as well as he could. 'The Emperor smiled, and said, "On s'agrandit toujours un peu, dans ce monde," and bowed; upon which I quitted him, and continued my walk.'[4] Ten years later Adams, now Secretary of State, was able to adopt a tone of moral reproof towards another great empire. He was discussing the American-Canadian frontier with the British ambassador, Stratford Canning, and said that the British claims were as reasonable as if the United States claimed the Shetland Islands or New South Wales. The following dialogue ensued:

Canning: 'Have you any *claim* to the Shetland Islands or New South Wales?'

Adams: 'Have you any *claim* to the mouth of the Columbia River?'

Canning: 'Why, do you not *know* that we have a claim?'

Adams: 'I do not *know* what you claim or what you do not claim. You claim India; you claim Africa; you claim – '

'Perhaps,' said he, 'a piece of the moon.'

Adams: 'No, I have not heard that you claim exclusively any part of the moon; but there is not a spot on *this* habitable globe that I could affirm you do not claim; and there is none which you may not claim with as much colour of right as you can have to Columbia River or its mouth.'[5]

Bismarck said that he could not imagine a great power not making its faculty for expansion a vital question, and defined a 'satiated' state as one whose requirements had either been satisfied already or could be satisfied without resorting to force of arms. The mandate system under the League of Nations and the trusteeship system of the United Nations enabled the victorious powers to redistribute the defeated empires among themselves under cover of a new principle of international accountability. But Stalin demanded a Soviet trusteeship over one of the Italian

4. J. Quincy Adams, *Memoirs*, Vol. II, Lippincott, Philadelphia, 1874, 6 May 1811, p. 261.

5. ibid., Vol. V, 27 January 1821, pp. 251–2.

colonies at the Potsdam Conference on the frank grounds that Russia 'would like some territory of the defeated states', and the claim was argued on the basis of Russia's need for an outlet into the Mediterranean.[6] The trusteeship system, indeed, in some way marks a regression from the principle of international account-ability compared with the mandate system, by providing for 'strategic trusteeships' where the administering power has a virtually free hand.

But the tendency to expansion is not only seen in the great colonizing and empire-building states. It can be found in the history of small powers as well, even among those which, like the states of Western Europe, are deservedly reckoned among the most civilized and unaggressive in the world. Switzerland, today the most peaceable member of international society, at the end of the fifteenth and the beginning of the sixteenth centuries was a leading military power, which destroyed the Burgundian power to the north and conquered Milan to the south. She produced the finest soldiers in Christendom; the Pope granted them the title of Protectors of the Liberties of the Church; and they still provide his guard at the Vatican in the uniforms designed by Michel-angelo. Sweden and Denmark were formerly great powers, ruling territories far beyond their present frontiers. Portugal and Holl-and amassed colonial empires many times greater than their own size. When Belgium acquired her independence by separating from Holland in 1831, she engaged in the partition of Africa and acquired a great African dominion; and when Norway similarly got her independence by separating from Sweden in 1905 her energies went into creating the world's third mercantile marine and annexing Spitzbergen in the Arctic and a large sector of the Antarctic continent. After the First World War many Belgians argued that as a reward for her heroic struggle Belgium should be allowed to incorporate Luxembourg; after the Second World War neither Holland nor Belgium were above seeking to annex various frontier villages at the expense of prostrate Germany. In 1941 the Finns gave flanking assistance to the German attack on Russia, justifiably eager to redress the wrongs committed against them by Russia's aggressive 'Winter War' of 1939-40; but they soon

6. J. Byrnes, *Speaking Frankly*, p. 76.

became captivated by the desire for the dismemberment of Russia and a vast territorial expansion up to the White Sea, which made Stalin insist on indicting a number of Finnish leaders as war criminals.

There are always economic or moral arguments for specific territorial annexations, whether these be 'frontier rectifications' or schemes of 'closer union' between a stronger power and a weaker. And in every country there are many individuals who feel personally magnified by an increase in the frontiers of the state. Thus nationalism, which is the will of a historically selfconscious people to attain self-government, inclines scarcely perceptibly through irredentism, which is the will to liberate peoples claimed to be of the same nationality, towards imperialism, which is the will to rule other peoples. No sooner had the Italians freed themselves from Austrian rule than they succeeded to the Austrian claim to dominate South Slavs. No sooner had the Serbs obtained a Yugoslav state than they forfeited the goodwill of their fellow Yugoslavs by establishing in the new state a harsh Serb predominance. There are many recent instances of the transition from nationalism to irredentism, and of the uncertain distinction between irredentism and imperialism. Eire claims Northern Ireland, and South Africa claimed the High Commission Territories,[7] as India claimed Portuguese Goa, and Indonesia claimed Western New Guinea, by appeal to some principle other than the wishes of the inhabitants, which were either unknown or hostile to the claim. Egypt hoped to absorb the Sudan, half of whose population are not Arab. Nkrumah sought a union of West Africa, which would reduce Liberia, with a hundred years experience in self-government, to a position subordinate to Ghana. The settlers of Southern Rhodesia, in their march towards independence, constructed a Central African Federation of which Nyasaland against her will was compelled to become a part.

When the territories of a state are geographically separated, there is a strong urge to complete their political union by the absorption of the intervening territory. In this way many states

7. The High Commission Territories were Bechuanaland, Basutoland and Swaziland (now respectively Botswana, Lesotho, Swaziland). They were administered by Britain. Eds.

have been built out of the scattered inheritance of a single dynasty. The German prince who reluctantly became George I of Great Britain was more interested in the slow aggrandizement of his native electorate:

... he had watched the Hanoverian dominions joining themselves together, like lakes and pools when the floods are out, spreading across the plains which lie between the rivers Ems and Elbe, encroaching upon the intermediate basin of the Weser, stretching out to the shores of the North Sea, pressing against Oldenburg, and threatening before long to overflow the coveted duchies of Bremen and Werden.[8]

A hundred and fifty years later Hanover herself was swallowed up in order to fill the gap between the east and west provinces of Prussia. Frederick the Great annexed certain Polish provinces in 1772 in order to link Brandenburg with East Prussia; when these provinces were restored to a newly independent Poland in 1919, the Germans refused to accept the separation of East Prussia from the Reich by 'the Polish Corridor', and brought about the greater injustice of Poland and Russia partitioning East Prussia between them. The same urge to territorial consolidation was seen on a world scale in the expansion of the British Empire. In the nineteenth century Britain collected all the naval bases and coaling stations she needed on the oceans between England and India; in the twentieth century she repeated the consolidation by land. The First World War gave her 'continuity of territory or of control . . . between Egypt and India'[9] through the acquisition under mandate of Palestine, Transjordan and Iraq, and also, through the acquisition of Tanganyika, a territorial sovereignty from the Cape to Cairo that had been beyond the dreams of Cecil Rhodes.

The converse of this tendency towards the combination of the scattered territories of a single power might be described as the precariousness of enclaves. A territorial property that is wholly or partially surrounded by lands of a stronger power is a poor risk for

8. F. S. Oliver, *The Endless Adventure*, Vol. I, p. 168.
9. L. Amery, *My Political Life*, Vol. II, Hutchinson, London, 1953, p. 102; also A. P. Thornton, *The Imperial Idea and Its Enemies*, Macmillan, New York, 1966, pp. 166–7.

its possessor. Louis XIV annexed the principality of Orange, whose sovereign had been his bitterest enemy, as soon as William III died; the French Republic annexed the Papal dominion of Avignon. It has been a *tour de force* to maintain the independence of West Berlin since 1945, and this outpost will be in danger of being absorbed by East Germany so long as East Germany itself is not absorbed in a reunited Germany.

It will be seen that the expansion of powers is a product of two causes: internal pressure and the weakness of surrounding powers. When an equilibrium is reached between the outward pressure and the external resistance, expansion stops. If the pressure of Persia upon Russia and the British Empire has been less than the pressure of Russia and the British Empire upon Persia, the reason lies in Persia's internal weakness. So long as China and India were impoverished and ill-organized, their capacity for expansion remained at a very low point. But if they now achieve an internal reconstruction comparable to that of Soviet Russia, they are likely to extend the frontier of their 'vital interests' to enclose the overseas populations of Chinese in South-east Asia, and of Indians in South and East Africa, through the successive stages of 'protection', 'liberation' and absorption. The encirclement of India by the two wings of Pakistan offered no threat to India, because she was the stronger power. On the other hand, the encirclement of Israel by Arab republics is a constant threat to Israel, because her strength in relation to her Arab neighbours may well decline.

The desire for access to the sea has sometimes been seen as the basic kind of expansion. The German political writer Arndt wrote that 'the first natural frontier that each country should get is the sea, the second is language'.[10] Russian history has been interpreted as a territorial movement towards warm-water ports. Mussolini told the Fascist Grand Council in 1939 that states were more or less independent according to their maritime position. 'That is to say, states which have oceanic coasts, or free access to the oceans, are independent; states which have no free communication with oceans and are enclosed in inland seas are semi-independent; continental states which have no outlet either to

10. E. M. Arndt, *Germanien und Europa*, Altona, 1803, p. 384.

oceans or to seas are not independent at all.'[11] The argument was designed to show that Italy was a prisoner in the Mediterranean, and must march towards the Atlantic, through French North Africa, or towards the Indian Ocean, by joining Libya with Ethiopia through the Sudan. It is true that landlocked states generally seek access to the sea. The War of the Pacific between Chile, Bolivia and Peru (1879–84), which is one of the five great South American wars, was fought by Bolivia to retain her Pacific littoral, and she has never acquiesced in the loss of it. The colony of British Honduras was separated from the independent Republic of Honduras by the Guatemalan outlet to the Atlantic, which Guatemala acquired from Honduras after failing to get it from Britain, at the cost of abiding resentment against Britain. The Afghan demand for independence for the Pathans at the expense of West Pakistan was bound up with the desire for a pathway to the ocean, from Kabul to Karachi. But it is a mistake to speak of expansion to the ocean as if the ocean is the final goal of expansion. The ocean is an avenue as well as a barrier. When Prussia obtained great seaports with the inclusion of Hamburg and Bremen in the North German Confederation in 1866, she soon renamed the North Sea the German Ocean, and within less than a generation was launched upon overseas expansion. When French expansion was blocked in the east, it moved south across the Mediterranean to the conquest of Algeria. And the course of American empire took its way westward from the Appalachians to the Pacific, and overleaping the ocean established American interests and power in East Asia. It would be naïve to suppose that if Russia obtained at last an oceanic outlet on the Persian Gulf, her territorial strivings would be accomplished.

There are always defensive arguments for territorial expansion. Gustavus Adolphus described the German coast of the Baltic which he conquered as the outworks of Sweden, her defence against Austria. There was a maxim of French policy, laid down by Turenne, repeated by Napoleon and remembered by Foch, 'If you would defend the left bank of the Rhine, cross to the right.' When the Allied campaign in Western Europe in 1944 had liberated the Channel ports from the Germans, an English news-

11. *Report to the Fascist Grand Council*, 5 February 1939.

paper wrote that Calais was more than a supply port: 'it is the traditional symbol of Britain's own freedom from Continental aggression. It means the freedom of the English Channel'[12] – though the French have a different memory of what Calais meant as an English possession. Thus there is a tendency towards cumulative expansion, one annexation making necessary another to complete or protect the first. This tendency is perhaps promoted by military strategists more than politicians. Lord Salisbury once wrote with his customary mordancy that one should not be too much impressed by the soldiers' strategic arguments: 'If they were allowed full scope they would insist on the importance of garrisoning the moon in order to protect us from Mars.'[13] This was in 1892, before space travel had got beyond the pages of Jules Verne. In 1958 an American general explained to the House Armed Services Committee the need to establish an American missile base on the moon, and when it was put to him that Russia might also establish bases on the moon 'the moral which he drew was that the United States must also occupy Mars and Venus'.[14]

The corollary of the expansiveness of powers is their general refusal to suffer territorial loss without a struggle. 'No nation', said Adam Smith, 'ever voluntarily gave up the dominion of any province, how troublesome soever it might be to govern it and how small soever the revenue which it afforded might be in proportion to the expense which it occasioned'.[15] After the retreat from Moscow, Napoleon played into the hands of the Allies by refusing to make the territorial sacrifices that might have undermined the unity of the Allied powers and thus preserved his throne; above everything he would not relinquish the natural frontiers of France, saying he could not leave France smaller than he had found it. Germany did not go to war in 1914 in order to conquer Belgium; but having occupied Belgium as a means of

12. *The Daily Express*, 2 October 1944, leading article.

13. Lady Gwendolen Cecil, *Life of Robert, Marquis of Salisbury*, Vol. III, Hodder and Stoughton, London, 1921, p. 218.

14. *The Manchester Guardian*, 8 January 1959, leader, p. 8.

15. Adam Smith, *The Wealth of Nations*, Vol. II, Book IV, Chapter VII, part 3, p. 116.

invading France, she refused to consider any peace that would not allow for the virtual annexation of Belgium, and this was perhaps the chief reason for the failure of the various peace negotiations of 1916–17. The schemes for disengagement in Europe that were put forward after Stalin's death took too little account of the political difficulty the Soviet government would have in abandoning East Germany (even if it so desired) because of the repercussions on the other People's Democracies of Eastern Europe. It may be guessed that a similar fear of unforeseeable consequences prevented the United States from compelling Nationalist China to abandon the offshore islands of Quemoy and Matsu and withdraw behind the barrier of the Formosa Strait.

The same reluctance to accept territorial diminishment is seen in the modern histories of Hungary and Poland. The Hungary of 1919 never renounced her hope of regaining all 'the lands of the crown of St Stephen', i.e. of ruling once more over Rumanians, Slovaks, Serbs, Croats and Ruthenes. The Poland of 1919 was never satisfied with not recovering the frontiers Poland had enjoyed before the Partition of 1772, i.e. with not ruling again over Ukrainians, White Russians and Lithuanians. This was why Pilsudski invaded Russia in 1920; and if at the end of the Second World War Russia deprived Poland of Lvov, the Polish capital of the Ukrainian province of Eastern Galicia, perhaps the deepest reason is that Poland had never truly reconciled herself to abandoning Kiev, the Ukrainian capital of the Ukraine itself.

There are two exceptions to this general rule of tenacity of territorial possession. One is territorial exchange, which is discussed in the chapter on compensation. Yet even a profitable bargain is likely to be hindered by the sentiment of dominion, especially when foreign policy is complicated by democratic government. When Britain and Germany made the agreement of 1890, exchanging the cession of Heligoland to Germany for Germany's abandoning her claims over Zanzibar, the public in both countries received it badly, caring for the interest that was sacrificed and not (like the two governments) for the greater interest that was secured. The other exception is when a power has attained the capacity for being content with an economic or moral equivalent for dominion. And this points to the possibility of moral limitation upon the rule of the expansiveness of powers.

Prudence will often make a power limit its liabilities, in accordance with its assessment of its special interests. When Charles V won his most splendid victory by the defeat and capture of his rival Francis I at the battle of Pavia in 1525, his chancellor Gattinara and his ally Henry VIII urged him to seize the opportunity of dismembering France; but caution or justice made the Emperor moderate, and he exacted nothing from his defeated enemy but the Burgundian territories to which inheritance entitled him. When the Russo-Turkish War of 1828–9 had made Russia mistress of the Balkans, Nicholas refrained from territorial aggrandizement and adopted a new policy of maintaining the Ottoman Empire in preference to the European complications of partitioning it. When Texas declared her independence of Mexico in 1836 and pressed for annexation by the United States, Jackson and Van Buren after him procrastinated for fear of disturbing the delicate balance of power within the United States. When the United States established a virtual protectorate over Santo Domingo in 1905, Theodore Roosevelt declared, 'As for annexing the island, I have about the same desire as a gorged boa-constrictor might have to swallow a porcupine wrong-end-to.'[16] These examples show a reluctance to pursue territorial expansion in very different political circumstances, for very different reasons. We have noticed others when discussing prestige.[17]

Correspondingly, there are examples of powers abandoning sovereignty over possessions, for motives in which calculation of interest may be mixed with considerations of justice. It has sometimes been done by a great power at its zenith. Thus in 1864 Britain abandoned her protectorate over the Ionian Islands and transferred them to Greece. The motive was to get rid of a troublesome and expensive dependency, and still more to draw Greece, an increasingly important Mediterranean power, into the British orbit. Thus again, the United States granted independence to the Philippines, in principle in 1935 and in fact in 1946, for much the same reason that Britain had returned the captured

16. Quoted in H. F. Pringle, *Theodore Roosevelt*, Harcourt, New York, 1956, p. 206.
17. See above Chapter 8.

French possessions in the West Indies to France at the end of the Seven Years War: to put a powerful competitor in the production of sugar outside the home market. But declining powers, which desire to end an unsuccessful war or recognize that certain territorial commitments are beyond their strength to maintain, afford the commoner instances. By the Treaty of Vervins of 1598, the beginning of the end of Spain's long struggle to dominate Europe, Philip II was reluctantly compelled to cede sovereignty over the Spanish Netherlands to his daughter and her husband the Archduke Albert; but the surrender was sweetened by the condition that if they had no children the Netherlands were to revert to the Spanish crown, and by the confidence that they were incapable of having children. With comparable reluctance Holland transferred sovereignty to Indonesia in 1949, and France to Vietnam in 1954, to Tunis in 1956, and to Morocco in 1956. Perhaps the sweetening afterthought here was that the liberated countries could not progress without the economic and technical help of their former rulers. If Britain seems to have given independence to India, Burma, Ceylon, Palestine, Ghana, Malaya and Cyprus with more readiness and candour, the reason is to be sought less in the transformation of the Empire into the Commonwealth, for the idea of the Commonwealth seems to have singularly little influence on British opinion, than in the long tradition in British politics of resistance to imperial expansion at all. Palmerston wrote in 1833 that Russia could not be trusted politically because she had 'not yet reached that point of civilization at which the government of a powerful country discovers that there are other objects deserving of attention, and other sources of glory for a sovereign, besides augmentation of territory and foreign conquest'.[18] This, it may be said, is all very well: Palmerston represents a period of satiated invulnerability in British foreign policy, and after his death Britain moved forward to vast augmentations of territory in Africa and the Middle East. He who praises Britain's unprecedented and unparalleled transfers of power to subject peoples would do well to remember that Britain had, after all, accumulated an empire unprecedented and unparalleled in

18. Letter to Esterhazy, 20 November 1833, in C. K. Webster, *Foreign Policy of Palmerston*, Vol. I, p. 313.

extent; but he who censures Britain's imperial appetite would do well to remember that there has been, in Britain, a more consistent tradition of hostility to colonial expansion than probably in any other country in the world.

Adam Smith's generalization was written at the beginning of the British attempt to prevent the secession of the American colonies, by a policy which he himself regretted. It was only the failure of that policy that enabled his generalization to be modified. 'That point of civilization' which Palmerston thought Russia had not yet attained has not been attained by any power except through bitter experience. The unity of a power, as we saw, is forged by struggle; the readiness of a power to set limits to its expansion is learned by defeat. The acceptance of the loss of America was the point at which Britain may be said to have become a mature power; for maturity in international politics might be described as the voluntary limiting of objectives. A mature power, for our purposes, would be one not with an internal regime we approve of, but which has been educated by adversity into being a good neighbour. And Britain may have learned a second lesson, a century and a half later, from the failure of her attempt to coerce Ireland, by the threat of 'immediate' and 'terrible war', into accepting a dominion status that meant nothing to the Irish as a whole and was soon quietly repudiated.[19]

There are powers that seem not to have acquiesced in a decline of status, and whose maturity in this sense seems doubtful. Thus Spain has always found it difficult to accept the loss of Gibraltar, and Franco grasped the opportunities that seemed to be offering in 1940 by demanding the return of Gibraltar and expansion at France's expense in North Africa. But there are other powers that have resigned themselves to the loss of great-power status without regrets or resentment: Venice, Portugal, Denmark, Sweden, Holland. A striking addition to their number was Turkey, when she based her national revival under Atatürk on a deliberate renunciation of all the non-Turkish territories of the old Ottoman Empire; but it must not be forgotten that she was able to assuage her national pride at the same time by inflicting a severe defeat on her traditional enemy Greece in the Anatolian War of 1919–22.

19. F. Pakenham, *Peace by Ordeal*, Cape, London, 1935, p. 324.

And if we are to define maturity in this way, we might conclude that the United States attained maturity, not as a result of the two World Wars, when she was able to deploy her prodigious resources and win victory at a sacrifice far smaller than her allies', but during the Korean War, when she bore nine-tenths of the burden and accepted at last a compromise peace. And its decisive incident in this respect would be President Truman's dismissal of General MacArthur.[20]

20. This draft was apparently completed in 1959 or the early 1960s. Eds.

15 : The Pattern of Power

Pure power politics would be a condition of what Hobbes called
'war of every man against every man',[1] in which each power
would depend wholly on its own resources and seek to 'go it
alone'. But no power is able to make its policy wholly without
reliance on some other powers, even if it relies only on their
neutrality. Dominant powers like Napoleonic France or Nazi
Germany acted with much arbitrariness and contempt for their
allies, but always took a certain trouble to ensure either a servile
compliance or non-interference. The United States at the
beginning of her history, predominant on a distant continent,
could repudiate European entanglements; but when there was a
danger of European intervention in South America she accepted
an entente with Britain as the basis of the Monroe Doctrine. No
power acts in complete detachment. All powers fall into one or
another of constantly changing alignments. These alignments are
formed under external pressure rather than from common sentiment, and their cohesion varies with the pressure. They range
from assurances of benevolent neutrality, through ententes and
alliances, to confederations and such a grouping as the North
Atlantic Treaty Organization. They are the lines of force that
compose the pattern of power.

It is a general rule that when powers are territorial neighbours
they are hostile. 'It has from long observation of the progress of
society become a sort of axiom in politics', wrote Hamilton, 'that
vicinity, or nearness of situation, constitutes nations natural
enemies.'[2] The rule has two exceptions. (1) When powers become
adjacent through partitioning a territory to which their right is
challenged, this challenge will tend to make them interdependent.

1. *Leviathan*, p. 66.
2. *The Federalist*, No. VI, p. 33.

Prussia and Russia established a common frontier by the Partition of Poland at the end of the eighteenth century, and a joint interest in suppressing Polish nationalism was the basis of their friendship for more than a hundred years. After the First World War Soviet Russia and Nationalist Turkey cooperated to eliminate the Transcaucasian republics that had sprung up between them when the Russian and Ottoman Empires collapsed, and this was an element (though weak in proportion to the weakness of Transcaucasian nationalism) in the good relations between Russia and Turkey between the wars. Israel and Jordan partitioned Jerusalem in 1948 in defiance of a United Nations resolution establishing it as a Free City, and partly for this reason Israeli–Jordanian relations have been less exacerbated than Israel's relations with the other Arab powers. Turkey, Iraq and Persia have a common interest in the partitioning of the Kurdish people, which will grow as Kurdish nationalism grows. (2) When a common frontier runs through undeveloped and sparsely populated territory, there will probably be slight pressure upon it, as has been seen with the colonial frontiers in Africa. The boundary between the United States and Canada is the classic example in the Western world of a disarmed and uncontentious international frontier; it was determined at a time when the Americans and the British were still moving westwards in two parallel streams of population and development. But it is worth remembering that this was not done without grave danger of war, and for all its being an unfortified frontier, the fear of United States annexation throughout the nineteenth century was one of the influences shaping Canadian nationalism.

If your neighbour is your 'natural enemy', the power on the other side of your neighbour is your natural ally. And what natural allies regard as a defensive alliance is likely to appear to the power between them as 'encirclement'. Thus Scottish policy, from John Balliol at the end of the thirteenth century down to Mary Queen of Scots at the end of the sixteenth, rested on the Auld Alliance with France against England, which ensured that England could always be threatened with a war on two fronts. Shakespeare makes Henry V and his advisers discuss this danger before invading France.

But there's a saying very old and true,
    'If that you will France win,
        Then with Scotland first begin'
For once the eagle England being in prey,
To her unguarded nest the weasel Scot
Comes sneaking, and so sucks her princely eggs . . .[3]

Thus France, in her turn, traditionally based her policy on alliance with the strongest states in the rear of the strongest German power, whether that power was Habsburg or Hohenzollern: Turkey, Poland, Sweden, Russia, the Little Entente. And the German power, in its turn, allied with Persia against Turkey in the days of Charles V, and with Russia against Poland in the days of Frederick the Great, the Weimar Republic and Hitler. The principle has been described by Sir Lewis Namier as 'the "sandwich system" of international politics'.[4]

The pattern of forces in international relations, then, resembles a chequer-board of alternating colours. But in practice it is indefinitely modified and complicated, becoming a *Looking-glass* chessboard, where the squares usually have less or more than four frontiers, and vary in size. The simple sandwich system is found only between powers of similar strength: that is to say, powers of which no one could conquer any other single-handed. If a sandwich system of small states comes under the direct pressure of a great power, it is apt to be gradually transformed. The great power itself will take part in the rivalries of the small powers, simultaneously encouraging and controlling them, on the principle of 'divide and rule'. This method of hegemony was employed by France in the seventeenth and eighteenth centuries among the German states, and by Germany between the World Wars among the states of Eastern Europe. There is evidence that Russia has had to pursue the same policy to control her East European satellites since the Second World War, in spite of their façade of Communist uniformity, and this in particular was why in 1948 it forbade the Yugoslav-Bulgarian federation desired by Tito and Dimitrov. When a sandwich system of small powers is

3. *King Henry V*, Act I, scene ii.
4. *Conflicts*, Macmillan, London, 1942, p. 14; also *Personalities and Powers*, Hamish Hamilton, London, 1955, pp. 111-12.

brought under pressure by two rival great powers at once, it tends to become obliterated. Thus the states of Renaissance Italy were fought over and divided by France and Spain, and at last reduced to a common dependence upon Spain. Thus Napoleon created the Confederation of the Rhine in 1806 in order to exclude Austria and Prussia from Germany; and the United States has similarly tried to promote Western European union by every means since 1947 in resistance to Russia. At this point local rivalries are largely ironed out by the pressure of greater rivalries; the small powers are reduced to a buffer zone between great powers; and the sandwich system is reproduced on a wider scale in the alignments of the great powers themselves.

A buffer state is a weak power between two or more stronger ones, maintained or even created with the purpose of reducing conflict between them. A buffer zone is a region occupied by one or more weaker powers between two or more stronger powers; it is sometimes described as a 'power vacuum'. Each stronger power will generally have a vital interest in preventing the other from controlling the buffer zone, and will pursue this interest in one of two ways, according to its strength. It will seek either to maintain the buffer zone as neutral and independent, or to establish its own control, which may lead in the long run to its annexing the buffer zone and converting it into a frontier province. Buffer states may therefore be roughly divided into trimmers, neutrals and satellites. Trimmers are states whose policy is prudently to play off their mighty neighbours against one another; the most famous of European trimmers was the Duchy of Savoy, which earned thereby first a kingdom and then the hegemony of United Italy; the neutralist states today are of their number. Neutral are states without an active foreign policy at all; their hope is to lie low and escape notice. Satellites are states whose foreign policy is controlled by another power. If the weaker state has formally conceded this control by treaty, so that in law as well as in fact it has surrendered a measure of its sovereignty, it is known as a protectorate. The gradation from trimmer to neutral, from neutral to ally, from ally to satellite, is obscure and uncertain. Fluctuations of power make most buffer zones unstable and ambiguous. A policy adopted by one great power to preserve the neutrality of a buffer state may be seen by its rival as reducing the buffer state to a satellite; and a buffer state may be regarded by the same statesman, in different circumstances, as either a defensive bulwark or a springboard for further expansion.

The most familiar examples of the neutral buffer state are the small powers established along the Franco-German and Franco-Italian frontiers, the main line of political cleavage and strife in Western Europe. Switzerland, after her brief career of military glory, settled down as a buffer state between France, the Habsburg Empire and the Spanish power in Italy, and has continued that role between France, United Germany and United Italy. Luxembourg is a buffer between France and Germany. Holland and Belgium are buffers between France, Germany and Britain. Britain has a traditional interest in their independence, for it is to be noticed that powers with sea frontiers seek to establish buffer states on the opposite shores from their own, and that these too may be either defensive outworks or bridgeheads for the penetration of the mainland.

Each of the dominant powers at its zenith has absorbed a buffer state, whose independence has afterwards, with the dominant power defeated, been re-established as necessary to the interest of other powers. Philip II attained the summit of his success when in 1580 he seized the crown of Portugal and united the Iberian Peninsula, together with the vast Spanish and Portuguese Empires overseas. In 1640, when Spain was greatly weakened by war with France and a revolution in Catalonia, Portugal revolted with French assistance and resumed her independence, which she confirmed by immediately renewing her alliance with England, 'the oldest of European alliances'. Portugal has ever since remained for Britain an indispensable seaboard buffer, whose independence guarantees the safety of the Atlantic routes; and she also served as a bridgehead for Wellington's expedition on the Continent against Napoleon. What Portugal was to Spain, Belgium was to France. It was a chief aim of the coalitions first against Louis XIV and afterwards against Revolutionary France and Napoleon, to prevent France from absorbing the Belgian Netherlands. This was brought about in 1815 by joining Belgium to Holland; and in 1830, when Belgium revolted, by erecting her into an independent state under international guarantee. And what Belgium was to France, modern Austria is to Germany. After 1918 Austria became the buffer state between Germany, Italy and the Little Entente (i.e. Czechoslovakia, Yugoslavia and Rumania). Hitler's conquest of Austria in 1938 was the great stroke that opened the way for Germany to the Mediterranean and the Black Sea. It made Czechoslovakia indefensible, which made Poland indefensible, which in its turn made all south-eastern Europe and the Ukraine indefensible; and at the same time it turned Italy into a German vassal. Germany had national claims to include Austria, as France had national claims to include Belgium; but in each case the security of international society has required the preservation of a buffer state.

The same pattern of power may be seen in Russia's advance westwards into Europe. Here there have been two chief buffer states, Poland and Turkey. Russian insistence on controlling Poland produced a crisis at the Congress of Vienna in 1815, and again at the Yalta Conference in 1945; and the other great powers were unable to save Poland from becoming a satellite. The recurrent Russian desire to control the Black Sea Straits has never been satisfied, and Soviet demands on Turkey caused another crisis in 1946, which led to the Truman Doctrine, which declared in effect that the United States had a vital interest in Turkish independence. Turkey remains one of the key buffer states whose independence cannot be lost without a general war.

In the nineteenth century the most important buffer zone in the world was that dividing the British Empire from Russia. Russia lay in the long curve of the British Empire rather like an egg in a spoon; but the two were separated by a layer of weak states stretching from the Near to the Far East – Turkey, Persia, Afghanistan and China, with her autonomous dependency Tibet and her frontier province Manchuria. It was Britain's great anxiety throughout the nineteenth century to keep this layer intact. There were four points along it at which she feared a Russian inroad: through Turkey to the Black Sea Straits and the Mediterranean, through Persia to the Persian Gulf and the Indian Ocean, through Afghanistan to the Punjab, and through Manchuria to the China Seas. This zone illustrates a wide variety of buffer states. Britain's historic policy in the Eastern Question was to preserve Turkey's independence as a bulwark against Russia; hence the Crimean War (1854–6) and the crisis which was resolved by the Congress of Berlin (1878). Persia, on the other hand, was partitioned into spheres of influence by Britain and Russia in agreement in 1907, a pattern repeated when the two great powers jointly occupied Persia during the Second World War. Afghanistan, an outpost of the Indian Empire, became a British protectorate as a result of the Second Afghan War (1878–80), conceding to Britain the control of her foreign policy; this was relinquished by Britain only after the Third Afghan War (1919), at a time when Russia had ceased to be a great power. China was too vast and important a region to be absorbed or made a protectorate by a single power, and here Anglo-Russian rivalry was complicated by the claims of other powers, France and Germany and Japan, with the United States as a watchful moderator. Britain's interests in China took the shape of trade and investments, and her traditional policy was to maintain China's integrity coupled with 'the open door' for all nations' commerce; but mutual jealousy in the end reduced the Chinese policy of all the great powers to a scramble for concessions, which might have led to partition if the First World War had not intervened. The outlying dependencies of China had already been more or less detached. Tibet, nominally under Chinese suzerainty, was neutralized by agreement between Britain and Russia in 1907, the two powers agreeing not to send diplomatic representatives to Lhasa, the Tibetan capital. It may be noted that Tibet was thus a buffer state without even possessing a common frontier with Russia. Manchuria and Korea are the Belgium and Holland of the Far East, the buffers between China, Japan and Russia.

The modern history of Korea illustrates how a buffer state that lacks internal strength and stability will gravitate, irrespective of its own wishes, away from a declining power towards an expanding power. Originally Korea was a tributary kingdom to China; by the first Sino-Japanese War of 1894–5 Japan compelled China to recognize Korean independence; in 1905 Japan asserted a protectorate over Korea; in 1910 she annexed Korea. Manchuria, which is of peculiar importance by reason of its industrial wealth, had a similar career. Russian ascendancy there was replaced by Japanese ascendancy as a result of Japan's defeat of Russia in the Russo-Japanese War (1904–5); in 1931–2 Japan conquered Manchuria and erected it into a satellite state, under the title of Manchukuo, as a prelude to the conquest of China itself.

This great buffer belt from the Mediterranean to the Pacific has undergone a threefold transformation as a result of the two World Wars. The Ottoman Empire has disappeared; the British Empire in the Indian Ocean has been dismantled, together with the other European Empires which it sheltered; and China has become a great power. The Middle East still remains one of the cockpits of international politics, not only as the strategic land-bridge between Europe, Asia and Africa, but also because of its oil resources. Here the Ottoman Empire, and the British and French spheres of influence that replaced it, have been succeeded by the independent states of the Arab League; but these have not yet established themselves as a stable buffer region, partly because of their internal weaknesses, partly because of their mutual rivalries, and partly because of the intrusion among them of the alien and detested state of Israel. Farther east, the disappearance of the British Empire in India, the Dutch Empire in the East Indies and the French Empire in Indo-China has produced a power vacuum throughout South and South-east Asia. Independent India, successor to the greatest of colonial empires, is, because of its military weakness, only the greatest of buffer states in the world pattern of power.

But the event that more than any other has changed the political pattern of Asia is the Chinese Communist Revolution. This has given China strong government for the first time since the Far East came under European ascendancy, and has shifted the battle-fields of Asia away from China herself to the countries on her borders – Korea and the former Indo-China and Burma. At the same time it has produced more of an equality of pressures along the longest land frontier in the world, that between China and Russia. Since the later nineteenth century Russia has been steadily encroaching upon the Chinese Empire. At one time it seemed that Manchuria might be detached and absorbed; Outer Mongolia has been detached and erected into a nominally independent state, and its northern province of Tuva has actually been annexed to the Soviet Union as an autonomous region; and the Russians after the Second World War penetrated deep into Sinkiang, by means of joint Sino-Russian companies to exploit the oil and minerals. But since Stalin's death in 1953 the Chinese reaction has gathered strength. Russia has withdrawn from Manchuria, the joint companies in Sinkiang have apparently been liquidated, and Mongolia alone has not yet been restored to the Chinese state. The frontier between the two Communist great powers in the 1950s enjoyed a tranquillity comparable to that between the United States and Canada. This may be partly ascribed to their absorption in what are called the tasks of socialist construction; but it is primarily to be understood as a feature of the world pattern of power, in which China and Russia stood back to back against a ring of enemies. At the same time China has brutally asserted her control of the fourth great frontier province, Tibet, ending its role as a buffer against India.

Throughout this Asiatic buffer belt, the United States took over the part played by Britain in the nineteenth century. It is the United States that now upholds the independence of Turkey, and gives arms to Pakistan for the defence of what used to be the North-west Frontier. But she also assumed the unprecedented role of maintaining the new buffer zone round the borders of resurgent China, which had become the principal Asiatic front in the cold war, and especially of trying to strengthen the weak states of South-east Asia, lying between China in the north, India in the west and Australia in the south.

No state can escape out of the pattern of power. A great power, however, has a certain freedom of choice in modifying the pattern, by its influence over the fate of its weaker neighbours. 'It is not an unreasonable generalization', says A. J. P. Taylor, 'that the Anglo-Saxons and perhaps the French believe in buffer states and the Germans and perhaps the Russians believe in partition as the best way to peace between the great powers.'[5] Differences of political tradition between the great powers will show themselves in different degrees of respect for the independence of smaller peoples, and perhaps here again a distinction can be seen between

5. Taylor, *The Struggle for Mastery in Europe*, p. 239, n. 1.

sea powers and continental powers. Small powers, on the other hand, have far less freedom of choice. It is broadly true that politics, like nature, abhor a vacuum; and a buffer state cannot achieve security on its own. The first condition of its stability is an equivalence of political pressure from the surrounding great powers; the second is a readiness on the part of more distant great powers to go to war in its defence; only the third is its own strength. This is illustrated by the history of Eastern Europe between 1919 and 1941. At the end of the First World War a buffer zone of small powers was able to appear between Germany and Russia, because these had temporarily ceased to be great powers. Even if Germany and Russia had been prepared to accept the existence of a buffer zone, its frontiers were swollen beyond their possible consent. It could not be maintained without reference to these adjacent great powers; still less could it be, as the Allies originally hoped, a wall to separate and confine them. France, following her traditional policy of seeking an ally in the rear of Germany, made military engagements with Poland and the powers of the Little Entente; but as Russia recovered strength, a Franco-Soviet alliance seemed a better alternative. But there was no possibility of cooperation between France's new great ally and her two smaller allies, Poland and Rumania, that themselves had disputed frontiers with Russia. When resurgent Germany expanded into the East European vacuum, the French system of alliances jammed in this contradiction; and Germany and Russia then partitioned the buffer zone as the prelude to conflict between themselves.

But a buffer state is not necessarily impotent. A small power with a strong and determined government can sometimes take advantage of an adjacent great power's readiness to protect it. A great power that lacks the will or the means to curb a small ally may find that its implicit guarantee of the small power's frontier leads insensibly into support of the small power's policy. Thus Piedmont, a buffer state between France and the Austrian power in Italy, had general encouragement in her Italian plans from Napoleon III; but when in 1860 Cavour conquered the Papal States he went much further than his patron had bargained for. In 1919 Britain established a veiled protectorate over Persia, and was at once embarrassed by Persian requests for support in an expansionist policy against Bolshevik Russia. South Korea under President Syngman Rhee sometimes seemed to enjoy a similar position in respect of the United States. The history of Europe since 1945 affords another illustration. The Second World War destroyed Germany, France and Italy as great powers, and turned the whole of Europe into a buffer zone between Russia on the one side and the English-speaking powers on the other. Russia transformed Eastern Europe into a frontier belt of satellite states, a glacis against invasion; the West European seaboard, with Britain as the great outpost, became equally vital to the United States. In between lay the vacuum of partitioned Germany. But the revival of western Germany has made her potentially the strongest power on the continent; and it has been a recurrent anxiety of American, British and French policy to harness this power to the North Atlantic alliance without at the same time harnessing themselves to a future West German expansionist campaign for the re-unification of Germany and perhaps for the recovery of the lost territories as well. The statesman has no harder problem of foreign policy than restraining an irresponsible small ally, whose security is a vital interest to his own country, and whose policies make an appeal, on grounds of justice or sentiment, to his own public opinion.[6]

6. This draft was apparently written in the late 1950s or early 1960s. Eds.

16 : The Balance of Power

The idea of a *pattern* of power enables us to generalize about international politics in relation to their geographical framework. At a higher degree of abstraction, we can interpret international politics by the idea of a *balance* of power. In doing so we think of the powers less as pieces on a chessboard than as weights in a pair of scales; we mentally pluck them out of their geographical setting and arrange them according to their alliances and affinities, with the underlying notion of matching their moral weight and material strength. The two ideas come very close to one another, and it is interesting to note that the famous chapter in the *Memoirs* of Philippe de Commynes, Louis XI's minister, which is usually credited with being the earliest account in modern European literature of the balance of power, is rather a vivid description of what we have called the pattern of power.[1] The pattern of power leads to considerations of strategy; the balance of power leads to considerations of military potential, diplomatic initiative and economic strength. The idea of balance arises naturally in considering any relationship between competing human units, groups or institutions: we talk of 'checks and balances' in a constitution, or of the balance of parties in a parliament. But the conception of the balance of power belongs especially to international politics, and it is in this connection that it has been most thoroughly explored. The balance of power is the principle of what might be called the mechanics of power politics; and the mechanistic metaphor is useful for describing international relations, provided that we do not suppose that it exhausts everything of importance that can be said about them.

The policy of the balance of power is founded, as Hume said,

1. Calmette (ed.), *Mémoires*, Vol. II, Champion, Paris, 1925, Book V, pp. 207–16.

'on common sense and obvious reasoning';[2] it is an application of the law of self-preservation. Let there be three powers, of which the first attacks the second. The third power cannot afford to see the second so decisively crushed that it becomes threatened itself; therefore if it is far-sighted it 'throws its weight into the lighter scale of the balance' by supporting the second power. This is the balance of power at its simplest. More generally, when one power grows dangerously strong the others combine against it. The balance of power is seen in full operation whenever a dominant power tries to gain mastery of international society, and momentarily 'overturns the balance'. Although the dominant power usually has a small following of vassal-states, too weak or too frightened to defend their independence, and of jackal-states,[3] with private local interests to pursue, nevertheless arrayed against them there arises a grand alliance of superior strength, whose victory 'restores the balance'. 'The balance of power,' said Stubbs, 'however it be defined, i.e. whatever the powers were between which it was necessary to maintain such equilibrium, that the weaker should not be crushed by the union of the stronger, is the principle which gives unity to the political plot of modern European history.'[4]

The system of the balance of power seems to follow a regular cycle, whose phases can be distinguished. When there are three or more great powers or blocs, not tied by rigid alliances, there may be said to be a multiple balance; the balance between the great powers resembles the equilibrium of a merry-go-round. This was the normal state of Europe in the eighteenth century. In Western Europe and overseas there was the balance between Britain, France and Spain; in Eastern Europe there was the

2. 'Of the Balance of Power', in *Essays Moral, Political and Literary*, Vol. I, T. H. Green and T. H. Grose (eds), Longmans, London, 1829, p. 352.

3. 'In a style less grave than that of history, I should perhaps compare the emperor Alexius to the jackal, who is said to follow the steps, and to devour the leavings, of the lion. Whatever had been his fears and toils in the passage of the first crusade, they were amply recompensed by the subsequent benefits which he derived from the exploits of the Franks.'
E. Gibbon, *The Decline and Fall of the Roman Empire*, Vol. II, The Modern Library, New York (no date), Chapter 59, p. 1047.

4. W. Stubbs, *Seventeen Lectures*, p. 258.

balance between Austria, Russia, Prussia, Sweden and Turkey; among the states of Germany and of Italy there were subordinate balances; and all these balances interacted. The great powers, when their interests shifted, changed partners as in a quadrille. In 1718 Britain, France and Austria were allied against Spain; in 1725 Spain and Austria were allied against France and Britain; in 1733 Spain and France were allied against Austria; in 1740 Britain and Austria were allied against France and Prussia; and in 1756 Britain and Prussia were allied against France and Austria. The multiple balance broke down, first with the American Revolutionary War, and then more decisively with the French Revolutionary War. The Vienna Settlement was an attempt to restore it. Britain had unchallengeable supremacy outside Europe, Russia took Poland, Austria was predominant in Italy, Prussia was given the Rhineland, and when after a few years of military occupation France resumed her status of great power, the multiple balance was complete.

The multiple balance lasts as long as no conflict of interests has arisen to make a decisive schism between the great powers. When this occurs, the powers divide into opposite camps. The multiple balance now resolves itself into a simple balance: it is no longer a merry-go-round but a see-saw. This is what happened in Europe when the Franco-Russian alliance was formed in 1892 against the Triple Alliance of Germany, Austria-Hungary and Italy; and again when the Berlin-Rome Axis was created in 1936 against the League powers. A period of simple balance is marked by heightened tension, a race in armaments, and the uneasy oscillations of the balance of power which are called crises. Sir Winston Churchill has inimitably described such a crisis in the years leading up to 1914:

The great powers marshalled on either side, preceded and protected by an elaborate cushion of diplomatic courtesies and formalities, would display to each other their respective arrays. In the forefront would be the two principal disputants, Germany and France, and echeloned back on either side at varying distances and under veils of reserves and qualifications of different density, would be drawn up the other parties to the Triple Alliance and to what was already now beginning to be called the Triple Entente. At the proper moment these seconds or supporters would utter certain cryptic words indicative of their state of mind, as a consequence of which France or Germany would step back or forward a very small distance or perhaps move slightly to the right or to the left. When these delicate rectifications in the great balance of Europe, and indeed of the world, had been made, the formidable assembly would withdraw to their own apartments with ceremony and salutations and congratulate or condole with each other in whispers on the result.[5]

There were similar crises in the 1930s, but the courtesies had worn thinner and the power was more naked – the Italian journalists hissing and catcalling when Haile Selassie rose to address the League Assembly in June 1936; Greiser, the president of the Danzig senate, giving the Nazi salute and thumbing his nose as he marched out of the League Council a few days later; Hitler's public threats and maledictions in 1938–9. And in due course the manoeuvring for position and for alliances cannot be prolonged, and the balance of power overbalances into general war.

A power that is in a position to contribute decisive strength to one side or the other is said to 'hold the balance'. The metaphor is seen at its simplest in a contemporary description of the foreign policy of Queen Elizabeth I:

There sat she as an heroical princess and umpire betwixt the Spaniards, the French, and the Estates [viz. the Dutch]; so as she might well have used that saying of her father, *Cui adhaereo, prae est*, that is, 'the party to which I adhere getteth the upper hand'. And true it was which one hath written, that France and Spain are as it were the scales in the balance of Europe, and England the tongue or the holder of the balance.[6]

Holding the balance of power is a policy specially suited to an insular power enjoying a certain detachment from continental rivalries, and it has been the traditional policy of Britain. It found

5. W. S. Churchill, *The World Crisis 1911–1914*, Vol. I, Butterworth, London, 1927, pp. 44–5.
6. W. Camden, *History of Elizabeth*, trans. 3rd edition, 1675, p. 223. It will be noted that the metaphor of 'holding the balance' is curiously inaccurate. The tongue of a balance is an index to show which way the scales incline, not a stabilizer. And a person who holds a pair of scales is, *ipso facto*, excluded from sitting in either of the scales.

expression in the preamble to the annual Mutiny Act, which from 1727 down to 1867 (with one or two lapses) described the function of the British army as 'the preservation of the balance of power in Europe'. The policy of 'splendid isolation' in the later nineteenth century was in truth no more than a negative aspect of holding the balance: it meant retaining freedom of action so long as it seemed unnecessary for Britain to commit herself. American isolationism between the World Wars had a similar character, though the Americans probably deluded themselves to a greater extent into thinking that their freedom of action was a permanent attribute instead of a temporary advantage.

A great power that holds the balance of power is perhaps usually a feature of the transition from a multiple to a simple balance. As Britain held the balance between the Triple Alliance and the Franco-Russian Alliance in the years before 1906, so Russia held the balance in the later years of the eighteenth century before the French Revolution and again when the League powers and the Axis powers were competing for her alliance in 1939. But it is sometimes a small power, through accident of strategic position or the energy of its people, that can contribute decisive strength to one side or the other; and indeed there is many a small power that likes to think that in some respects it holds a balance, if only between its allies. For the notion of holding the balance shades easily into the hope of contributing *some* strength, whether decisive or not, which is almost the equivalent of possessing some degree of freedom of action. If a power is courted by both sides, this suggests that it holds the balance. Thus Savoy used to hold the balance on the Alps. Thus the Iroquois in the first half of the eighteenth century held the balance between French and English in North America.[7] And thus Yugoslavia holds a balance in Europe between the Western and Communist blocs. Indeed, the policy of trimming, which we noticed earlier, is in essence an example of holding the balance, even if what is to be offered to either side is not decisive strength but only moral influence.

Enough has been said to show that 'the balance of power' is a

7. W. C. Macleod, *The American Indian Frontier*, Kegan Paul, London, 1928, pp. 272–7; Appendix VIII, pp. 555–7.

confusing and ambiguous term, and it is necessary to distinguish the various senses in which it is used. There are five or perhaps seven. The reader will notice how the various senses slide into one another, and how difficult it has been to choose examples of usage which illustrate a single sense only. For if the balance of power is a confusing term, it is also a very rich one; and the difficulty of describing international politics adequately without resorting to this metaphor is perhaps explained by its being flexible and elastic enough to cover all their complexities and contradictions.

1. The original meaning of the phrase is *an even distribution of power*, a state of affairs in which no power is so preponderant that it can endanger the others. When Machiavelli said that, before the French invasion of 1494, 'Italy was in a way balanced',[8] he was describing such a condition of things. Here is a description of the states-system a little over a hundred years later, in 1609, when the Spanish attempt at predominance had been defeated:

It is first to be considered that this part of Christendom is balanced betwixt the three Kings of Spain, France, and England; as the other part [is] betwixt the Russian, the Kings of Poland, Sweden, and Denmark. For as for Germany, which if it were entirely subject to one Monarchy, would be terrible to all the rest: so being divided betwixt so many Princes and those of so equal power, it serves only to balance itself, and entertain easy war with the Turk; while the Persian withholds him in a greater.[9]

By a similar use of the metaphor, Sir Winston Churchill describes the European situation brought about by the Locarno Treaties in 1925: 'Thus there was a balance created in which Britain, whose major interest was the cessation of the quarrel between Germany and France, was to a large extent arbiter and umpire.'[10] And the same notion of even distribution is seen in Lester Pearson's celebrated dictum that 'The balance of terror has superseded the balance of power'.[11] In this usage the word 'balance' has its

8. *The Prince*, Dent, London, 1960, Chapter 20, p. 119.

9. Sir Thomas Overbury, 'Observations on his Travels', in *Stuart Tracts 1603–1693*, C. H. Firth (ed.), Constable, London, 1903, p. 227.

10. *The Second World War*, Vol. I, p. 24.

11. Speech at San Francisco, 24 June 1955, *Commemoration of the Tenth Anniversary of the Signing of the UN Charter*, UNP, Sales No. 1955 I 26.

primary meaning of 'equilibrium', and it is perhaps most likely to appear as the object of such verbs as maintain and preserve, upset and overturn, or redress and restore.

2(a). From this, almost insensibly, the phrase comes to mean *the principle that power ought to be evenly distributed*. It passes from a descriptive to a normative use. When during the American Revolutionary War George III was seeking the assistance of Catherine the Great, she replied on one occasion: 'Her ideas perfectly correspond with his, as to the balance of power; and she never can see with indifference any essential aggrandizement, or essential diminution, of any European state take place.'[12] Here we see sense 1 leading into sense 2. In the eighteenth century the balance of power was generally spoken of as if it were in some manner the unwritten constitution of international society. 'The balance of power had been ever assumed as the known common law of Europe . . .,' said Burke; 'the question had only been (as it must happen) of the more or less inclination of that balance.' And he went on to describe it, in a passage that might be chosen to illustrate sense 1.[13] In this sense the phrase 'the balance of power' was frequently written into international treaties from the Treaty of Utrecht in 1713 down to the time of Bismarck; and legal writers have laid down that the balance of power is the indispensable condition of international law.

'The balance of power in Europe', said Lord John Russell, to cite one from innumerable examples, 'means in effect the independence of its several states. The preponderance of any one power threatens and destroys this independence.'[14] The shadowy system of cooperation between the great powers in the nineteenth century, known as the Concert of Europe, was indeed in its origin and essence a common agreement on the principle of the balance of power. Most states at most times seek to maintain the balance of power, and the balance of power conceived as a policy derives naturally from this sense. 'If there is to be coexistence there must be a balance of power,' wrote the *Manchester Guardian* in 1954,

12. *Diaries and Correspondence of the Earl of Malmesbury*, Vol. I, p. 396.
13. 'Letters on a Regicide Peace: III', in *The Works*, Vol. V, p. 441.
14. H. Temperley and L. M. Penson, *Foundations of British Foreign Policy*, C.U.P., Cambridge, 1938, p. 205.

'for if power is unbalanced the temptation to Communism to resume its crusade will be irresistible.'[15] In this sentence there seems a coexistence of sense 1 and sense 2.

2(b). However, the principle of the balance of power has a kind of demonic vitality and changeableness, because it is the policy by which most states at most times seek their security. Its protean quality becomes most apparent in the circumstances of a simple balance, when each of two powers or coalitions is trying to maintain an even distribution of power between them by a competition in armaments or a diplomatic struggle for alliances. In these circumstances it becomes equivalent to *the principle that my side ought to have a margin of strength so as to avert the danger of power being unevenly distributed.* Here the word balance acquires the sense it has when we say we have a balance in the bank, i.e. a plus, not an equality of assets and debits. Sir Norman Angell has recorded how, as a young man, he heard Churchill, as a young politician, declare that peace depended on the British navy keeping its superiority over the German navy, and he asked a question to which there was no answer. Thus American policy after 1947 was seeking at the same time to restore the balance of strength against Russia by rearmament, and to be able, in Dulles's words, to 'negotiate from a position of strength'. This is indeed a fundamental conundrum of international politics.

3. It is the trouble about international politics that the powers are frequently in disagreement on the distribution of power being an even distribution, and that any distribution of power does not long remain constant. Most arrangements of power favour some countries, which therefore seek to preserve the *status quo*, and justify it as being a true balance in the sense of an equilibrium; and are irksome to other countries, whose policy accordingly is revisionist. Thus the idea of an even distribution is drained out of the phrase 'the balance of power', and it comes to mean simply *the existing distribution of power.* This linguistic process can be seen at work in a discussion between Sir Stafford Cripps and Stalin in July 1940. Cripps had been sent to Moscow as British ambassador with the task of persuading Stalin that Germany's victories endangered Russia as well as Britain. 'Therefore both

15. 21 August 1954, leading article on Lord Attlee's visit to Peking, p. 8.

countries', he argued, 'ought to agree on a common policy of self-protection against Germany and on the re-establishment of the European balance of power.' Stalin replied that he did not see any danger of Europe being engulfed by Germany. 'The so-called European balance of power', he said, 'had hitherto oppressed not only Germany but also the Soviet Union. Therefore the Soviet Union would take all measures to prevent the re-establishment of the old balance of power in Europe.'[16] When the spokesman for the Admiralty told the House of Commons in 1951 that 'the balance of sea power has tilted away from us dramatically during the last ten years',[17] he was using the phrase in this neutral sense. And by a natural extension it comes to mean any possible distribution of power, future as well as present or past. Thus Churchill wrote to Eden in 1942: 'No man can see how the balance of power will lie or where the winning armies will stand at the end of the war.'[18] This is probably the most frequent usage of the term, as the relationship of power prevailing at a given time. The word 'balance' has entirely lost its original meaning of 'equilibrium'. There is less notion of stability about it, more of perpetual change than in sense 1; and it will more frequently be found as the subject of a sentence (to be said to 'have changed' or to 'be appearing'), as though it lies largely beyond human control.

4. The fourth sense of the phrase is when we speak of 'holding the balance'. This means that a power possesses *a special role in maintaining an even distribution of power*. The earliest known use of the phrase in English illustrates this sense. It appears, appropriately enough, in the dedication of a book to Queen Elizabeth in 1579: God hath 'put into your hands the balance of power and justice, to appease and counterpoise at your will the actions and counsels of all the Christian kingdoms of your time'.[19] Here is another fuller example, from a letter written by Palmerston to

16. *Nazi-Soviet Relations 1939–1941: Documents from the Archives of the German Foreign Office*, Department of State, Washington DC, 1948, p. 167.

17. L. J. Callaghan's speech in the House of Commons, 12 March 1951, *Parliamentary Debates*, Fifth Series, Vol. 485, col. 1093.

18. W. S. Churchill, *The Second World War*, Vol. III, p. 616.

19. Geffray Fenton, 'Epistle dedicatorie to the Queen', in *The Historie of Guicciardin . . . reduced into English*, 1579, part iv.

William IV in 1832. Palmerston is explaining the quarrels that occurred between France on the one side and Austria, Prussia and Russia on the other about fulfilling the treaty that established Belgian independence, and British policy with regard to them:

Upon the occasion of all these pretensions the British government brought the three powers to bear upon France, and France was upon all compelled to yield; latterly the three powers have in their turn been unreasonable and deficient in good faith, and have endeavoured, under false pretences, to defeat the treaty they had ratified and to mar the arrangement they had guaranteed. The British government then brought France to bear upon the three powers, and it is to be hoped with ultimate success. Rivals in military strength, as France and the three powers are, Your Majesty may be said practically to hold the scales of the balance of Europe. France will not venture to attack the three powers, if she is also to be opposed by England; and the three powers will pause long before they attack France, if they think that France could in that case reckon upon the support of England.[20]

But this usage too is equivocal. If he who holds the balance is weaker than either of the powers which make the scales, his function will be only that of mediator; but if he is as strong as either of them, or stronger, he will tend to become an arbiter. A power in this special role may not play it in a way that other powers regard as just; it may be concerned less to maintain an even distribution of power than to improve its own position. Thus holding the balance of power in sense 1 passes over into holding the balance of power in sense 3, and what the holder possesses is simply *a special advantage within the distribution of power*. When an English politician in 1704 rejoiced that the battle of Blenheim 'has given the balance of Europe into the Queen's [sc. Anne's] hands',[21] he meant that it had made England the strongest power on the Continent, with a freedom of action greater than that of other powers. Continental powers have always noted that while Britain traditionally claimed to hold the balance in Europe with her right hand, so to speak, she was establishing with her left hand an oceanic and colonial hegemony which refused for two centuries to recognize the principle of equilibrium. Thus holding the

20. C. K. Webster, *The Foreign Policy of Palmerston*, Vol. II, pp. 801–2.
21. G. M. Trevelyan, *Blenheim*, Longmans, London, 1930, p. 419.

balance comes to mean possessing a decisive advantage. In this sense Chester Bowles wrote in 1956 that 'the two-thirds of the world who live in the undeveloped continents . . . will ultimately constitute the world balance of power'.[22] And possessing a decisive advantage comes to mean possessing a predominance. In this sense Bonaparte wrote enthusiastically to the Directory in 1797, the year that saw the collapse of the first coalition against Revolutionary France: 'We hold the balance of Europe; we shall incline it as we wish.'[23] And, more dramatically, the Kaiser boasted to the British Foreign Secretary in 1901 that the traditional English policy of upholding the balance of power was exploded: 'The balance of power in Europe is *me*.'[24] Here at last the word balance has come to mean the opposite of its original sense: equilibrium has become preponderance, balance has become overbalance. And the verbs that govern the phrase pass from possession to identification: from holding and inclining to constituting and being.

5. There is a fifth and final sense of the phrase balance of power, when it describes *an inherent tendency of international politics to produce an even distribution of power*. This is a general statement of how the groupings of powers fall into ever-changing equilibria. It asserts a law of international politics that underlies and reinforces the principle of the balance of power, in sense 2(a), so that even if powers neglect or repudiate the principle, the law will be seen at work overruling them. Rousseau already saw it in this light when he wrote, 'Let us not think that this vaunted balance of power has been achieved by anybody, and that anybody has done anything with a view to maintaining it . . . Whether one is conscious of it or not, this balance exists, and can well maintain itself without outside interference.'[25] In the later nineteenth century, says A. J. P. Taylor, 'it seemed to be the political equivalent of the laws of economics, both self-operating. If every man followed his

22. *Christianity and Crisis*, 15 October 1956, p. 137.

23. A. Sorel, *L'Europe et la Révolution Française*, Vol. V, p. 185.

24. *Die Grosse Politik*, Vol. XVII, p. 28; also H. von Eckardstein, *Ten Years at the Court of St James*, Butterworth, London, 1921, p. 194, and H. H. Asquith, *Genesis of the War*, Cassell, London, 1923, pp. 19–20.

25. E. M. Nuttall (trans.), *Projet de paix perpétuelle*, Cobden-Sanderson, London, 1927, p. 26.

own interest, all would be prosperous; and if every state followed its own interest, all would be peaceful and secure.'[26] In modern political writings the balance of power as political law has tended to replace the balance of power as moral and legal principle. 'The balance of power', says Professor Toynbee, 'is a system of political dynamics that comes into play whenever a society articulates itself into a number of mutually independent local states.' It 'operates in a general way to keep the average calibre of states low in terms of every criterion for the measurement of political power . . . a state which threatens to increase its calibre above the prevailing average becomes subject, almost automatically, to pressure from all the other states that are members of the same political constellation'.[27]

5(a). But the balance of power as a political law, like the balance of power as a descriptive phrase, moves from the idea of even distribution. It becomes a statement of the endless shiftings and regroupings of power, the scales perpetually oscillating without coming to rest. When a great historian of antiquity writes, 'The complicated political situation which constituted the balance of power among the Hellenistic states gave rise to almost uninterrupted warfare,'[28] the notion of long perspective loses sight of recurring equilibria. Here the phrase becomes synonymous with the states-system itself.

A political law is a generalization about how political events recur. It may be a satisfactory generalization within a limited context, but become dubious in a wider context. The law of the balance of power is fascinating, but possibly misleading if we do not take account of contrary indications. It may be that it works with progressively diminishing force. We have already seen that while international society has widened from Europe to cover the whole world, there has been a steady reduction in the number of great powers: though the field of the balance of power has expanded, the number of decisive weights has decreased. We have

26. A. J. P. Taylor, *The Struggle for Mastery in Europe*, p. xx.
27. A. J. Toynbee, *A Study of History*, Vol. III, O.U.P., London, 1934, pp. 301–2.
28. M. Rostovtzeff, *Social and Economic History of the Hellenistic World*, Vol. I, Clarendon Press, Oxford, 1941, p. 36.

also noticed that the very idea of the balance of power has a mobility that tends to defeat its own original purpose, so to speak, so that the phrase comes to mean predominance instead of equilibrium. If we consider this, together with the record of other states-systems, such as those of ancient China before the establishment of the Han Empire or of the Hellenistic world before the Roman Empire, we may wonder whether it is not necessary to frame a wider generalization. There may be another law of international politics, slower in operation than the balance of power, and ultimately overriding it: a law of the monopoly of concentration of power. Professor Barraclough has argued that the law of the balance of power has been good for Europe, but that 'outside Europe, the principle of preponderant powers is securely established'.[29] This is an over-simplification. The balance of power has worked itself out in Europe (considered by itself) by the end of the Second World War. And outside Europe the balance of power is evident enough. In North America there was a kind of balance of power for two hundred years before the American Republic finally achieved predominance. In India there was a balance of power for a hundred years before the British became predominant. In China there was a balance of power between the European powers for a hundred years before it was overthrown by Japan. In the Middle East the Eastern Question was an essay in the balance of power, only ending when Britain acquired the lion's share of the Ottoman Empire. And in Africa, a balance was finally achieved between French and British power. In all these regions the balance of power is discernible, as well as in the world as a whole. What we need to do is to get clear the limits, geographical and historical, within which the balance of power works. And this seems to be the same thing as defining the field of international politics themselves.

But it is impossible to separate the balance of power as law, as something that happens in politics, from the balance of power as policy, as something that politicians make happen. 'No political law', as Collingwood remarked in another connection, 'enforces

29. G. Barraclough, *History in a Changing World*, Blackwell, Oxford, 1955, p. 176.

itself automatically . . . it is for the community to invent measures which are feasible . . . and will secure the result aimed at.'[30] Rulers often make mistakes in their estimates and forecasts of power, and sometimes indeed have stronger motives than the interests of the states they govern. There is an example of the bungling of the balance of power in Mussolini's policy in 1940. The German conquest of Western Europe placed Italy, as well as Britain, in mortal danger. At this juncture Italy might have chosen to throw herself on the side of Britain and the exiled governments of the overrun states, in order to create a balance against the dominant power. But Mussolini hated Britain so vehemently that he eagerly assumed her defeat, and he also saw the chance of immediate gains from France; he therefore entered the war on what he thought was the winning side. Nevertheless he had no illusions about the nature of his voracious ally, and he was concerned to establish a private balance between Italy and Germany. Accordingly he launched his contemptible invasion of southern France, in order to earn prestige with as many casualties as possible before France surrendered, and so be able to treat with Germany more as an equal. The final result of this futile policy was that while Britain survived, Italy was occupied and ruined. This has been a common fate of jackal powers; the history of Prussia's relations with Napoleon before the battle of Jena and of Rumania's relations with Russia in the Russo-Turkish War of 1877-8 afford other examples. For we may notice that the law of the balance of power is true of states in proportion to their strength, confidence and internal cohesion. Weak and corrupt states, and especially those ruled by an unrepresentative despot or clique, tend to gravitate *towards* the dominant power. It is popular states without deep social cleavages (whether their governments be democratic or dictatorial) that tend to gravitate away from the dominant power.

The principle of the balance of power has been repudiated from opposite sides. It is always rejected by dominant powers, and in the past two centuries it has been rejected by a large body of

30. R. G. Collingwood, 'The Three Laws of Politics', in *Hobhouse Memorial Lectures 1941-50*, O.U.P., London, 1952, pp. 8-9.

radical opinion, both liberal and socialist. But both kinds of critic have in the end found themselves entangled in what they disbelieved.

Instead of the independence of nations based on a system of equilibrium, dominant powers assert some ideal of solidarity and unification, from the Counter-Reformation Catholicism of Philip II down to Hitler's New Order in Europe. 'What Britain called the balance of power', said Hitler, 'was nothing but the disintegration and disorganization of the Continent.'[31]

'. . . as for the balance of power,' said Burke of the French Revolutionaries, 'it was so far from being admitted by France . . . that, in the whole body of their authorized or encouraged reports and discussions upon the theory of the diplomatic system, they constantly rejected the very idea of the balance of power, and treated it as the true cause of all the wars and calamities that had afflicted Europe; . . .

'Exploding, therefore, all sorts of balances, they avow their design to erect themselves into a new description of empire, which is not grounded on any balance, but forms a sort of impious hierarchy, of which France is to be the head and the guardian.'[32]

But when facing defeat by a grand alliance, a dominant power hastens to seek the protection of the principle it has formerly neglected. George III, writing to Catherine the Great for her assistance in the American Revolutionary War, said that a mere naval demonstration by her 'will be able to restore the repose of the whole of Europe, by breaking up the coalition that has been formed against me, and upholding the system of equilibrium which this coalition seeks to destroy'.[33] After the battle of Stalingrad, German propaganda began appealing to the principle of the

31. Speech in the Berlin Sportpalast, 30 January 1941, in *The Times*, 31 January 1941, p. 3.

32. 'Letters on a Regicide Peace: III', in op. cit., pp. 442–3.

33. *Diaries and Correspondence of the Earl of Malmesbury*, Vol. I, p. 265. Cf. the complaint of a patriotic historian: 'Thus, the trend of European politics in the East, in Germany, and in the Netherlands told heavily against England and increased the natural reluctance of any power to seek the friendship of a beaten nation. It is at such times that the artificiality of the idea of the balance of power is seen. No state took the slightest interest in restoring the islanders to their rightful position in the world.' J. Holland Rose, *William Pitt and National Revival*, Bell, London, 1911, pp. 300–301

balance of power against the overmighty strength of Russia, just as Napoleon at St Helena sometimes argued that his own policy had been directed by the same principle against the same danger.

Nor was it simply idealism that made the United States in her earliest years repudiate the balance of power along with entangling alliances. From the moment of independence, she was potentially the dominant power of the New World, as Hamilton clearly saw. 'We may hope, ere long,' he wrote in 1787, 'to become the arbiter of Europe in America, and to be able to incline the balance of European competitions in this part of the world as our interest may dictate . . . Our situation invites and our interests prompt us to aim at an ascendant in the system of American affairs.'[34] An inter-American balance of power has always been impossible, however much the Latin American countries have desired it, because of the overwhelming preponderance of the United States; and not until the twentieth century was the European balance of power understood as essential to the security of America.

On the other hand, there were those who thought that though the balance of power might be desirable, the price to be paid might be too high. At the end of an exhausting war which, from a political viewpoint, had restored the balance of power, Pope wrote his caustic epigram with more wit than political truth:

> Now Europe's balanc'd, neither Side prevails;
> For nothing's left in either of the Scales.[35]

Men who were told that taxation and wars were necessary to maintain the balance of power naturally blamed the balance of power when they were tired of taxation and wars. The example of the United States, serenely aloof from the ordinary rules of foreign politics, had a powerful influence on English radicals in the nineteenth century. The policy of the balance of power was criticized by Cobden and Bright, mainly on practical grounds, as a source of endless wars and unnecessary entanglements; partly on intellectual grounds, as a mischievous delusion which meant so many different things that it meant nothing at all. 'So far as we

34. *The Federalist*, No. XI, pp. 65 and 69.
35. N. Ault and J. Butt (eds.), 'The Balance of Europe', in *Minor Poems*, Vol. VI, Methuen, London, 1954, p. 82.

can understand the subject,' said Cobden, 'the theory of a balance of power is a mere chimera – a creation of the politician's brain – a phantasm, without definite form or tangible existence – a mere conjunction of syllables, forming words which convey sound without meaning.'[36] The English tradition of idealist internationalism and the American tradition of detachment from the balance of power converged in the First World War and produced the League of Nations. Nevertheless, President Wilson was able to repudiate the conception of the balance of power in 1918–19 with such immense authority only because the United States had already been drawn into the balance. The First World War transformed her into the holder of the balance. It was still against her will, so that when she abandoned neutrality and intervened to tip the scales, she still sought to preserve a moral detachment by calling herself only an 'associated power', not an ally. The Second World War has completed the involvement by making the United States into one of the weights of a simple balance. And the hope of holding the balance flickers in the minds of Japanese and Germans as they recover from their defeat.

Is then the balance of power the guarantee of the independence of Nations? Or is it the cause of war? The only answer is that it is both. History plainly shows that the balance of power is the policy by which most powers have pursued self-preservation in most cases. And so long as the absence of international government means that powers are primarily preoccupied with their survival, so long will they seek to maintain some kind of balance between them. It is easy to point to occasions on which the final move in the rectification of the balance has been war. It is not remembered how often the balance of power has averted war. For the balance of power is not 'the cause' of war; the cause of war, however one chooses to identify it, lies in the political conditions which the balance of power in some degree regulates and reduces to order. The alternatives to the balance of power are either universal anarchy or universal dominion. A little reflection will show that the balance of power is preferable to the first; and we

36. 'Russia' (1836), in *The Political Writings of Richard Cobden*, Vol. I, Ridgway, London, 1868, p. 263.

have not yet been persuaded that the second is so preferable to the balance of power that we shall submit to it.[37]

37. This draft, which was probably written in the late 1950s, represents an intermediate stage in the author's analysis of the balance of power, between that of the corresponding chapter in the original *Power Politics* and that of the paper with the same title in *Diplomatic Investigations* (H. Butterfield and M. Wight (eds.) Allen & Unwin, London, 1966, pp. 149–75). While the latter chapter, which in large part rests on this chapter, distinguishes nine senses of the term, this chapter presents seven. Eds.

17 : Compensation

There are two usages in international politics which deserve to be discussed separately. These are compensation and intervention. Compensation is a principle governing the relations on the whole between powers of comparable strength; intervention is a principle governing the relations on the whole between stronger powers and weaker. Compensation is essentially a mode of operation of the balance of power; intervention is not.

There are several kinds of compensation; one of them is the economic indemnities or reparations which victorious powers impose on defeated powers. But in its strictest sense, which became established in the eighteenth and nineteenth centuries and with which we are here concerned, compensation means a method of regulating the balance of power by agreed territorial exchange. We may call it bilateral compensation when there are only two parties to the transaction, multilateral when there are more than two.

Bilateral compensation is seen at its most elementary when a state loses territory in one place and gains equivalent territory elsewhere. There are examples of a simple swop, especially in the eighteenth century, as when in 1720 the Duke of Savoy exchanged the Kingdom of Sicily for the Kingdom of Sardinia with the Emperor. Generally, however, the material of compensation on one side or the other is provided by a state which is not party to the agreement. Thus, at the Peace of Loeben in 1797, Bonaparte agreed to deliver Venice to Austria (although Venice happened to be a neutral independent state) in compensation for the Austrian Netherlands; the bargain was afterwards confirmed as part of the multiple compensation arranged by the Congress of Vienna. In 1878 Russia deprived Rumania of Bessarabia, which was inhabited by Rumanians, and gave it in exchange the northern

Dobrudja, which was inhabited by Turks and Bulgars. Similarly, in 1945 Russia deprived Poland of the territory east of the Curzon Line and gave it German territory up to the Oder-Neisse Line instead.

Compensation of this kind is usually the consequence of war in which both parties have been engaged; and it registers a degree of strength on the part of the compensated power somewhere between complete victory and decisive defeat. Wholly victorious powers are unaccustomed to surrender territory, even for compensation; decisively defeated powers are accustomed to be deprived of territory, without compensation.

But territorial compensation is sometimes claimed, not for territory forfeited, but for more intangible damage, such as loss of prestige or of security through a shifting of the balance of power. (In diplomacy, it has been said, it is always useful to assume the role of the injured.) Thus Napoleon III obtained the cession of Savoy from Piedmont in 1860, in compensation for the Piedmontese annexation of the states of central Italy, which he had wanted to prevent. He sought a similar compensation for the aggrandizement of Prussia during and after the Austro-Prussian War, either German territory on the Rhine or Luxembourg or Belgium; Bismarck contemptuously described it as a policy of *pourboires*. In the same way, when Bulgaria acquired Eastern Rumelia in 1885, both Serbia and Greece demanded compensation, though they failed to get it. Mussolini seized Albania in April 1939 to compensate himself for Hitler's seizure of Czechoslovakia in March, and invaded Greece in October 1940 to compensate himself for Hitler's occupation of Rumania. Here, however, though the intention was to rectify the balance between Italy and Germany, there was not agreement with Hitler, which would have made it compensation in the sense we are discussing.

If the balance of power is strictly interpreted, one great power cannot increase its territorial strength without all the other great powers claiming a corresponding increase; if the claim is accepted, there follows multiple compensation, based on the principle of equality of aggrandizement. It was on this principle that the great powers in the later nineteenth century managed the Eastern Question, partitioned Africa, and established spheres of influence in the Far East. Thus at the Berlin Congress in 1878 Russia obtained Rumanian Bessarabia and Batum, Austria-Hungary obtained Bosnia and Herzegovina, Britain obtained Cyprus, and France three years later acquired Tunis. It was the same in the scramble for concessions in China in 1897–8. Germany seized Kiaochow as a coaling-station, in quick succession Russia took Port Arthur, France took Kwangcho-wan, and Britain took Weihaiwei. Each was at first alarmed by the other's aggrandizement, and then (as the Russian Foreign Minister said) 'grateful to Germany' for having given the opportunity for general aggrandizement in the name of compensation. The same principle was seen at work when the Potsdam Conference in 1945 began discussing the future of the Italian colonies. Stalin, who saw only Anglo-American preponderance in the Mediterranean and not the niceties of the trusteeship system, said bluntly that Russia 'would like some territory of the defeated states'.[1]

The classic example of multiple compensation is the Partition of Poland in 1772, which was conducted on the basis of exactly equal acquisitions by Prussia, Russia and Austria. The same example shows that the principle of compensation can compel a power to take part in an international transaction against its will. Frederick the Great and Catherine the Great had agreed on the partition of Poland; Maria Theresa could not afford to be left out. She opposed it on moral grounds, but her ministers did not, and reasons of state were paramount. 'Elle pleurait, et prenait toujours,' said Frederick cynically.[2] Something comparable occurred when in August 1918 America joined the Allies in intervention in Russia. Wilson had steadily opposed intervention; but Britain, France and Japan forced his hand by sending troops themselves. America could not afford to allow the Japanese a free run in Siberia; Wilson at once reversed his policy and dispatched American troops, at the same time issuing a statement of the moral objections to intervention which was the Wilsonian equivalent of Marie Theresa's tears. Similar considerations make it very difficult for a single great power to remain neutral in a war between

1. J. F. Byrnes, *Speaking Frankly*, p. 76; also p. 96.
2. A. Sorel, *La Question d'Orient au dix-huitième siècle*, Plon, Paris (no date), p. 254.

other great powers and when such a great power enters the war with the promise of territorial gain and the intention of maintaining the balance of power between itself and its allies, the principle of compensation is at work. Such was the case with the entry of Italy into the World Wars in 1914 and 1940, and with the entry of Russia into the Anglo-American-Japanese war in 1945.

It will be seen that compensation usually presupposes an impotent state, like Poland, the Ottoman Empire or the Chinese Empire, which is not a party to the arrangement but provides the material of compensation. Nothing has discredited the balance of power more than this, by making it appear the excuse for partitioning and despoiling defenceless peoples. On the other hand, it must be remembered that the principle of compensation has often introduced an element of restraint into the rivalry of the great powers. It has meant that at least one of the powers concerned has foregone the aggrandizement that might otherwise have been open to it, and that territory which was likely to be redistributed anyway was redistributed by some measure of agreement without unilateral violence and without recourse to war. Thus compensation raises the same moral problems as appeasement, if that word is used in its strict sense to describe such a policy as that of the British government towards the Axis powers between 1935 and 1939. Appeasement indeed was inverted compensation. Powers have demanded territorial compensation for alleged harm to their interests through a shifting of the balance of power, claiming substantial indemnity for shadowy injury. Chamberlain endorsed Hitler's role of the injured instead of contesting it, and gave him territorial payment in advance for entirely insubstantial future returns. It is not thus that the balance of power is maintained.

The division of defeated Germany into occupation zones in 1945 was the most recent example of the compensation principle in practice. The rigid partition of Europe since then has meant that the principle has appeared only in the negative sense, in proposals for withdrawal of Russian and American forces from Germany by equal stages. Moreover, doctrinal conflict tends to limit the possibilities of compensation, which presupposes a certain degree of moral unity and common agreement between the powers concerned. But in Asia, where the frontier between the two blocs is still undefined, there is scope for regulating the balance of power by means of territorial compensation, and it is not impossible that this practice may play a part in the settlement of such long-term questions as the transfer of Formosa to Communist China and the unification of Korea and Indo-China.[3]

3. This draft was apparently written in the 1950s or early 1960s. Eds.

18 : Intervention

Intervention may be defined as forcible interference, short of declaring war, by one or more powers in the affairs of another power. In principle, every state is independent in the management of its own affairs (except in so far as it may be limited by some treaty), and foreign interference is a violation of its rights. This principle is enshrined in the articles of the League Covenant and the United Nations Charter which preclude the international organization from intervening in a matter which lies within the domestic jurisdiction of a state.[1] In practice, intervention occurs more commonly than war, and raises questions of the utmost moral complexity: adherents of every political belief will regard intervention as justified under certain circumstances.

An act of intervention may be regarded from several points of view. Is it intervention in the external or the internal affairs of the country concerned? The one is a less flagrant interference than the other. Is the object of intervention a great power or a small power? In the first case, the danger of war resulting from the intervention will be greater than in the second. Is the purpose of the intervention to maintain or to alter the status quo? The former may be called defensive intervention, the latter offensive. Is the intervention imposed by the intervening power, or is it invoked from the country intervened in? If it has been solicited from within, does the invitation come from the government of the country or from an anti-governmental faction or group of rebels? Each of these cases makes a different legal and moral situation.

In its strict sense, intervention means coercion short of war. The intervening power does not immediately intend war; it may, indeed, be aiming to avoid war; but it is usually ready for war, and war may be the result, if the state against which the intervention is

1. Article 15(8) of the Covenant; Article 2(7) of the Charter.

directed chooses to resist, or if other powers counter-intervene. Thus intervention is always dictatorial, involving the threat if not the exercise of force. It is quite distinct from diplomatic protest, or mediation, or an offer of friendly assistance. But an offer of friendly assistance may be suspected of sinister motives and denounced as intervention, as the Soviet government denounced the offer of Marshall Aid to the countries of Europe in 1947.

There is a looser usage of the word, when we say that the French intervened in Italy in 1494, or the United States intervened in the First World War in 1917. Intervening here is a synonym for going to war, but implies greater freedom of decision in the matter than is possessed by other powers. (We say intervention of the United States' entry into the First World War, not into the Second.)

Intervention may occur either in a country's foreign policy or in its domestic arrangements. In 1742 a British naval captain demanded to see the King of Naples, with a message that, if the King did not agree within half an hour to recall Neapolitan troops from the Spanish army in central Italy, the waiting British squadron would lay Naples in ashes by bombardment from the sea. In February 1945 Vyshinsky demanded to see the King of Rumania, and told him that he had two hours and five minutes in which to dismiss his Prime Minister and find another; implying that otherwise Vyshinsky would not be responsible for the continuance of Rumania as an independent state. These two incidents, which have a certain dramatic resemblance, illustrate intervention in the external affairs and the internal affairs respectively of another state.

Intervention against a great power necessarily implies a direct threat of war, for a great power is more likely to resist intervention than a lesser power. In 1850, by the treaty of Olmütz, Austria compelled Prussia to abandon the new union of German states which Prussia had fabricated after the revolution of 1848, and to return to the German Confederation of 1815; this humiliation left Prussia, as Bismarck long afterwards said, a great power only *cum grano salis*.[2] In 1895, Russia, Germany and France jointly demanded that Japan should give back to China the Liaotung Peninsula with Port Arthur which China had just been compelled

2. *Reflections and Reminiscences*, Vol. I, p. 302.

to cede to Japan by the treaty of Shimonoseki; it is perhaps a sign that Japan was not yet fully recognized as a great power that no means of saving face were provided. When Britain intervened between Russia and Turkey in 1878 by protesting against the Treaty of San Stefano, Russian prestige could be saved by a European Congress, just as when the United States intervened in the frontier dispute between Britain and Venezuela in 1895, British prestige could be saved by an arbitral award.

If intervention in the external affairs of a great power is likely to produce a war crisis, intervention in the internal affairs of a great power is unlikely to be attempted. A great power is a power that will not be dictated to in its domestic arrangements. The generalization is confirmed by the few instances history affords of attempted intervention in the internal affairs of a great power. When Louis XIV recognized the Old Pretender as rightful King of England on the death of the exiled James II in 1701, the outburst of patriotic anger he produced in England, as seeming to dictate about the succession to the English throne, was the occasion of the general war in which he himself was finally humbled. A similar role in the origin of the French Revolutionary War was played by the half-hearted proposals of Austria and Prussia for intervening to rescue Louis XVI from the revolutionaries, and by the suspicion that Louis XVI and Marie Antoinette were intriguing to bring this about. The Allies were able to intervene in Russia in 1918–19 only because Russia had temporarily ceased, in the convulsions of revolution and civil war, to be a power at all. The example of Communist China shows that when a civil war has led to the establishment of a strong government, that government will regard continued relations between foreign powers and the defeated party as bordering on intervention; just as in the American Civil War, the federal government considered British relations with the Confederates as bordering on intervention. But there is an exception to this rule, when intervention is requested by the government itself of the great power. In 1849 the Austrian government accepted the offer by the Tsar Nicholas I of help in repressing the Hungarian revolution; the Russians reconquered Hungary without asking any reward and restored Austria to its status of great power, 'the greatest service', as Bismarck afterwards said, 'that a sovereign of a great power has ever done to a neighbour'.[3] It will be noted that in all these examples, except that of the American Civil War, the purpose of the intervention was to reverse a revolution. The only intervention likely to be practised against a great power is something falling short of the name, a covert intriguing with potential rebels, which can be disavowed if circumstances change.

It is in the relations between great powers and weak powers that intervention most frequently occurs. And here we may consider two kinds of defensive intervention: intervention to preserve the balance of power, and intervention by a great power in the affairs of its client-states, which is intervention to preserve an imbalance of power. A sphere of interest is one where an international police authority is assumed by the presiding power and exercised by means of intervention. It is not the refusal altogether to intervene by which the character and policy of a great power can be judged, for intervention will sometimes be necessary in the interests of peace and good government, but the tact and reluctance with which intervention is conducted. The brutal and humiliating fashion of Russian intervention was shown when the Prince of Bulgaria was kidnapped and compelled to abdicate by Russian hirelings in 1886; and again when in 1947 Stalin insisted that Czechoslovakia should withdraw its acceptance of the Franco-British invitation to a conference in Paris about the Marshall Plan, and moreover demanded that since the Czechoslovak Cabinet had accepted unanimously, so it should reverse its decision unanimously. It is possible that British interventions in the Near East have shown more restraint, and a large part of British public opinion has been quick to condemn them, even in wartime. British intervention in Iraq to frustrate Rashid Ali's coup d'état in 1941 was accepted by British opinion as necessary to prevent Iraq from coming under German control; but the intervention in Egypt in February 1942, when British tanks burst through the gates of the palace and forced the King to appoint Nahas Pasha as Prime Minister, was censured throughout the war and has never been officially explained or defended; and Churchill's intervention in Greece in 1944, to prevent the Communists

3. *Reflections and Reminiscences*, Vol. I, p. 236.

from seizing Athens and establishing themselves in power, was strongly attacked at the time in Parliament and the press, though its wisdom has since become plain.

Intervention of this kind has been most nearly erected into a system in the relations between the United States and Latin America. The United States laid down the Monroe Doctrine in 1823 to prevent the European powers from intervening in Latin America; but at the beginning of the twentieth century the Doctrine was turned inside out to justify intervening in Latin America by the United States.

Such intervention was usually to protect United States investments and economic interests, the policy which became known as 'dollar diplomacy'; but it was also presented in moral terms, as aimed against misgovernment, civil discord and dictatorship. It received its extreme statement in Theodore Roosevelt's 'corollary' to the Monroe Doctrine:

Chronic wrongdoing, or an impotence which results in a general loosening of the ties of civilized society, may in America, as elsewhere, ultimately require intervention by some civilized nation, and in the Western Hemisphere the adherence of the United States to the Monroe Doctrine may force the United States, however reluctantly, in flagrant cases of such wrongdoing or impotence, to the exercise of an international police power.[4]

Roosevelt had already carried out the most daring, important and successful intervention in American history when in 1903 the United States encouraged the revolt of Panama from Colombia and prevented Colombia from suppressing it, in order to acquire the future Canal Zone from the newly formed Panamanian Republic. By 1916 the United States had undertaken a military occupation in San Domingo, Haiti and Nicaragua, and intervened with a powerful army in Mexico. This imperialist tradition caused intense resentment in Latin America, and was gradually abandoned in the later 1920s in favour of what Franklin Roosevelt called the 'good neighbour policy', which meant above all a policy of non-interference. But the cold war after 1945 created con-

4. Annual Message to Congress, 6 December 1904, in R. J. Bartlett (ed.), *The Record of American Diplomacy*, Knopf, New York, 1964, p. 539.

ditions in which the United States felt its interests endangered by events in Latin America far more acutely than had ever been the case in the heyday of economic imperialism, and therefore felt once more impelled to intervene.

International lawyers have held that intervention is excusable, if not strictly legal, when it is undertaken to preserve the balance of power. Collective interventions by the great powers in the nineteenth century generally had this object. Sometimes such intervention resulted in the establishment of a new state, usually intended as a buffer: in 1827 Britain, France and Russia intervened in the Greek War of Independence against Turkey, and afterwards recognized Greek independence; in 1830 Britain and France intervened in the Belgian revolt against Holland, and established an independent Belgium; in 1913 they intervened in the Second Balkan War, and established an independent Albania. Sometimes such intervention has aimed at maintaining an existing buffer state, like Turkey. The Eastern Question in the nineteenth century was largely an attempt by the powers to ensure that if there were intervention in Turkey, it should be collective intervention, not sole intervention by Russia. Sometimes collective intervention has been competitive intervention and has led, as we saw in the last chapter, to multiple compensation. At its worst, collective intervention has degenerated into pillage of the weak by the confederated strong: an international lawyer has said that the intervention of the great powers to punish China for the Boxer Rising in 1900 had no essential characteristics to distinguish it from the Norse invasions.

Intervention by a great power in the affairs of a weak power usually engenders resentment and xenophobia: anti-Russian feeling in Poland and the Balkans, anti-Yankee feeling in Latin America, anti-British feeling in Egypt, anti-Western feeling in China are sufficient examples. Nevertheless, to invoke foreign intervention has always been the last resource of warring factions in weak states and of governments themselves, although history has often shown that this is to invoke King Stork as an ally against King Log. It was the intrigues of Italian powers that brought the French into Italy in 1494, with the disasters that followed. In the domestic struggles in the Balkan states, each party has traditionally looked beyond the frontiers to some great power as patron. In Persia, a successful politician is automatically regarded as the client of some foreign power; how else could he have got where he is? The confusion of domestic and international politics has perhaps gone farthest in Latin America, where the nationalities are not sharply distinguished, and opposition leaders in one country habitually take refuge in a neighbouring country, from which they conspire against the government at home. Intervention by a Spanish-speaking sister republic does not arouse patriotic scruples and indignation in the same degree as intervention by the United States.

Most intervention is defensive, with the aim of preserving the *status quo*; but there is also offensive intervention, designed to change it. In times of doctrinal conflict, offensive intervention is a regular method of international revolution. The most famous example is afforded by the French Revolution; proclaiming principles of universal scope, it was led by an inherent logic to the decree of the French Convention of 19 November 1792, which offered 'fraternity and assistance to all peoples wishing to recover their liberty'. This was a proclamation of universal intervention, holding out, as Pitt said, 'encouragement to insurrection and rebellion in every country in the world'. The Holy Alliance adopted the same principle, though in the opposite sense, when at the Troppau Conference in 1820 it declared that it would intervene anywhere to suppress revolution. It was at this point that Britain parted company with her former allies against the French Revolution. Castlereagh argued that organized intervention on abstract principle could not be regarded as truly defensive; and might indeed endanger the liberties of the world; and that intervention could only be regarded as truly defensive if the territorial balance of Europe were disturbed. It is a question whether Soviet foreign policy, though its development has been historically different and more cautious than that of French Revolutionary policy, is not fundamentally based on a corresponding principle of offensive intervention. Certainly all movements of national unification (or 'reunion' as it is often called, sacrificing historical accuracy to moral fervour) tend to regard offensive intervention not as an instrument of policy only but as a duty. At the same time, offensive intervention usually differs from defensive intervention in being unofficial and underhand: it works by fomenting revolution abroad. A government will tacitly encourage the nationalist movement, both within its own frontiers and beyond; if insurrection abroad is a failure, it can be disavowed; if it is successful, its fruits can be reaped, and usually the frontiers of the intervening power are extended. Garibaldi's invasion of Sicily in 1860 with an army of volunteers, Cavour's manufacture of a 'spontaneous' incident in the Papal States, and the subsequent Piedmontese invasion and annexation of the Papal and Neapolitan dominions, were perhaps the supreme example of offensive intervention in time of peace, and were indistinguishable from war in all but diplomatic forms. Cavour's methods were condoned by liberal opinion because it welcomed the unification of Italy; but Hitler's policy towards Austria and Czechoslovakia up to 1938, and German and Italian intervention in the Spanish Civil War (1936–9), showed totalitarian governments using the same methods.

We defined intervention as forcible interference, short of war, in the affairs of another power. It might be said that the definition does not extend to an international revolutionary movement in the service of a particular power, such as Nazi Germany's fifth column of Germans abroad and Fascist sympathizers, and the Communist International, which represent the most insidious technique of offensive intervention. But at this point precision in political analysis becomes as difficult as exact knowledge of whether the power controls the international movement. Here we are compelled to define intervention in terms of motive rather than action: there cannot be serious argument about the aim of Communist parties in countries which have not yet gone Communist, though their activities may be outside the view of diplomacy. This is the twilight region where international and domestic politics become indistinguishable.

The opposite of intervention is, in theory, non-intervention. Non-intervention in general was proclaimed by British radicals in the nineteenth century as the aim of sensible policy. They meant that Britain should not mix herself up in other people's quarrels. This assumed that other people's quarrels did not affect Britain's interests, and was the equivalent of the isolationism of the United States before 1941, an expression of unshaken security and confidence. Non-intervention in particular cases may be as positive a policy as intervention. British policy towards Garibaldi's invasion of Sicily in 1860 was formally one of non-intervention; in effect Britain held the ring in favour of one of the combatants and prevented other powers from intervening. Hence the truth of Talleyrand's sardonic remark, that 'non-intervention is a term of political metaphysics signifying almost the same thing as intervention'. The Non-Intervention Agreement of 1936 was a diplomatic fiction whereby the Western powers refrained from supplying help to the legitimate government of Spain and the Axis powers supplied the help to the Nationalist rebels without which they would probably not have won. In times of doctrinal conflict it may be thought that non-intervention is wrong, because it is in effect intervention against the right. The conflict or tension between the general principle of non-intervention and the desirability of collective action against tyranny and persecution is sharpened when there is danger of subversive doctrines gaining ground. At the Caracas Conference of the Organization of American States in March 1954, John Foster Dulles was concerned to stress the danger of Communism in Latin America. 'The slogan of non-intervention', he said, 'can plausibly be invoked and twisted to give immunity to what is in reality flagrant intervention.'[5] Five months later the United States non-intervened decisively against the left-wing government of Guatemala, and Dulles's observation was bitterly remembered by Latin Americans.[6]

5. Speech of 8 March 1954, in *The New York Times*, 9 March 1954, p. 1.
6. This chapter was probably written in the mid 1950s. Eds.

19 : The League of Nations

The First World War ended with a revolution of nationalities throughout Central and Eastern Europe, as first the Russian Empire and then Austria-Hungary collapsed in the last two years of the war; with the defeat of Germany; and with the most elaborate attempt yet made at a rational reordering of international relations. The first two of these happenings were given legal form in the various peace treaties collectively known as the Versailles Settlement, of which the Treaty of Versailles with Germany was the most important. The third was enshrined in the Covenant of the League of Nations, which on Wilson's insistence formed Part I of the Treaty of Versailles. Both the Treaty and the Covenant became the subject of great political controversy, and the controversies were intertwined.

What was least discussed was what was in a way the most important matter – the new balance of power that underlay the treaty and the Covenant. The balance of power had become a dirty word. In one of his famous speeches in 1918 Wilson spoke of 'the great game, now for ever discredited, of the balance of power'.[1] The balance of power, as we have seen, is inherently unstable, because powers are not static societies, but are constantly growing or declining in relation to one another. And it is essentially competitive: it leads to rivalry of power, which leads to war, as a consequence of which one side is temporarily eliminated and the other has a temporary monopoly of power. At the end of the First World War it was widely hoped that this system could be transformed or replaced by something better.

But this hope was itself the product of a peculiar and transient balance of power. The situation at the end of the war was in two

1. Speech to Congress, 11 February 1918, in *The Messages and Papers of Woodrow Wilson*, Vol. I, Review of Reviews, New York, 1924, p. 478.

respects unprecedented. The Versailles Settlement was the only general peace settlement that has given the defeated dominant power a greater potential ascendancy in Europe than that which led to the war. For it was a paradox of national self-determination that it could not have been put into effect without the defeat of Germany, and that if put into effect it gave Germany a preponderance greater than she had had before the war.[2]

In 1914 Germany was an empire of 65 millions surrounded by a France of 40 millions, an Austria-Hungary of 50 millions and a Russia of 111 millions. In 1920 Germany was a national state of 65 millions, capable of rising to 75 millions if she absorbed the adjacent Germans in Austria and Czechoslovakia, and surrounded by a France of 40 millions, a Poland of 33 and a Czechoslovakia of 15. She was the greatest industrial power in Europe, with enormous capital equipment and unrivalled technical skill. Her territory had suffered none of the destruction of war, and she was reluctant to recognize that she had undergone military defeat. This preponderance could only be controlled by a firm and effective system of counter-balance.

But for the first time the European balance of power had ceased to be self-regulating, and a European conflict had been decided, very belatedly, by a great power outside Europe – the United States. International society still had its centre in Europe, but the centre could not be kept functioning without the aid of its extra-European members. On the Continent of Europe, to offset German preponderance, there were only the two weakest of the great powers, Italy and France. France was Germany's oldest and most consistent enemy, but she had barely escaped total defeat and she was more exhausted, perhaps, than any nominally victorious great power has ever been. She could only survive if Germany was decisively weakened, or if she had the assured support of the two great powers that had fought with her, Britain and the United States.

2. It had long been seen, before 'Germany' meant a national Germany, that the German disunion was a condition of the European balance, and that a united Germany 'would be terrible to all the rest'. See above Overbury, 'Observations on his Travels', pp. 183–4; also Rousseau, *Projet de paix perpétuelle*, pp. 32–4.

In February 1917, just before the fall of the Tsarist regime, France and Russia agreed to detach the Rhineland from Germany and make it a buffer state, with French garrisons. The acquisition of the Rhine frontier, by annexation or by making a buffer state, was France's highest hope of safety. But the United States and Britain would not agree to so flagrant a violation of the national principle, and France had to be content with a permanent demilitarization of both banks of the Rhine, together with a joint Anglo-American guarantee of the French frontier. Then the United States repudiated both the Versailles Treaty and the guarantee, and Britain also withdrew. Abandoned by her allies, France made new allies among the new states of Eastern Europe, in the rear of Germany. The failure of the Anglo-American guarantee to France was the decisive and symbolic event of the inter-war years. It was a declaration of political irresponsibility whose effect was never undone. Britain had followed America half-way into isolation, which did much to excuse later French obstinacy. Britain, half in and half out of Europe, and the greatest gainer from the war, had the greater responsibility.

In 1922 Britain refused to guarantee the French frontier; in 1925 she gave the desired guarantee, but refused to guarantee the frontiers of Eastern Europe. In 1939 she gave a guarantee to Poland and Rumania, and went to war in fulfilment of it. If she had given the guarantee to France in 1922, and had extended her guarantee to Eastern Europe at Locarno, the war would not have occurred. Britain pursued a false balance of power, a mechanical application of the principle between a naturally preponderant and potentially aggressive power and a temporarily dominant and deeply defensive power.

The political controversies of the past can be studied in two ways. The historian will point out the reasons why decisions were taken or avoided, and will tend to argue that it is futile to imagine that things could have been otherwise. He is not on the whole concerned with contingencies. The political scientist is more concerned with the abiding rules of political action that are illustrated by these controversies, and he is freer to point out that if policies had been different the consequences might have been different too. 'Example', as Burke said, is 'the only argument of effect in civil life.'[3] The way to learn from political study is to analyse the political mistakes of the past, provided that there is sympathetic understanding for the reasons for the mistakes, since an attitude of easy condemnation can cloud the political judgement itself and narrow its range. It is desirable too to avoid the easy and insidious tendency to suppose that decisive responsibility lay with some other country than one's own.

The Versailles Settlement did not, as is sometimes said, create the new states of Eastern Europe. They had already asserted or reasserted their existence in 1917 and 1918. But it recognized their existence, and its achievement in doing so seems (in so far as this can be said of anything in international politics) broadly irreversible. Only the three weakest of them, Estonia, Latvia and Lithuania, have since gone back into the darkness; the map of Eastern Europe is still the map of 1919 modified; the Versailles Settlement marks the point from which we measure the retrogression of national freedom since 1945. More than any previous general peace settlement, it was a direct expression of the wishes of peoples (whether or not this is a good thing in international relations). But the same liberalism that approved a settlement of national self-determination itself began to undermine the settlement. No previous general peace settlement has so quickly been subjected to critical attack and widespread discredit. The desire for justice, which had tinged the settlement, overreached itself and became a subversive sentimentality.

The public of the English-speaking world came to believe that the treaty was harsh to Germany. This belief was the result, not of a sober judgement of the provisions of the treaty, but of an emotional reaction from the vindictiveness inspiring the reparations clauses. In the flush of victory, with an ignorance and extravagance that seem the mark of democratic foreign policies when contrasted with the moderation of the monarchical and aristocratic victors of 1815, the Allies had hoped to make Germany pay for the war. The attempt to exact reparations had two effects. It encouraged the Germans to evade their treaty obligations when possible and when not possible to live with a

3. 'Thoughts on the Cause of the Present Discontents', in *The Works*, Vol. I, p. 499.

financial recklessness and extravagance that contributed to the economic crisis of 1930. And it encouraged British opinion, instructed by J. M. Keynes, to believe that since the economic clauses of the treaty had been harsh, such arrangements as the Polish Corridor, the Bohemian frontier and the prohibition of union between Germany and Austria were equally harsh. But these measures struck a balance between the national principle and the need to safeguard international society against German predominance. (The balance has had to be tilted much further against Germany: she has now lost East Prussia altogether, and Germans have been expelled from the Sudetenland.) The Germans did not, in fact, rebel against the injustices of the peace treaty; they resented having lost the war. The peace they had imposed on defeated Russia at Brest-Litovsk a year earlier was incomparably harsher than the Versailles Treaty, and when they had recovered their strength they set out, not to recover the frontiers of 1914, but to conquer the whole of Eastern Europe and Russia. 'We are too timid and modest about our own achievements; there is too much criticism and not enough defence,' wrote the historical adviser to the British Foreign Office in 1925. 'Cannot we recognize that the settlement of 1919 was an immense advance on any similar settlement made in Europe in the past? In broad outline, it represents a peace of reason and justice, and the whole fabric of the continent depends on its maintenance.'[4]

The treaty imposed several kinds of limitation on Germany's freedom besides the demand for reparations, but none of them was unprecedented. The Rhineland was demilitarized; as France was compelled to demolish the naval base of Dunkirk under the Treaty of Utrecht, and Russia was compelled to demilitarize the Black Sea under the Treaty of Paris of 1856. The German army was limited, as Napoleon had limited the Prussian army after Tilsit. It was easy to misinterpret the wording of this limitation as implying a contractual obligation on the Allies to disarm themselves as they had disarmed Germany.

The system for maintaining peace set up by the Covenant of the League of Nations had four main elements. 1. *The peaceful*

4. Sir James Headlam-Morley, *Studies in Diplomatic History*, Methuen, London, 1930, pp. 184–5.

settlement of disputes. It was supposed that many wars occurred because of inadequate arrangements for international litigation. The Hague Peace Conferences of 1899 and 1907 had already devised elaborate legal procedures for conciliation and arbitration; these were embodied, with some improvements, in Articles 12–15 of the Covenant. They remained almost entirely a dead letter, and on the whole no disputes were settled by means of them which would not have been settled if they had never existed. 2. *Disarmament.* It was supposed that armaments, or more precisely the competition in armaments, had been a main cause of the First World War. Germany was disarmed by the Versailles Treaty. By Article 8 of the Covenant, the members of the League recognized 'that the maintenance of peace requires the reduction of national armaments to the lowest point consistent with national safety and the enforcement by common action of international obligations'. Accordingly the League Council was to make plans for reducing armaments, and after these limits had been accepted by the several powers they were not to be exceeded without the Council's permission. 3. *Collective security.* This was the principle to replace the discredited balance of power. The central article of the Covenant, No. 10, took the form of a general mutual guarantee: 'The members of the League undertake to respect and preserve as against external aggression the territorial integrity and existing political independence of all members of the League.' Article 11 declared that any war or threat of war was a matter of concern to the whole League, and that the League should take any action deemed wise and effectual to safeguard the peace of nations. Article 16 provided that if a member of the League resorted to war in disregard of the procedures for the peaceful settlement of disputes, 'it shall *ipso facto* be deemed to have committed an act of war against all other members of the League'. The other members undertook, in these circumstances, to subject the Covenant-breaking state immediately to a complete economic, financial and social boycott; and the Council was to recommend to the powers concerned what armed forces they should contribute 'to protect the covenants of the League'. 4. *Peaceful change.* If collective security was seen as a means of law-enforcement in international society, it was necessary to balance it by some means of adapting the law to changing needs. If forcible change was forbidden, peaceful change must not be blocked. When treaties were manifestly obsolete or unjust, they should be subject to revision. Article 19 therefore provided that the Assembly might recommend the reconsideration of treaties which had become inapplicable. Lord Robert Cecil had wanted to combine this provision closely with the general guarantee, by writing it into Article 10; but owing to French opposition the idea was emasculated and embodied in a separate article. But if the League powers had desired peaceful change the procedure was entirely adequate. These four elements were combined in a Covenant which was simple and flexible, the first written constitution agreed to by the great majority of the members of international society.

The history of the League was to a large extent the history of the interpretation of this instrument and of the attempts to amend and improve it. Throughout the period between the World Wars there was a great debate about the merits and application of the Covenant, not a sterile and destructive debate, like the controversy about the treaty, but a debate concerning abiding and fundamental issues of politics. It may be described as a debate about the relative importance and priority of the four elements in the Covenant. Each had its protagonists; but the protagonists of disarmament, the peaceful settlement of disputes and peaceful change were largely the same people, who found themselves arguing with the protagonists of collective security. This debate in the end tore the fabric of the Covenant apart, leaving nothing at all.

The first and deepest issue was between the peaceful settlement of disputes and collective security. Collective security means internationalized defence. The powers at the heart of the League system, France and her allies in Eastern Europe, regarded the League as part of their own defence; that is to say, they meant to have 100 per cent security without the Covenant, and 200 per cent security with it. The powers at the periphery of the League system, especially the members of the British Commonwealth and the Scandinavian states, assumed that the Covenant added little or nothing to their own safety, which could be attained by more traditional means. They saw the League as a benevolent charitable institution for composing the disputes of other less fortunate and probably more cantankerous powers.

. . . we have never believed very strongly in the League as a police-man. What we looked for . . . was rather the machinery which should enable the governments of the world, by frank discussion, to devise before it was too late, some peaceful means of settling every dispute in which in most cases there is a good deal of right on either side and in which in any case butchery settles nothing.[5]

Here are the detachment and pacifism of the British view, which to other powers, who did not forget that the First World War had settled for Britain that the German navy should be sunk and Britain should add the Middle East to her Empire, seemed like complacency and hypocrisy.

The balance of power was also at issue in the debate about collective security. For some of the founders of the Covenant, especially Wilson, the Covenant was to abolish the balance of power and replace it by a 'community of power'. But there were others, of whom Cecil and belatedly Churchill were the greatest, who saw it in a different light: rather as an attempt to institutional-ize the balance of power, to make it work more automatically, more effectively and more rationally, to enable it to forestall more wars and to end the wars it could not forestall by a more decisive combination of power against the aggressor, wielded with a more coherent purpose. The balance of power worked traditionally by *ad hoc* alliances against a known enemy; the League, as Sir Arthur Salter said, was to be a permanent potential alliance 'against the *unknown* enemy'.[6] This uncertainty and impartiality was always inherent in the notion of a guarantee, and there was a model, the guarantee of the Franco-German frontier given by Britain and Italy at Locarno. There was much legalistic discussion about how to define the unknown enemy, i.e. the aggressor; but in practice it never presented the slightest difficulty, the great dis-turbers of the peace could be distinguished and isolated as easily as France in 1840 or Russia in 1878, and one of the merits of the

5. *Documents on British Foreign Policy 1919–1939*, Second Series, Vol. VI, H.M.S.O., London, 1956, No. 196, p. 301.
6. Sir Arthur Salter, *Security*, Macmillan, London, 1939, p. 155.

Covenant was to give a definition in terms of a power violating its covenants under Articles 10, 11 and 16.

British opponents of the idea of collective security made play with the distinction between 'producers' of security, of whom Britain herself was regarded as the great example, and 'consumers' of security, e.g. France and her allies. (A little later the same people prided themselves that Britain was 'standing alone' against Hitler between 1940 and 1941.) It was true that if the wrath of Mussolini's fleet fell upon the coalition of sanctionist states in 1935–6, it was the British navy that would have the task of sinking it, but it was Yugoslavia who suffered a permanent dislocation of her trade by loyally applying sanctions. It was true that if pressure had to be brought upon Japan when she conquered Manchuria in 1931–2, it would have had to be the British fleet (with or without American cooperation) that did it. This was sometimes said to be intrinsically impossible, because the Washington Treaty of 1922 had frozen British and American bases as far away as Singapore and Pearl Harbor, giving Japan unchallenged mastery of the western Pacific. But when Japan threatened British and American interests in Shanghai, Britain and the United States found themselves able to bring pressure upon her by fleet movements, and in the end they found themselves waging a war against her when the fleet at Pearl Harbor had been destroyed and the naval base at Singapore had been lost.

It was impossible to avoid the impression that the failure to impose effective sanctions against Italy in 1935–6 was a turning point in international history that has conditioned everything since, a seminal failure, the generator of a whole series of other failures. There could scarcely have been a clearer test case. The Japanese attack on Manchuria was more complicated. Japan had complicated legal rights in Manchuria, which gave her good cover for defensive argument; the scene of the war was geographically remote; it was easier to argue that action was impossible without the cooperation of a power outside the League, the United States or even Russia. The Italian attack on Abyssinia happened in a part of the world where the British and French spheres of influence met, and no other great power had ever been concerned; the illegality of the attack was more flagrant; strategically it was immensely vulnerable, because Britain could blockade the Suez Canal, as she had done in the First World War and was to do again in the Second. The preponderance of power that could be mustered by the League against Italy was overwhelming; the support for sanctions from the small powers was remarkably unanimous; of the three great powers outside the League, Japan was remote and preoccupied, the United States was benevolently neutral, and Germany, the most important, was hesitant. It was fear of German action in Europe that inhibited Britain and France from preventing the Italian conquest of Abyssinia. But it was not until after the League had shown itself impotent that Hitler took his decisive action, ending the demilitarization of the Rhineland and preparing his expansion in Eastern Europe. It is possible to argue, of course, that the consequences of having defeated Italian expansionism separately, of having an Italy more resentful externally or gravely weakened internally, would have been very difficult. They could not however have been more difficult than the consequences of not doing so.

The possibility of collective security constantly came back to the balance of power on which the League was based. The defeat of Germany enabled it to be founded; the Russian Revolution and the withdrawal of the United States into isolation conditioned its working. Of these the most discussed was the refusal of America to join, which is commonly said to have given the League its death-blow. There is much to be said against this view. The heart and test of the League system was in Europe, where the United States had never been a regular power. A semi-isolationist United States in the League might well have minimized its obligations and destroyed it from within more quickly than did a semi-isolationist Britain. The abiding effect of America's withdrawal was to give Britain a constantly repeated excuse for belittling the Covenant. The absence of Russia might be regarded as more important than the absence of the United States, because without Russian cooperation there could be no stable European balance. In 1934 Russia entered the League. But with Bolshevik Russia was real cooperation possible? Two hypotheses have to be weighed against one another: whether the United States, if she had joined the League, would have wanted to enforce the Covenant, and whether Russia, if she had had British and French confidence when she was in the League, would have tried to overreach them for her own revolutionary ends. Perhaps history will never be able to decide whether the genial but distant gestures of Roosevelt were more useless than the bland declarations of loyalty to the Covenant by Litvinov.

The disarmament of Germany in the Treaty of Versailles was prefaced by the phrase, 'In order to render possible the initiation of a general limitation of the armaments of all nations',[7] and the Covenant implied that members of the League were to give up the right to be sole judges of what armaments they needed. When disarmament negotiations started in earnest after Locarno, the French insisted that no disarmament arrangement was satisfactory which did not provide an effective system of international supervision to make certain it was not being violated, a point of view only reached by the United States and Britain after a second World War. But the British and Americans were reluctant to consider, not only international supervision, but even a level of armaments implying cooperation in defence between themselves. 'Each discussed its naval needs as if they were something absolute . . . The British cruiser programme was calculated as though it might have to protect British commerce single-handed on all the oceans, the United States' programme as though the American navy would have to operate entirely from its own bases.'[8] There was a long and futile attempt to classify armaments as defensive and offensive, known as qualitative disarmament. It had been easy to deprive defeated Germany of 'offensive' weapons in 1919; but when the other powers came to discuss it as regards themselves, it was found that tanks, heavy artillery, bombing planes, battleships and submarines were defensive if you possessed or hoped to possess them, offensive if not. The fundamental reason for the failure of the disarmament negotiations, which dragged through six years as the Preparatory Commission (1926–32) and

7. H. W. V. Temperley (ed.), *A History of the Peace Conference of Paris*, Vol. III, p. 187.
8. F. P. Walters, *History of the League of Nations*, Vol. I, pp. 367–8.

two as the Disarmament Conference (1932–4), can once again be explained in terms of the balance of power.

For every power the main consideration about disarmament proposals is the effect they are likely to have upon the relationship of power. It is perhaps generally true that satisfied powers will welcome a limitation of armaments, since this will freeze a balance of power that favours them. Thus Britain desired a limitation of armaments at the Hague Conference in 1907, since this would have confirmed her naval preponderance and relieved her from the threat of German naval competition, and the United States in 1946 put forward the Baruch Plan, which would have put her atomic supremacy into commission and relieved her of the threat of Russian nuclear competition. Correspondingly dissatisfied powers resist a limitation of armaments, which will hamper them in altering the balance of power more to their advantage, and improving their relative position. A Serbian statesman said, of the Hague Conference in 1899:

> The idea of disarmament does not please our people in any way. The Servian race is split up under seven or eight different foreign governments and we cannot be satisfied so long as this state of things lasts. We live in the hope of getting something for ourselves out of the general conflagration whenever it takes place.[9]

But different proposals for the reduction of armaments strike in different ways, and most are influenced by the hope of mitigating the weakness of the proposer or reducing the striking power of his rivals. And some relate to advantages which a power enjoys irrespective of the temporary balance of armaments. Thus it is that France, a satisfied power, did not see disarmament as a way of protecting herself against Germany, because every tendency towards a levelling of armaments would increase the advantage Germany possessed through greater population and industrial resources, and she saw her own military preponderance as the way of maintaining a precarious balance against these more substantial and long-term advantages of her enemy. And thus it is, on the other hand, that Litvinov came to the Preparatory Com-

9. Headlam-Morley, *Studies in Diplomatic History*, p. 268.

mission with his famous proposal for the abolition of all armaments, the most dissatisfied of all powers proposing total disarmament. It was logical for the revolutionary power to propose, in effect, the abolition of the balance of power. Since she depended on propaganda and her Communist fifth column in every country, her proposal, if she had been taken at her word, would only have enhanced her relative power.

Disarmament would itself have been a kind of peaceful change, by improving Germany's position in the balance of power relative to other powers. The failure of disarmament diverted those who believed injustice had been done to Germany to seeking peaceful change, and Germany's successful violation of the treaty in the matter of armaments suggested that change was bound to come about and might as well be made a matter of discussion. But the argument about peaceful change suffered from two radical vices. The first was a practical one: that it was seriously begun only after change was conceded, not by the strong to the weak on grounds of justice, but by the comfortable to the violent because of alarm. It is possible, though very arguable, that if disarmament or peaceful change had been conceded to Germany when she was represented by Stresemann, in the years after Locarno, German democracy would have been strengthened sufficiently to avert the Nazi Revolution. Once the Nazis were in power, peaceful change acquired the appearance of sacrificing small powers to the aggressor. But there was a deeper issue, on the level of principle. Centuries earlier the German international lawyer Pufendorf had argued that a state which has gone to war without seeking to settle the dispute pacifically must accept 'the dice of Mars'; even an unjust peace is an approximation to justice, and has to be accepted as final if international society is to have any order at all; hence the general rule that peace treaties must be performed in good faith. Here however was a case, not only where the defeated party was reluctant to accept the dice of Mars, but the more powerful of the victors too began to have scruples. This was a credit to their sense of justice, perhaps, but neglected the fundamental political law that the first condition of justice is an enforced order. It is possible to conceive an unjust order; it is possible to conceive, and even slowly to create, a just order; it is impossible (except for the theoretical anarchist) to conceive a just disorder. This, however, was the direction in which the protagonists of peaceful change set themselves, as they dismantled the rude scaffolding of international order set up in 1919. Henry II was able to introduce the grand and petty assizes, which were procedures for peaceful change in a feudal society, only because his predecessors had already established a strong central government which vigorously enforced the King's peace; nor did Lincoln attempt to meet the grievances of the Southern States by revising the terms of the Union in accordance with the doctrine of state sovereignty and the Dred Scott decision.

The deficiency of appeasement was not that it sought agreed change in the international order; this was a function of diplomacy and the balance of power. It was a threefold deficiency, part moral and part intellectual. 1. *A misjudgement of the nature of Nazism*, despite the fullest evidence and ample warnings. There is an easy doctrine that a country's internal practices are no concern of other powers; but ever since the murder of Dollfuss in 1934 the international implications had been clear. 2. *A misjudgement about the balance of power*. The function of the balance of power (sense 2) is to protect the independence of small powers. Peaceful change that endangers them is likely to be peaceful change in the wrong direction. The appeasement of Nazi Germany by the Western powers was the first time that the principle of 'peaceful change' was used to please a dominant power, and it was ironical that the beneficiary was the most barbarous of all dominant powers. Not since Charles II's policy towards Louis XIV had there been a precedent. It is interesting that the precedents appealed to by E. H. Carr in *The Twenty Years Crisis* are the Congress of Berlin in 1878, which was a change against the potentially predominant great power, the rebellions of the Americans and the Irish against the British, and the rejection of the Treaty of Sèvres by Turkey. 3. *A misjudgement about morality*. The Western powers, and particularly Britain, had adopted a high morality in subscribing to the Covenant, and now argued that the Covenant was unworkable and must be put aside in the name of the higher morality of peace. The issue between Chamberlain and Hitler at Munich was that Hitler wanted a violent alteration of the status quo, while Chamberlain insisted that alterations must come about by peaceful means. But he had just recognized a violent change brought about by the conquest of Abyssinia by Italy, and the participation of Mussolini in this example of peaceful change could not be without its effect on the moral credit of the British.

The system known as appeasement had already begun functioning behind the façade of the League; it was in a sense a continuation of the old system of the Concert of Europe, whereby the great powers settled matters by private bargains among themselves at the expense of small powers. The first instance was in 1923 when Italy used a dispute with Greece to bombard and occupy Corfu. Anxious to secure the evacuation of Corfu and restore the balance of power in the Mediterranean, Britain and France appeased Italy by preventing the League from handling the affair and agreeing to Italy's extortion of a large indemnity from Greece. In 1933 Mussolini proposed a Four Power Pact, under which the four European great powers (excluding Russia) were to undertake the revision of the Peace Settlement, with the implication that they would impose their views on the minor powers. This was frustrated for the moment by the Little Entente. There followed the Hoare-Laval Plan (1935) to bring the Abyssinian War to an agreed end by partitioning Abyssinia in Italy's favour; the establishment of the Non-Intervention Committee in London (1936), which removed the issues of the Spanish Civil War out of the hands of the League; the Anglo-Italian Agreement of April 1938, which adjusted Anglo-Italian interests in the Mediterranean and the Near East at the price of British recognition of Italy's conquest of Abyssinia; and the fulfilment at last of the idea of the Four Power Pact at Munich (September 1938), where the four powers agreed to the partitioning of Czechoslovakia by Germany (with Poland and Hungary coming in as jackal states) in order to preserve the peace.

Appeasement had formerly been an honourable word; it became infamous because, as the name of Western policy in the 1930s, it acquired the sense of seeking to buy off an expansionist great power by the sacrifice of small allies whom there was a pledge to defend.

Up to this point the four-power directorate had excluded Russia, to whom all the four powers (except in some degree France) were inflexibly opposed on ideological grounds. Thus Russia, the last great power to seem to champion the League system, was driven into isolation, and herself resorted to appeasement. The Nazi-Soviet Pact of August 1939 was Russia's Munich. The second article of the Pact stated that if either power 'should become the object of warlike action on the part of a third power', the other would in no way support the third power. Germany forthwith became the object of warlike action on the part of Poland and of most of the self-defending nations of Europe; while Russia hastened to transform the Baltic states into frontier provinces, and became the object of warlike action on the part of the self-defending Finns. The same method of arriving at international settlements by the great powers over the heads of the small powers concerned was seen at Yalta in 1945, when the Polish question was settled by the three Allied great powers without Polish representation, as the Czechoslovak question had been settled at Munich without Czechoslovak representation. These instances of appeasement are not necessarily all on the same moral level. The appeasement of a predatory power with whom you shortly afterwards find yourself at war may appear in a different light from the appeasement of a heroic ally in whose company you have just won an exhausting victory. But what we are here concerned to note is that the method throughout was the same – the great powers acting as a directorate. This is the system of power politics that the League of Nations was designed to supersede, but failed to do.[10]

10. This draft was completed in the early 1960s, probably in 1960. Eds.

20 : The United Nations.

If we entitle a chapter dealing with international politics between the World Wars 'The League of Nations', this is, so to speak, only by courtesy. The League of Nations, as we have seen, never controlled the politics of the period. The present chapter deals with international politics since 1945, and it is still more a courtesy to entitle it 'The United Nations', since the United Nations Organization has had less influence over international politics since the Second World War than the League of Nations had over international politics before it. Nevertheless, the two international organizations provide convenient labels; they are important though rudimentary developments; and interested students of international relations consistently overrate their importance.

The period of the United Nations is a continuation of the period of the League of Nations; that is to say, the historical break represented by the First World War was greater than that represented by the Second. 1945 was less of a new beginning than 1919. Three elements of continuity may be noted. The first is a renewed attempt to establish an effective international organization for international security: the United Nations was the formal successor of the League of Nations. The second is the resumed conflict, on a larger scale and a wider stage, between Communist Russia and the Western powers. The third is the working out of the principle of national self-determination beyond Europe, in Asia and Africa. Nevertheless, these elements of continuity do not make for resemblance between the two post-war periods. Perhaps the most striking of many differences is that the period after 1919 saw the greatest attempt ever made to provide international society with an effective constitution and to establish international law and order by cooperation between states. But the period after 1945 has shown, by contrast, a reversion to revolutionary power politics. It has been marked by a diminished concern for legality and order. It has seen the failure of general international cooperation and the development instead of rival hemispherical defence blocs. It has been compelled to abandon general security as a political objective, and has assumed that this will be given through mutual terror of nuclear armaments.

The Charter of the United Nations, which was drafted by the United States, Britain and Russia at Dumbarton Oaks in 1944, and completed by an international conference of all the Allied powers at San Francisco in April 1945, established a more authoritarian organization for world security than the League had been. The League had been able to do nothing except by the free cooperation of its members. The United Nations had the qualities of a governmental organization, that could in some respects order and override its members and perhaps even alter their legal rights. 1. Its coercive powers were vested in the Security Council. The signatories of the Charter empowered the Security Council to act on their behalf in maintaining peace and security (Art. 24), bound themselves to accept and carry out its decisions (Arts. 25 and 48), and undertook to provide it with armed forces and assistance (Art. 43) and to hold air forces immediately available for sanctions (Art. 45). 2. By a striking innovation, the traditional rule that international bodies can decide only by a unanimous vote (which is the legal principle that a power cannot be bound by a decision to which it has not itself consented) was modified. The Security Council, a body fixed at eleven members, decides by a majority of seven. The General Assembly decides by a two-thirds majority.

These developments seemed to go in the direction of constitutionalism. But they were offset by the great powers assuming for themselves a more irresponsible position under the Charter than they had had under the Covenant. The majority of seven by which the Security Council decides must include the five permanent members, viz. the great powers themselves (Art. 27 (3)). Thus, each of the great powers can veto any decision. It is to be noted that the veto was desired independently by each of the great powers at Dumbarton Oaks. The small powers in the Assembly were deprived of what was traditionally regarded as the protection of the unanimity rule; the great powers alone retained it. Moreover, in the Covenant the principle had been established that a state might not be judge in its own case, so that in reckoning unanimity the votes of the parties to an international dispute were not to be counted (Art. 15 (6); cf. Art. 16 (4)). In the Charter this principle virtually disappears (Art. 27): it survived with respect to the pacific settlement of disputes, but at Stalin's demands was erased from where it was most needed, with respect to threats to the peace and acts of aggression (Art. 27 (3)). The assumptions beneath the Covenant were those of free cooperation and mutual good faith between sovereign states consenting to limit their freedom of action for the sake of order and peace. The assumptions beneath the Charter were those of the unrestrainable power of each of the victor states and renewed aggression to be feared only from the ex-enemy states. The effect was to place the great powers outside the organization in all matters which they were likely to regard as their vital interests, and to place them above the law which, if they could agree among themselves, they could impose on smaller powers.

The consequences were unforeseen except by the most far-sighted. The great-power veto, exercised repeatedly by Russia, made the Security Council unworkable, and within a couple of years what had initially been regarded as the most important parts of the Charter were obsolete. The value was now seen of an escape-clause added at San Francisco: Article 51, which recognizes the right of individual or collective self-defence in the event of the Security Council failing to fulfil its function. The right of individual self-defence is the basic principle of international anarchy; the right of collective self-defence is the basic principle of the balance of power; and these survived with unimpaired vigour beneath the fictions of the Charter. Article 51 'turned the veto inside out' (to use a phrase of Sir Charles Webster's) by recognizing that a majority of powers cannot be prevented from cooperating to pursue *outside* an international organization a policy which the unanimity rule prevents them from pursuing *inside* the organization. For the same reason, the veto possessed by every member of the League had not seriously obstructed the League's purpose. In the supreme crisis of Italian aggression in

1935, the Assembly could not formally vote sanctions, because Italy voted against and her three satellites, Albania, Austria and Hungary, abstained. But Beneš, the President of the Council, pointed out that the application of sanctions was a matter for each member of the League individually, and if fifty of them had agreed in condemning Italy's aggression, the same fifty were within their rights in setting up a standing conference (which was euphemistically entitled the Coordination Committee) to concert their measures against Italy. It was to Article 51 of the Charter that the Brussels Treaty establishing Western Union and the treaty establishing NATO expressly appealed (North Atlantic Treaty, 1949, Article 5). By a parallel development, the General Assembly was to enter upon a boisterous career by trying to take over some of the functions which the Charter had carefully withheld from it.

The Charter of the United Nations thus showed a reversal of a faltering trend towards international constitutionalism which could be traced from the Concert of Europe in the time of Castlereagh down to the League Covenant. A corresponding and more notable reversal appeared in respect of a peace settlement. The Covenant of the League had been an integral part of the peace treaties of 1919, and had thus suffered along with the peace settlement from the attacks of revisionists. The Charter of the United Nations was thought to escape this disadvantage, since it was agreed before the Second World War had come to an end, and was attached to no peace settlement. But one of the most extraordinary consequences of the Second World War was that a peace settlement was not arrived at. The peace conferences at the end of general wars had steadily grown more comprehensive; and resembled the great legislative gatherings of international society.[1]

1. After the first period of the Italian Wars was the double pacification of Noyon (1516) between France, Spain and the Emperor, and London (1518) between France and England; after the second period of the Italian Wars the peace of Cateau-Cambrésis (1559) between Spain, France, England and Savoy; after the general war against Philip II there was the triple pacification of Vervins (1598) between France, Spain, Savoy and Switzerland, London (1604) between Britain and Spain, and Antwerp (1609). After the Thirty Years War was the double pacification of Westphalia (1648) and the Pyrenees (1669). After the Spanish Succession War was the Peace of Utrecht (1713).

Now they ceased. In 1946 there was a diminutive Paris Peace Conference, which made treaties between the twenty-one chief Allied powers and the minor enemy states of Europe – Italy, Hungary, Rumania, Bulgaria and Finland. A corresponding treaty with Austria was delayed till 1955. But the victorious powers were unable to agree on a peace settlement with their two principal enemies. With Japan, the United States and forty-seven of her associates signed a peace treaty at San Francisco in 1951; but this was rejected by the Communist powers, India and Burma, and was signed by neither Chinese government since the Western powers could not decide which of these ought to be represented. Russia made peace separately with Japan in 1956. With Germany, a peace treaty was impossible, in the Western view, until Germany was reunited; and the reunification of Germany was the most intractable of all post-war diplomatic problems. The economic success of federal Germany, and her adoption into the defensive system of the Western powers, seem to show that a peace treaty can be dispensed with. But the chronic weakness of Eastern Germany, the Russian need to give this satellite power some legal status, the unconfirmed frontier between Eastern Germany and Poland, and above all the dangerous and anomalous position of West Berlin, were directly connected with the absence of a peace treaty.

The Security Council broke down, and a comprehensive peace settlement was not made, because of the cold war. Victorious allies had always in the past fallen apart when the danger from the common enemy had been removed, but never before had conflict between the victorious allies broken out so quickly and implacably: another sign of the general deterioration in international relations. For the cold war was only a new phase of the doctrinal conflict between Bolshevik Russia and the rest of the world that had gone on since 1917. In the 1930s, as we have seen, there was a triangular struggle of the League powers, the Fascist Anti-Comintern powers, and the Soviet Union. After the Nazi Revolution, Russia joined the League to cooperate with the Western powers in self-defence. In the period of appeasement, the Western powers cooperated with the Axis to exclude Russia from Europe. After the Nazi-Soviet Pact, Germany cooperated with Russia to partition Eastern Europe. After the German invasion of Russia, Russia cooperated with the Western powers to destroy the Axis powers. The Second World War eliminated one party to this triangular conflict. In the retrospect of twenty years, Fascism looks (perhaps mistakenly) like an irrelevant intrusion into the course of history, which in 1945 could resume the fundamental debate between the Communist power and the Western world. Western fear and hatred of Communism had been seen when Russia was expelled from the League for her attack on Finland in December 1939, a punishment not inflicted on Japan and Italy for their aggressions. Soviet distrust of the West had been seen throughout the diplomacy of the Second World War. But while the springs of Russo-Western hostility lie in the nature of Communism itself, which is dedicated to the total destruction of its neighbours' ways of life, and rejects the bourgeois convention of an international order as it rejects bourgeois morality and bourgeois democracy, it is perhaps another mistake to see the conflict as predetermined, and to forget the occasions when an intelligent Western trustfulness towards Russia was lacking.

On the Russian side, the beginnings of the cold war were perhaps seen in a suspicion that the Western powers were in collusion with the Germans during the last months of the war, in the abrupt and unfriendly ending of Lend-Lease by the United States in the summer of 1945, and in the dropping of the two atomic bombs on Japan, which showed that the United States no longer needed the Soviet help in defeating Japan that had been promised at Yalta, and that she had suddenly acquired a new and vast military superiority over her exhausted ally. On the Western side, they were seen in the ruthlessness and chicanery with which Stalin imposed a Communist government on Poland. The first effect of the cold war[2] was the division of Europe and the Middle East between the Soviet and Western blocs. The states of Eastern Europe, which had been conquered or reduced to satellites by Nazi Germany, were now swiftly Communized by Russia. Czechoslovakia maintained a precarious balance between East

2. The name was apparently coined by Bernard Baruch, in his speech of 16 April 1947 at the unveiling of his portrait in the South Carolina House of Representatives. *New York Times*, 17 April 1947, p. 21.

and West under Beneš; and Greece, a Mediterranean not a Balkan state, which had been liberated by the British, had a conservative royalist regime. Russia pushed heavily against her southern frontier, trying to detach Azerbaijan from Persia, demanding territory and a revision of the Straits regime from Turkey, and allowing the Greek Communists to start a guerrilla war in Greece. The United States replied in 1947 with the Truman Doctrine, the first example of the policy of containment, which advanced American lines of defence to embrace Greece and Turkey, promising them the aid that Britain had become too weak to give. Three months later the United States took the diplomatic initiative with the Marshall Plan, which offered economic aid to Europe in general provided the European nations agreed on a joint programme. Russia rejected the Marshall Plan for herself and her satellites, thus demonstrating the division of Europe; and the Marshall Plan became, what perhaps its authors had wanted it to be, a revival of the economies of Western Europe under American guidance, and a move in the policy of containment.

Russia retaliated in September 1947 by establishing the Cominform, an organization of the European Communist parties whose main purpose was probably disruptive action in Western Europe through the powerful Communist Parties of France and Italy. She also destroyed the coalition government in Prague in 1948 and imposed Communism on Czechoslovakia, which had wanted to accept the Marshall Plan and had been compelled to reverse her policy in a humiliating manner. This violent coup, which recalled the Nazi seizure of Prague in March 1939, hastened the establishment of Western Union between Britain, France, Belgium, Holland and Luxembourg by the Brussels Treaty of March 1948, a pact of mutual defence and economic cooperation for fifty years. A year later they were joined by the United States in the North Atlantic Treaty Organization, embracing the five Brussels powers, the United States, Canada, Italy, Norway, Denmark, Iceland and Portugal, who agreed that an attack on one was an attack on all. This was the first alliance formed in time of peace providing for an organized military force with a unified command. In 1952 Greece and Turkey joined the alliance.

These developments were reflected and exaggerated in the mirror of Germany. Germany had been divided into four zones of occupation, subject to an agreement to preserve German unity and govern through an Allied Council of Four; Berlin, an enclave within the Soviet Zone, was correspondingly divided into four sectors. Almost from the moment of victory, each had become more afraid of the other than it was of Germany. Russia's ultimate goal was probably to transform a united Germany into a Communist satellite (Germany had once had the largest and strongest Communist Party in the world). The West's ultimate goal was to re-educate Germany into a law-abiding and democratic member of international society, who might freely choose to cooperate with the West against Communism. Through interminable meetings of their Foreign Ministers, Russia, the United States, Britain and France failed to agree on a common policy for Germany. The Marshall Plan stimulated the Americans and British to fuse their zones of occupation so that German industry might contribute to European recovery, and the French, after failing to mediate, joined the Western powers. Russia retaliated by stopping land communication between Western Germany and Western Berlin. The Berlin blockade was a bloodless battle, waged from June 1948 to May 1949, and won by the airlift and a counter-blockade of the Eastern Zone. The raising of the blockade, and the ending of guerrilla war in Greece the same autumn, marked the failure of the Russian attempt to alter the *status quo post bellum* in Europe. Germany was now irretrievably divided: the Western Zones rapidly united to form the Federal Republic, the Soviet Zone developed into a Communist satellite. The balance of power in Europe, created when the Soviet and Western armies met in the heart of defeated Germany in May 1945, and endangered by the rapid demobilization of the Western powers, had been restored. The only change had been Yugoslavia's secession from the Soviet camp in 1948. In 1949 Russia had acquired the atomic bomb, but once again had found herself technologically outdistanced because by that time the United

States was developing the hydrogen bomb, which it first tested in 1952.

As after the First World War, the Soviet Republic had failed in an attempt to invade and Communize Europe (though it had advanced its power from Lake Peipus and the Pripet Marshes to the Baltic Sea and the Elbe); and now again, though more effectively than in the 1920s, it turned to the road via Peking and Calcutta. The attempt to re-divide the territories that had formed the Nazi New Order in Europe was followed by an attempt to re-divide the territories that had formed the Japanese Co-Prosperity Sphere in eastern Asia. When Japan surrendered, Japan herself was occupied by the United States alone, in contrast with Germany; China resumed her civil war, suspended or soft-pedalled since the Japanese invasion of 1937, between the Kuomintang government and the Communists, with the United States as an ineffective mediator; Korea was occupied by the Russians north of the 38th parallel and the Americans south of it, in preparation for forming an independent government for Korea for the first time since Japan had annexed her in 1910; and Holland, France, Britain and the United States resumed or attempted to resume the administration of the South-east Asian territories that Japan had conquered from them.

This distribution of power was overthrown when in 1949 the Chinese Communists finally conquered the whole of the Chinese mainland. It did not end the Chinese civil war, since the defeated Nationalist government still held Formosa and certain other islands. But the establishment of the Chinese People's Republic with its government at the old imperial capital of Peking in 1949, and its military alliance with Russia in 1950, decisively changed the balance of power in Asia and the world, and offset the formation of NATO. The original Communist great power was now joined by a second. It was natural to compare the new military alliance with the Rome–Berlin Axis that had confronted the Western powers in the 1930s. But it had never been in question which of the two Axis powers was the stronger and the leader. With the two Communist powers this was in question, in proportion to the timespan considered. At the moment China was much the weaker, a potential great power only, with no heavy industry, and dependent on Russia for armaments. But she possessed the most numerous, diligent and disciplined population in the world, the fourth largest extent of territory (after the USSR, Canada and Brazil), all the resources for heavy industry, large Chinese communities overseas, especially in Siam, Malaya and Indonesia, resembling strategically the German minorities in Eastern Europe which had been instruments of Nazi expansion, and a claim to the oldest continuous civilization in the world. She was traditionally the Middle Kingdom, the empire to which all the peoples of the world were tributary barbarians. Moreover, China was no Russian satellite. Yugoslavia had been able to withstand the Soviet Union in 1948 because she was the only country since Russia herself where the native Communist party had gained power without Soviet supervision. China was now a third, and Mao owed even less to Stalin's support than Tito. The Chinese Revolution was a new and independent application of Marxist principles, different in important respects from the Bolshevik Revolution; and after Stalin's death Mao became the senior Communist revolutionary and could claim to be the most authoritative Communist theorist. These considerations raised Western hopes that China and Russia might be encouraged to fall out.

The invasion of South Korea by Communist North Korea in June 1950 began the greatest war since 1945, and gave United Nations procedures an unexpected exercise. President Truman, remembering the failure of the League of Nations to resist Italian aggression, summoned the Security Council, and committed American forces to battle. Till now, the Russian veto in the Security Council had been excused or explained by the American domination of the United Nations, which made it part of the diplomatic equipment of the cold war. Russia was at the same kind of disadvantage in the United Nations, under American leadership, as Prussia had been in the German Confederation, under Austrian leadership, before Bismarck took office. The uses of the United Nations had been illustrated during the Greek civil war, when the United Nations Special Commission on the Balkans, using planes with UN markings, could report on the aid the Greek rebels were receiving from Albania, Yugoslavia and Bulgaria, and the General Assembly conferred a kind of international approval on United States support of the Greek government. In the General Assembly, before 1955, the Western and Latin American groups numbered thirty-eight votes, the Communist bloc and the uncommitted powers only twenty-two; though of course it was only the Communist bloc that rigidly followed these alignments. In the Security Council, Russia was in a constant minority of one among the five permanent members; her positive motions could never attain the requisite majority of seven, and were thus stillborn. The veto, said Vyshinsky, the Soviet representative at the United Nations, was the weapon of the minority. He also proclaimed that the majority in the United Nations represented only a minority in the world, and that the majority throughout the world stood behind the minority in the United Nations.[3] In the hope of seducing this vast audience, Russia developed the World Peace Movement between 1948 and 1952, as a potential alternative international organization, dominated by herself as the United Nations was dominated by the United States. And at the beginning of 1950, having been defeated in a proposal to transfer the Chinese seat in the United Nations from the Nationalists to the Chinese People's Republic, the Soviet Union began a boycott of the United Nations.

Russia's absence from the Security Council (and the Chinese seat being occupied by Formosa not Peking) allowed the Security Council to vote assistance to South Korea without a veto. But still the Security Council was not working according to the Charter. Its resolution was a recommendation to member states, not a direction; it was working as the Council of the League had worked, and the sanctions it prescribed were optional, like those under Article 16 (2) of the Covenant. When, after the outbreak of the Korean War, Russia returned to the Security Council to condemn what had been done in her absence and prevent further action, the United States sought to transfer as much as possible of the Security Council's functions to the General Assembly. The

3. United Nations General Assembly: *Official Records of Ad Hoc Political Committee*, Third Session, 24 November 1948, p. 125; UNGA: *Official Records of the Plenary Meetings*, Part I, Third Session, 4 November 1948, p. 408.

Uniting for Peace resolution of 3 November 1950 provided that when the Security Council failed to take action through lack of unanimity among its permament members, the General Assembly should be summoned in emergency session to take action in its place. But the General Assembly could only take action within its powers: it could only recommend, not direct. In practice, the collective security that could be organized in the United Nations was proving legally indistinguishable from the collective security which could be organized under the Covenant of the League: it was the voluntary cooperation of sovereign states whose common interest and sense of obligation led them to unite. It seems that this is the highest degree of cooperation that the nature of independent powers permits.

But politically, as distinct from legally, the collective security illustrated by the Korean War was very different from the collective security provided under the League Covenant and dishonestly attempted by Britain and France against Italy in 1935.[4] The makers of the League had envisaged a multiple balance of power, in which an aggressor would be faced by a preponderant coalition of great powers who were determined to uphold the Covenant. In 1935, despite the aloofness of the United States, Japan and Germany, these circumstances still were granted. The Korean War, however, was a crisis of a simple balance of power, a struggle between the two great coalitions into which international society was divided; of the nominal great powers, the United States, Britain and France were ranged against Russia and China; in military terms, the attempt by one half of partitioned Korea to unify the country turned into a Sino–American War. Though eighteen members of the United Nations had armed contingents in Korea,[5] the United States supplied 50 per cent of the ground forces (American-trained South Koreans providing

4. Dishonestly, because while in the League Assembly they proposed and led sanctions against Italy, they had already privately agreed not to impose sanctions which Italy might retaliate against by military measures. See F. P. Walters, *A History of the League of Nations*, Vol. II, p. 670.

5. The United States, Britain, France, Australia, New Zealand, Thailand, Canada, South Africa, the Netherlands, Belgium, Greece, Turkey, the Philippines, Panama, Costa Rica, Bolivia, Colombia, Nationalist China. See *Survey of International Affairs 1949–50*, p. 482, n. 5.

another 40 per cent), 86 per cent of the naval forces and 93 per cent of the air forces. The United Nations Command for Korea was virtually identical with the United States Far East Command. On the Communist side, Russia provided the North Koreans and Chinese with military equipment and diplomatic support, but did not commit her forces: this was the chief reason why the fighting could be confined to the Korean peninsula. And the experiment in collective security ended, not by restoring legality and vindicating the authority of the United Nations, which had decreed as its war aims the reunification of Korea under a government chosen by free elections under United Nations auspices, but by an armistice that restored the original line of partition – a realistic compromise that registered the balance of military force.

When North Korea invaded South Korea, the United States feared a more general Communist attack on American interests in the Pacific, and intervened immediately in the Chinese civil war, by ordering the US Seventh Fleet to neutralize Formosa. This, followed by the UN conquest of North Korea, led to Chinese military intervention in the Korean War. The whole of the strategic battlefront in eastern Asia was now agitated. The military struggle between the Communist and Western powers shifted south from the civil war in Korea, even before the Korean armistice, to the civil war in Indo–China. In 1950 Chinese aid to the Vietminh in Indo–China became apparent, by giving asylum across the frontier, training troops and providing military materials. The war in Indo–China became a second theatre to the Korean War in the struggle between the Communist and Western powers, with France taking the leading role as the United States did in Korea, but with no native equivalent of the sturdy South Koreans to make it a genuine civil war, partly because the French grant of independence to Vietnam, Laos and Cambodia was slow and reluctant and clumsy. By 1954 France was utterly defeated and the United States on the point of intervention. On the initiative of Russia and Britain a conference met at Geneva (April–July 1954) to settle Indo–China and Korea, the first at which Communist China appeared. The conference failed to agree on how Korea might be unified; but it ended the war in Indo–China by agreeing to neutralize Laos and Cambodia, and by fixing an armistice line in Vietnam along the 17th parallel, which conceded the northern half of the country to the Vietminh. Vietnam thus joined Korea, China, and Germany as one of the states partitioned by the boundary between the Communist and Western powers. The Geneva Conference was a success for the Communists, but it was the only conference since 1945 at which all the great powers were present and a great issue was settled by diplomatic negotiation and compromise. One reason was the mutually deterrent effect of the hydrogen bomb: Russia had announced her possession of it in 1953, though she still had not the means of making it reach America. Another reason was that the conference was held outside the confusing procedures of the United Nations.

The wars in Korea and Indo–China had shown the Western powers the need both for mutual security and for finding allies in the Pacific region. In 1951 the United States sought to transform Japan from an occupied ex-enemy state into an anti-Communist ally by a peace treaty granting Japan freedom to rearm and a security pact allowing United States forces to remain in and about Japan. But the new ally disturbed older friends. Australia and New Zealand were reluctant to consent to the rearming of Japan, and several months before the Japanese Peace Treaty obtained guarantees in a mutual defence pact with the United States. The ANZUS Pact, as it came to be called, was the first diplomatic arrangement to show that the British Commonwealth was no longer a defensive unit, and that the old Pacific Dominions must look for protection to the United States. The need for another Pacific security arrangement to include Britain and France was met, in September 1954, by the South-east Asian Collective Defence Treaty, signed at Manila by eight powers.[6] Each recognized an attack on any of the others as endangering itself, and all agreed to consult in the case of subversion. Laos, Cambodia and South Vietnam were designated as within the protection of the treaty, and its area included Pakistan, but excluded Hong Kong and Formosa. The South East Asia Treaty Organization was not, like NATO, a grand alliance of like-minded and contiguous

6. The United States, Britain, France, Australia, New Zealand, Pakistan, Thailand, the Philippines.

powers to defend their common culture and homeland. Its sources of strength lay outside the region that it was created to defend. Of the three Asian members, only Pakistan had an effective army, and she was more afraid of aggression from India than from the Communist powers.[7] Of the Western members (including Australia and New Zealand under that name) none had forces to spare for East Asia except the United States. Strategically, SEATO was a patchwork of weak bridgeheads; its members possessed only one common land frontier, the Kra peninsula between British Malaya and Thailand. It could not therefore develop a common army with an integrated command, but depended upon limited local forces for internal security, and the American Seventh Fleet for retaliating against serious aggression.

The weakness of SEATO reflected the political Balkanization of Asia. Here the course of the cold war is broadened and complicated by the third stream of continuity between the new beginnings of 1919 and the world of the United Nations: the working out of the principle of national self-determination beyond Europe. The rearrangements after the First World War applied self-determination only in Ireland, in Eastern Europe, and in a rudimentary way in the Near East, where the Ottoman Empire was dismantled and semi-independent Arab states appeared. But the Second World War led immediately to the dismantling of the Japanese, United States, British, Dutch and French Empires in Asia, and more slowly to the dismantling of the British, French and Belgian Empires in Africa. Only in the case of the American dependency of the Philippines was independence granted with entire spontaneity by the imperial power.[8] The British emanci-

7. The only other two Asian powers on the Western side with substantial military forces were South Korea and Nationalist China. These were a political liability, since in Asia they were seen as Western satellites and in the West as irresponsible and bellicose autocracies. Nevertheless, the United States concluded a defensive alliance with each of them at the turn of 1954–5.

8. The process of enfranchisement was at work among the other dependencies of the United States, but only in the case of the Philippines did it produce a new member of international society. Puerto Rico was given home rule without full independence; Alaska and Hawaii were admitted to the Federal Union.

pation of India was long prepared, but had to be repeatedly accelerated by violent explosions of Indian nationalism, which provided the psychological equivalent of a war of independence. Elsewhere the surrender of British power kept pace with local demands, but the states that thus came into being saw the surrender as due to the demands. 'Liberated nations', as Bismarck said of Russian experience in the Balkans in the nineteenth century, 'are not grateful but exacting.'[9] The Japanese conquests that swept away the European empires in eastern Asia had found support from local nationalists, who had then had to resist by force the Dutch and the French when they tried to reimpose their rule over Indonesia and Indo–China.

The result was the formation of a group of states in Asia and Africa who stood consciously apart from the cold war. They were politically aloof, because they were preoccupied with their sense of independence and the difficulties of their own economic development; they thus reproduced the attitudes seen more than a century earlier in the history of the United States. They were militarily ineffective, but so long as the Western and Communist blocs were matched in the balance of atomic power, they could hope in some sense to hold the balance. But they were more censorious of Western imperialism, which they had experienced, than of Soviet imperialism, which they had only heard about. They tended to identify the Western powers with the past, and the Communist powers (for all their faults) with the future, to which they themselves belonged. They too were revolutionary, demanding a change in the status quo, resenting the increasing gap in living standards between themselves and the privileged minority of mankind dwelling in Western Europe and North America, who form one-sixth of the world's population and possess two-thirds of its wealth. This gave them a community of outlook with the Communist powers against the conservative West, and a double standard in judging the two great powers, which itself became a factor in the cold war.

Two events in 1955 marked the appearance in international politics of this third group. The first was the Bandung Conference of Asian and African powers in April 1955. It was summoned by

9. *Reflections and Reminiscences*, Vol. II, p. 292.

India, Indonesia, Pakistan, Burma and Ceylon, and attended by twenty-four other powers.[10] They included Communist China, which here had as much success in influencing opinion as she had had at Geneva the year before in securing political gains. The members of the conference had many differences among themselves, but presented a united front by attacking the colonialism and imperialism of the West; a resolution condemning Soviet imperialism in Eastern Europe was dropped. The second event was the admission of sixteen new powers to the United Nations in December 1955. An international political organization can aim either at effectiveness, in which case it will restrict its membership to like-minded states capable of agreeing upon and pursuing a common interest, and will resemble an alliance, or at universality of membership, in which case it will include so many diverse interests that it will be incapable of political cooperation on major issues. The League of Nations began with the first conception (which was Wilson's) and gradually slid into the second by ceasing to scrutinize the qualifications of new applicants for membership. But the absence of the United States from the League gave currency to the doubtful belief that its lack of universality was the cause of its failure; and the United States was a member of the United Nations from the beginning. When the original conception of the United Nations was destroyed by the failure of the permanent members of the Security Council to be unanimous, the universality of the United Nations became a compensatory aim, and it was indeed remarkable and unprecedented how capacious its membership became. In 1961 it admitted its hundredth member. But perhaps the most striking contrast between the United Nations and the League of Nations is least often mentioned. The aggressor powers, Japan, Germany, Italy, one after another quit the League, because they feared that League membership might hamper their freedom of action. No

10. Afghanistan, Cambodia, the Chinese People's Republic, Egypt, Ethiopia, the Gold Coast, Iran, Iraq, Japan, Jordan, Laos, Lebanon, Liberia, Libya, Nepal, the Philippines, Saudi Arabia, Sudan, Syria, Thailand, Turkey, the Vietminh, Vietnam, Yemen. The Central African Federation refused an invitation; Israel, Formosa, Korea and South Africa did not receive one.

power has yet resigned from the United Nations.[11] This may be partly because the Charter, unlike the Covenant, does not allow for withdrawal, but it is also because membership of the United Nations does not hamper the freedom of action of any state, save the minority of states where political opposition is tolerated.

The three-cornered power struggle between the World Wars was not confined within the framework of the League. The League never included more than two points of the triangle. In the 1920s, before revisionism grew strong, it included victors and revisionists and excluded Bolshevik Russia. In the 1930s the revisionist powers walked out – Japan, Germany, Italy – and Russia came in under the name of collective security, herself to be expelled in 1939, leaving Britain and France alone as the rump of the League. The United Nations, on the other hand, is a body within which the tripartite struggle of the Communist powers, the status quo powers and the have-not powers can go on. This might almost be said to define its nature.

It is convenient to view the tripartite struggle in the United Nations as passing through three phases up to the present time. The first phase runs from 1945 to 1947. This saw the collapse of the original organization, the breakdown of the assumption of great-power unanimity on which the Charter was based, as a result of Russia's use of the veto for purposes of obstruction.

In the second phase which runs from 1947 to 1953, the United Nations, as we have seen, becomes part of the diplomatic equipment of the cold war. In the constitutional history of the United Nations, this phase is marked by the transfer of authority from the Security Council to the General Assembly, which of course is a constitutional development or a violation of the Charter, according to the point of view. This transfer of authority was only possible because, during the first and second phases, the United Nations was a piece of diplomatic machinery controlled by the United States. This power could indulge the illusion that the United Nations was a natural expression of her own interests. When a conflict appeared between the United Nations and

11. Indonesia withdrew from the United Nations in January 1965 and returned in September 1966. Eds.

American interests, American enthusiasm for the United Nations at once evaporated. The classic illustration is the Guatemalan case in 1954. Guatemala, menaced by armed intervention, appealed to the Security Council. Cabot Lodge, the representative of the United States, declared in the strongest terms that the United Nations must keep out of this affair, which was to be settled by the Organization of American States. This was the moral equivalent of a veto. To the parties not immediately concerned, the Guatemalan episode appeared quite as shabby a betrayal of the United Nations as the Anglo–French intervention in Suez did, but because of the differences in circumstances the United States was able to dispose of the threat to her interests more tidily and with less fuss.

The third phase, which may appropriately be named the Bandung period, starts in 1953. That date saw the Korean armistice. More important, it saw the death of Stalin. In one aspect, the third phase is the post-Stalin era. Soviet diplomacy now showed less rigidity and more flexibility in its use of the United Nations. The World Peace Movement faded into oblivion; Russia joined the ILO, she returned to UNESCO. But the basic reason for her renewed interest in the United Nations was that it was moving increasingly in a direction that suited her. The head-on conflict between Russia and the West, in which Russia was at a disadvantage, was gradually ceasing to be the dominant theme of United Nations politics. It was being replaced by the anti-colonialist campaign.

The anti-colonialist campaign was rooted in earlier phases. It had first made its mark on United Nations machinery as early as 1946, when the Committee on Information was set up. Article 73 of the Charter declares the obligations of powers which administer non-self-governing territories, and it lays down that, in respect of these territories, such powers shall 'transmit regularly to the Secretary General for information purposes, subject to such limitation as security and constitutional considerations may require, statistical and other information of a technical nature relating to economic, social, and educational conditions'. The Charter says nothing about how such information shall be handled, nor whether it shall be debated. Accordingly, in 1946 the General Assembly set up an *ad hoc* committee for the job, which the colonial powers received with grave reserve and which France claimed was a violation of the Charter. Here one sees the pattern appearing: when the peace and security arrangements of the United Nations were amended or developed, Russia claimed the Charter was being violated; when the arrangements concerning trusteeship and non-self-governing territories were amended or developed, the colonial powers claimed the Charter was being violated.

From now on, the Committee on Information and the body to which it reported, the Fourth Committee, or Trusteeship Commitee, of the General Assembly, became the grand annual battleground for the struggle between the status quo and the have-not powers. The battle did not draw blood; it only caused irritation rising into exasperation. Russia judiciously stimulated it when occasion served, but in general she could sit back and watch its progress with satisfaction. From the outset, the have-not powers sought to widen the scope of Article 73 by demanding the transmission, not only of technical information about economic, social and educational conditions, but of *political* information also. This was hotly resisted by the colonial powers. In 1949 the General Assembly passed a resolution making it obligatory to submit political information. The British delegate condemned the resolution as an illegal and 'backdoor' effort to amend the Charter, and declared that Britain would not comply with 'misguided and sometimes incompetent policies' urged by countries 'actuated by emotion and envy'.[12] But a couple of years later, with what was perhaps a tardy access of wisdom, the colonial powers, deciding that they had nothing to conceal but much to be proud of, began submitting political information voluntarily, and did some useful counter-propaganda with it.

During these debates the United States tended to sit on the fence, trying to mediate between the two sides. In 1952 she announced that she was about to cease transmitting information on Puerto Rico, which was about to cease being non-self-governing. This threw the Fourth Committee into consternation: how could

12. UNGA: *Official Records of the Plenary Meetings*, Fourth Session, 1 December 1949, pp. 455–6.

it prevent a colonial power from escaping its clutches by the mean subterfuge of announcing that a non-self-governing territory had become self-governing? With the crazy logic of political passion it began a search for a list of factors or criteria of self-government, as a guide to determine when the interesting condition of non-self-government under the supervision of the United Nations has not yet been outgrown. In their violence and abstraction, the debates of the Fourth Committee now resembled those of the legislative assemblies of the French Revolution. The search for the 'list of factors' produced a grandiose essay in half-baked political philosophy, adopted in October 1953. But two months earlier Belgium had finally withdrawn from the Committee of Information on the grounds that it abused its powers, nor has she since returned to it.

Meanwhile the anti-colonialist campaign had widened. It was moving from the Fourth Committee to the General Assembly itself, from the question of non-self-governing territories to the question of domestic jurisdiction. The Charter is an ill-drafted document, full of potential contradictions. Perhaps the most famous is the contradiction between Article 2, Paragraph 7, which precludes the United Nations from intervening 'in matters which are essentially within the domestic jurisdiction of any state', and the tenor of much of the rest of the Charter.

The limits of Article 2, Paragraph 7, were first explored in the case of South Africa. The question was this: if South Africa infringes human rights, can the General Assembly infringe South African domestic jurisdiction? The Afro-Asians argued that respect for human rights overrides juridical limitations. 'It is better to be carried away by emotions', said the Pakistani delegate in 1952, 'than bogged down by legal sophistications'[13] – a highly revolutionary sentiment. Accordingly in that year the General Assembly began debating South Africa's policy of racial discrimination, and it established a three-man committee of inquiry under the title of the United Nations Commission on the Racial Situation in the Union of South Africa. Since UNCORSUSA was flatly refused entry into South Africa, it set up shop in the summer of 1953 in Geneva, and held public hearings of critics of

13. UNGA: *Official Records of the Ad Hoc Political Committee*, **Seventh Session**, 13 November 1952, p. 76.

South African policy. It became an open tribunal for propaganda against South Africa. Dr Malan responded by describing the United Nations as 'a cancer eating at the peace and tranquillity of the world',[14] the closest thing yet in the history of the United Nations to what Hitler used to say about the League. UNCOR-SUSA continued its activities until 1955, when in a dramatic debate the South African delegate accused India of conducting a 'vendetta' against his country, and withdrew from the General Assembly. Immediately afterwards UNCORSUSA collapsed, to the chagrin of the Afro-Asians, for the quite undramatic reason that the Budgetary Committee refused to provide funds for continued trips to Geneva.

It was in the same assembly that the campaign against French domestic jurisdiction came to a head. Already in 1951 France had withdrawn from the Fourth Committee because Egypt discussed French rule in Morocco. In 1955 the General Assembly put on its agenda the question of Algeria, which was part of Metropolitan France. The French thereupon withdrew from the Assembly. This caused some scandal: France was a great power, and she had traditional admirers among the Latin Americans. The Afro-Asians reluctantly climbed down and allowed Algeria to be removed from the agenda. The package deal for the admission of new members was being negotiated, and France on the Security Council might have vetoed the whole bargain. So the Afro-Asians sacrificed the Algerian issue, for one year, in order to become the largest bloc in the United Nations.

The development of the United Nations in these directions is remarkable. It was not contemplated at San Francisco that the United Nations should be an organization for collective intervention in the domestic affairs of its members. Yet, as the Holy Alliance was a coalition of kings for suppressing revolutionary movements, so the United Nations is tending to become an instrument of the have-not and Communist powers for promoting revolutionary movements. It has sometimes been argued that revolutions, by being brought into the United Nations, are controlled and rendered bloodless. But it is arguable whether the

14. Speech at Bloemfontein, 21 October 1953, in *The Times*, 22 October 1953, p. 8.

activities of the General Assembly either control revolutionary movements or reduce their violence: the annual debates may be themselves an inflammatory factor. And indeed, these interminable debates sometimes seem to be the diplomatic equivalent of brain-washing – an adaptation of that new revolutionary technique in domestic affairs to international relations. The reiterated oratorical denunciations of colonialism suggest a desire to convert the victim for his own good. In international politics the victim has an advantage over his domestic counterpart, in that if driven beyond endurance he can walk out of the United Nations. This of course spoils the fun, and it is amusing to see the Afro–Asian inquisitors pleading with him to come back, so that the process of his enlightenment may be continued.

The important feature of the United Nations is not that it has dramatized the *entente* of sympathy and perhaps of interest between the proletarian nations, who believe they have nothing to lose but their backwardness, and the Communist powers, who offer the most highly coloured diagnosis and remedy for this condition. Such an *entente* existed irrespective of the United Nations. Nor is it that the United Nations has played only a small part in the power struggle between Russia and the West. This was predictable and in accordance with all historical experience. It is rather that the United Nations has enhanced the power struggle between the have-nots and the status quo powers. The existence of the United Nations has exaggerated the international importance of the have-not powers, enabling them to organize themselves into a pressure group with much greater diplomatic and propaganda weight than they would otherwise have had. The paradoxical consequence has been that powers which, taken collectively, exhibit a low level of political freedom, governmental efficiency, public probity, civil liberties and human rights, have had the opportunity to set themselves up in judgement over powers which, taken collectively, for all their sins, have a high level in these respects.[15]

15. This chapter presents the author's draft chapter on the United Nations, followed by edited extracts from 'The Power Struggle within the United Nations', a paper the author read to the Institute of World Affairs in Pasadena, California, on 12 December 1956, and published in *The Institute of World Affairs Conference Proceedings*, 33rd Session, 1956. Eds.

21 : The Arms Race

An arms race is the competitive amassing of troops or armaments, whereby each side tries to gain an advantage over its neighbour or at least not to remain at a disadvantage. The race can be pursued by two rival powers or many; it can be local or general. Arms races have been a recurrent though not a continuous feature of international history, and they have become more intense as the states-system has coalesced.

New powers will sometimes amass armaments and soldiers without having a coherent foreign policy. The intrinsic efficiency of weapons is attractive; they are useful to maintain internal power, or for prestige. Renaissance princes valued firearms, fortresses and warships for their beauty as well as their utility. Franz von Sickingen recruited his landsknechts and gangster knights for random purposes, as Frederick William I of Prussia collected his tall Potsdam grenadiers for show. When Italy was recognized as a great power after her unification in the nineteenth century, national vanity made her aim at a front-rank army and navy, on which she spent a greater proportion of her slender national income than Germany. The new states of Africa after 1945 acquired what they could of aircraft, anti-tank guns or frigates, irrespective of external threats, for reasons of internal security and as insignia of independence.

The development of a foreign policy brings self-comparison with other powers, and especially with potential enemies. 'All states are considered strong and feeble only in comparison with the strength or weakness of their neighbours,' wrote the Huguenot statesman Du Plessig-Marly in 1584.[1] Self-comparison with

1. 'Discours au roi Henri III, sur les moyens de diminuer l'Espagnol', 14 April 1584, *Mémoires de Messire de Mornay*, Vol. I., J. Daillé (ed.), Amsterdam, 1624, p. 357.

other powers is the subjective prompting for an arms race. But in European history it has been reinforced by objective changes in military organization and technology. The arms race marks the point at which the free play of international rivalries, the endless repetitive fluctuations of the struggle for power, become geared into the forward thrust of social and scientific advance. Thus we may speak of 'the arms race' as an abiding feature of international society, of which particular arms races are acute temporary manifestations.

The arms race begins with the invention of new weapons, at first condemned as shocking and barbarous, and then increasingly adopted because of their superior efficiency. In the eleventh century the Normans invented the crossbow. The Third Lateran Council in 1139 anathematized it, and perhaps helped the English preference for the shortbow and afterwards the longbow.[2] But the Church later allowed the use of the crossbow against the infidel, on the vicious principle, which readily corrodes the society that adopts it, that a holy cause justifies an unjust means of warfare. In the thirteenth century gunpowder was discovered, and by the end of the fifteenth century cannon had mastered the medieval fortification and portable firearms were ousting the bow. Their appearance, it has been said, 'brought about Europe's first important proliferation controversy'.[3] It was not an arms race between powers, but a debate cutting across the internal frontiers of Christendom, and thereby bearing some witness to its continued unity, between conservative advocates of the traditional restraints of chivalry (some of whom conveniently attributed the invention of firearms to infidels like the Chinese or the Moors), and the moderns, who took pride in technical expertise and professional efficiency.[4] The tempo of technical innovation

2. Sir Henry Maine, *International Law*, J. Murray, London, 1888, p. 139; H. Delbrück, *Geschichte der Kriegskunst*, Vol. III, G. Stilke, Berlin, 1925, p. 389n.

3. J. Larus, *Nuclear Weapons Safety and the Common Defense*, Ohio State U.P., Columbus, 1967, p. 101.

4. For a recent survey of the debate, see J. R. Hale, 'Gunpowder and the Renaissance: An Essay in the History of Ideas', in *From the Renaissance to the Counter-Reformation: Essays in Honour of Garrett Mattingley*, C. H. Carter (ed.), Cape, London, 1966, pp. 113–44. More generally, J. U. Nef,

seemed at that time as rapid as it afterwards seemed in the twentieth century. In 1559, the year after her accession, Queen Elizabeth's envoy in Brussels asked the President of the Netherlands Council of State, the Bishop of Arras, whether in the event of renewed war with France England might expect help from her traditional Spanish ally. Granvelle replied harshly that the whole world knew England's weakness. 'Is there one fortress or hold in all England that is able one day to endure the breath of a cannon? Your men are hardy and valiant; but what discipline have they had these many years? And the art of war is now such that men be fain to learn anew at every two years' end.'[5] And already during the Thirty Years War we find military innovation linked with the idea of competition in armaments. 'We see the face of war and the forms of weapons alter almost daily, every nation striving to outwit each other in excellency of weapons,' wrote an English soldier when the Civil War broke out in 1642.[6]

The first great military change in modern history is the development of standing armies in the seventeenth century, which accompanied new conceptions of the state as a military and economic power unit and of war potential.[7] 'When the expedient of a standing army had once been adopted by one civilized nation', says Adam Smith, 'it became necessary that all its neighbours should follow the example. They soon found that their safety depended upon doing so, and that their own militia was altogether incapable of resisting the attack of such an army.'[8] A

War and Human Progress, Routledge, London, 1950, Chapter 2. For the English debate in Elizabeth's reign, which ended with the Privy Council decision in 1595 no longer to enrol archers, see Sir Charles Oman, *A History of the Art of War in the Sixteenth Century*, Methuen, London, 1937, pp. 380–85.

5. Sir Thomas Chaloner to Cecil, 6 December 1559, in J. A. Froude, *History of England from the Fall of Wolsey to the Defeat of the Spanish Armada*, Vol. VI, Longmans, London, 1893, p. 286. I owe this and the next quotation to Nef, op. cit., pp. 30–31.

6. D. Lupton, *A Warlike Treatise of the Pike*, 1642, p. 131, quoted in H. C. Firth, *Cromwell's Army*, Methuen, London, 1902, p. 12.

7. See M. Roberts, *The Military Revolution 1560–1660*, Boyd, Belfast, no date.

8. *The Wealth of Nations*, Vol. II, Book V, Chapter I, part I, p. 199.

general arms race became noticeable in the eighteenth century, and was first described perhaps by Montesquieu, who wrote this passage in the period of the Polish Succession and Austrian Succession Wars (1733–5, 1740–48):

A new disease has spread across Europe; it has smitten our rulers, and makes them keep up an exorbitant number of troops. The disease has its paroxysms, and necessarily becomes contagious; for as soon as one power increases its forces, the others immediately increase theirs, so that nobody gains anything by it except common ruin. Every sovereign keeps in readiness all the armies he would need if his people were in danger of extermination; and peace is the name given to this general effort of all against all.[9]

'It is true', he adds in a footnote, 'that this general effort is the chief thing that preserves the balance, because it is breaking the backs of the great powers.'

What Montesquieu described, with some ironical exaggeration, was a competitive augmentation of troops by rival monarchs. But the arms race was given a sinister propulsion by a threefold development that became apparent during the French Revolutionary Wars. The first was the mobilization of manpower, through compulsory enlistment. There had been gropings towards conscription in several countries during the eighteenth century, notably in Prussia and Russia; but it was the French Revolution that introduced the nation in arms, the *levée en masse*. Compulsory universal service was introduced by all the great powers in the course of the nineteenth century (Britain lagging behind until 1916), accompanied by its two handmaids, compulsory universal education and universal manhood suffrage. The second development was the mobilization of opinion. The growth of a public opinion about foreign policy took chiefly a nationalist and militarist form, concerned that the defences of the country for which it spoke were being outstripped by rival powers. But we may remember that there was also a steady current of pacifist and internationalist opinion, giving rise to an international peace movement of lofty aims and negligible influence. The third development was the industrialization and mechanization of war,

9. *De l'esprit des lois*, Garnier, Paris, no date, Book XIII, Chapter 17, p. 203.

producing an independent momentum of technical innovation in armaments. Here the important changes came after the Revolutionary Wars. Nevertheless, the Revolutionary Wars saw the introduction of the explosive shell, the incendiary rocket and the first submarine; the French Convention began the mass-production of cannon, and Napoleon invented the massed artillery barrage.

By the end of the nineteenth century the bases of military power in Europe were army reserves and strategic railways. The American Civil War and the Prussian Wars of 1866 and 1870–71 first showed the use of railways for transporting armies with speed. Under the German Empire, the railways system was virtually a civil section of the army. The military arms race between 1871 and 1914 was seen chiefly in the extension of strategic railways and the competitive increase in the term of national service.

But it was in the naval sphere that the intensity of the arms race could best be seen. In the middle of the nineteenth century the revolution in naval armament from sail to steam, and from wooden ships to ironclads, promoted a naval race between Britain and France. In 1845 Palmerston, in an alarmist speech from the opposition, said that steam navigation had made England vulnerable by throwing a steam-bridge across the Channel.[10] There followed a succession of 'panics', when an influential part of British opinion believed that the country was falling into a position of inferiority compared to its rival, and the government increased the defence estimates. A similar panic was occasioned a hundred years later by the Western belief in 'the missile gap' between 1958 and 1962. After the first Soviet sputnik was launched in October 1957, it was feared that the United States was lagging behind the Soviet Union in missile science and production, and that there was consequent danger of a surprise attack. The missile gap came to an end in 1961 with an admission by Kennedy's administration that a false assessment of Soviet missiles had been made. The Anglo–French naval race petered out because British opinion was unable to persist in a false assess-

10. House of Commons, 30 July 1845 in *Parliamentary Debates*, Third Series, Vol. 82, col. 1224; see also 3 April 1852 in ibid., Vol. 120, col. 1104.

ment of French policy. Disraeli and Gladstone had successively favoured and imposed a reduction in naval estimates, even before France was defeated and humiliated in the Franco-Prussian War by a new enemy, whose menace Britain was slow to recognize.

In the Anglo–French naval race, the political conflict was subordinate to the alarms created by the technical revolution. In the Anglo–German naval race, at the beginning of the twentieth century, the relationship of the political and the technical was reversed. British opinion had recognized the German naval menace before, in 1902, the Admiralty did; in 1903 the government announced a new naval base in the Firth of Forth, across the North Sea from the German bases; in 1904 the Home Fleet was concentrated in the North Sea. In 1905 Britain took the bold decision to build the *Dreadnought*, an all-big-gun battleship with greater speed and range of fire than any existing warships. This was a leap in naval armaments that made existing fleets virtually obsolete – the British first of all. But it was known that other powers were contemplating such a vessel, and it was vital 'not to permit the Germans to get the jump'.[11] From then on Dreadnoughts became the units of the accelerating competition between Britain and Germany.

As one of the main causes of the First World War was the German threat to British naval supremacy, so one of the main consequences was a new American threat to it. In 1905 the British had recognized that an Anglo-American war was not 'a contingency sufficiently probable to need special steps to meet it', and in 1909 the American navy was explicitly excluded from the calculation of the two-power standard. In 1916, when the United States was still outside the war but as alarmed by Japanese expansion in eastern Asia as by the danger of a German conquest of Europe, she passed a Naval Act with the purpose of building 'a navy second to none'. This construction was half completed by the end of the war, when the American navy was second only to the British. And already before the Armistice each was thinking of the balance of strength between them when the war ended, and there was tension between the two associated powers, comparable

11. A. J. Marder, *British Naval Policy 1880–1905 : The Anatomy of British Sea Power*, Putnam, London, 1941, p. 538.

244

to, though less acute than, that between the Western powers and the Soviet Union in the last year of the Second World War. The German fleet itself now became a pawn in the struggle. The Americans wanted it not to be surrendered to Britain, to augment British superiority. Under American pressure, the Supreme War Council decided in October 1918 that the Germany navy should be interned in neutral ports. No neutral was willing to accept the embarrassment, and the decision was amended to include designated Allied ports. But the British Commander-in-Chief, Beatty, was made responsible for carrying out the naval clauses of the Armistice; and the splendid ceremony, unparalleled in naval history, which he organized ten days afterwards, when the greater part of the German High Seas Fleet steamed into the Firth of Forth under the escort of the British Grand Fleet, 'surrendering under the eyes of the fleet it dared not encounter', to be interned until the peace treaty was signed, strained the terms of the Supreme Council's decision and put a weighty bargaining counter in British hands.[12]

But there was a deeper conflict between the two associated powers. Before she entered the war the United States had asserted the principle of the freedom of the seas, and Wilson had just enunciated it as the second of his Fourteen Points, which he meant to govern the peace terms. It was the historic American claim that neutral shipping should not be searched, nor private property at sea captured, in war any more than in peace. Britain asserted far older belligerent rights, which allowed her to use her naval preponderance, as they had just done once again, to defeat a great Continental enemy by measures of contraband and blockade. She expressly dissociated herself from the principle of the freedom of the seas when she agreed to the Fourteen Points (about which she had not been consulted) as the basis of peace terms.[13] But Wilson came to the Peace Conference at Paris with two particular aims: that it should include both the freedom of the

12. W. S. Chalmers, *Life and Letters of Beatty*, Hodder and Stoughton, London, 1951, pp. 341–9; S. Roskill, *Naval Policy between the Wars*, Collins, London, 1968, pp. 73–5.

13. Lord Hankey, *Supreme Command 1914–18*, Vol. II, London, 1961, pp. 859–63.

seas and a League of Nations. And he was prepared to coerce the European powers with the threat of unlimited American naval expansion. The United States Navy, for their part, wanted equality with Britain for its own sake.

There followed at the Peace Conference what afterwards got the name of 'the naval battle of Paris'. The British were determined to oppose the freedom of the seas as Wilson understood it; the Admiralty hoped to stabilize naval armaments in the ratio of the existing strength of the British and American navies. The crunch came when the First Lord of the Admiralty suggested to the American Secretary of the Navy that Lloyd George would be unable to support the League of Nations if the American building programme continued. Wilson came to terms. On 10 April 1919 there was a highly confidential exchange of notes between Lord Robert Cecil and Colonel House, employing the urbane understatements used between English-speaking gentlemen, by which it was understood that Wilson would postpone the naval building programme, and in return Lloyd George would support the plan for a League of Nations, and also raise no objection to a clause in its Covenant to affirm the validity of the Monroe Doctrine. This gave Wilson some of the political support he needed against his critics at home, established a truce in naval building, and left Britain with her precarious preponderance.[14]

The United States also tacitly abandoned the principle of the freedom of the seas. It was not discussed at the Peace Conference, found no place in the Covenant, and disappeared forever, even from the populous underworld of international fantasies, when in the Second World War the United States succeeded by right of strength and inheritance to the British use of naval mastery.[15] Germany's unrestricted submarine campaign had brought the United States into the First World War; in the Second World

14. See C. Seymour (ed.), *Intimate Papers of Colonel House*, Vol. IV, p. 431–9; D. H. Miller, *My Diary at the Conference of Paris*, Vol. VIII, 1924, pp. 138–47; H. and M. Sprout, *Towards a New Order of Sea Power*, Princeton U.P., New Jersey, 1940, pp. 62–72; Roskill, *Naval Policy*, p. 91; R. S. Baker, *Woodrow Wilson and World Settlement*, Vol. III, Doubleday, New York, 1922, pp. 206–17.

15. P. E. Corbett, *Law in Diplomacy*, Princeton U.P., New Jersey, 1959, pp. 133–5.

War the United States waged an unrestricted submarine campaign from the outset. But the British on their side also recognized the force of circumstances, and soon abandoned their claim to naval supremacy. Not only was the balance of economic and financial resources between the two powers unequal; Britain was also financially exhausted by the war, while American strength had been whetted. 'By the autumn of 1919 the British government was in no mood to contest the American claim to parity, and even the Admiralty had come round to accepting it as inevitable.' In 1920 Britain consequently enunciated a one-power standard, which meant parity with the United States in general, but a two-power standard in European waters. In 1921 it was accepted as the basis of imperial defence.[16]

The history of how Britain surrendered her secular claim to the mastery of the seas has not yet been fully written. The composure with which she accepted new circumstances here is as remarkable as that with which, after the Second World War, she acquiesced in the dismantling of the Empire. It was a suspended arms race, not exacerbated by technical innovations, in which the stronger power was able to gain its end without racing. It was tempered by the ties between the two countries and by the refusal on the British side to consider the possibility of war with the United States. On the American side there was no such general inhibition, and navalists spoke freely of the logic of history that would either bring a war between the old dominant power and her younger stronger rival, or allow the rival to seize the trident from the old one's weakening grasp. House could write to Wilson in July 1919 that 'the relations of the two countries are beginning to assume the same character as that of England and Germany before the war'.[17]

The parity of naval strength between the two powers was made formal by the Washington Naval Treaty of 1922, to which we shall return in the next chapter. The celebrated ratio of 5: 5: 3 between the United States, Britain and Japan marked Britain's open acquiescence in the abandonment of her supremacy. The treaty

16. Roskill, *Naval Policy*, pp. 21, 216, 230–31.
17. Seymour (ed.), *Colonel House*, Vol. IV, p. 510; Sprout, *op. cit.*, pp. 77–85.

had unintended consequences. Not till after the economic crisis, in 1934, would Congress vote the funds to allow the United States navy to attain the equality with Britain that was its right. And the Washington agreement being limited to capital ships had the effect of stimulating competition in the unrestricted classes of warship, cruisers, destroyers and submarines. Britain claimed superiority in light cruisers on the grounds that her commerce and imperial communications presented special needs. The United States demanded parity at a lower level of heavier cruisers. Each argued as if it would have to defend its interests single-handed, and the American navy, at least, as if Britain might be an enemy. The conflict wrecked the Three-Power Naval Conference (United States, Britain, Japan) at Geneva in 1927, after which the chief British delegate, Lord Cecil, resigned from his government in protest against his country's obstinacy. As late as 1928 President Coolidge could find it necessary to say to the British ambassador, as late as 1929 King George V to the American ambassador, that it was deplorable to talk of the possibility of war between the two countries.[18] Agreement was at last reached at a third naval conference in London in 1930, partly through Ramsay MacDonald's diplomacy. The ratification of the London Naval Treaty of 1930 in Tokyo brought the constitutional crisis that ended with the army gaining control of Japanese policy, and beginning the conquest of Manchuria; but although the United States and Britain ceased their competitive arming, it was another ten years before they recognized a common interest in the world.

The Anglo–German naval rivalry before 1914 has resemblances to the American–Russian nuclear rivalry since 1945. The object of the race was the greatest engines of destruction then available to man; the two rivals easily outdistanced other competitors (but in the first race, only so long as the United States remained too proud to fight); the race was exacerbated by technical innovations, ensuring a high rate of obsolescence, but was governed by political antagonism. But there are important dissimilarities; the development of military technology, and the place of public opinion.

18. Roskill, *Naval Policy*, p. 549; H. Nicolson, *King George V*, Constable, London, 1952, p. 438.

248

With the progress of military science, the arms race has proceeded by the improvement of weapons rather than by their increase. From being quantitative, it has become qualitative. Within a year of its first use the atomic bomb had been called 'the absolute weapon',[19] a description that perhaps fostered the dangerous misconception that it did not simply take its place as an addition to the immemorial range of weapons, but made all other weapons unnecessary. But the nuclear bomb was the absolute weapon in the sense that, because of its destructive power, a relative advantage in its possession was without military value. It was the first weapon in history that its possessors decided that, after accumulating a certain stock, they had enough of. This conclusion was being approached by both parties in the race, from 1958, when the Soviet Union led the way in suspending tests, to the final Test-Ban Treaty of 1963. But already the competition had been diverted into the methods of delivering the bomb. The superfortress that dropped the first atomic bomb on Hiroshima had been superseded by the B 47 jet bomber; this by the B 52; this by the intercontinental ballistic missile. Competition then moved to making the weapons invulnerable, and produced the missile base buried in a deep silo and destructible only by a direct hit, and the mobile base carried on a submarine. It was at about this stage, in 1960, that Herman Kahn estimated that a contemporary weapons-system lasted about five years before a new technical revolution made it obsolete, recalling Tirpitz's remark about the Anglo-German naval race that 'Every ship became obsolete by the time it was finished'.[20]

From here the race may be seen as diverging simultaneously along three separate tracks. One was the search for a defence against missiles, through the development of an anti-ballistic missile. A second was to improve methods of offence, with guided and homing missiles, multiple warheads, submarine-destroying

19. The phrase may have originated with the wise and perspicacious book edited by Bernard Brodie, *The Absolute Weapon: Atomic Power and World Order*, Harcourt Brace, New York, 1946.

20. Herman Kahn, *On Thermonuclear War*, Princeton U.P., New Jersey, 1960, p. 315; Alfred von Tirpitz, *My Memoirs*, Vol. I, Hurst & Blackett, London, 1919, p. 141.

missiles and attack submarines (to kill the missile submarines). A third was space exploration.

Public opinion constitutes a second difference between the earlier naval races and the American–Russian nuclear race. The earlier races occurred before the totalitarian revolutions of the twentieth century, and the Anglo–American was unaffected by them. Public opinion was tolerably free on both sides in the race, and on each side tended to encourage its government not to allow the nation's defences to fall behind the supposed increasing dangers. In the nuclear race, public opinion has a modified role. 1. Public opinion is effective only on one side of the race. The Soviet political system, with its total control over the population and its extreme secrecy of administration, is only remotely influenced by what faint and inchoate public opinion exists in the USSR. Still more is this the case with China. It is customary in the West to believe that a free society is intrinsically stronger than a despotism, and that it has higher chances of survival. The two World Wars seem to have confirmed this belief. But it is by no means certain that it will always hold good. Two developments within the democratic states might gravely weaken them *vis-à-vis* a ruthless and controlled despotism. One was a partial loss of faith in representative government and economic free enterprise, because of the inefficiencies and injustices inherent in all political life, but open in this system to view and to debate (and to correction). The other was a rise in the political moral standards of the democratic states that contradicted and censured the unchanging violence and ruthlessness of power politics. 2. And this was due to the increasing influence of that stream of opinion, pacifist and internationalist, which we noticed earlier. Before 1914 its influence on governments was negligible. Between the World Wars, Western governments had to take more account of it for electoral purposes, and it made its contribution to the imbecility of British and American policy in the face of the Axis powers. After 1945 it became a useful weapon in the hands of the Soviet government, which organized the World Peace Movement of 1948–52, culminating in the Stockholm Peace Appeal of 1950. This did not much embarrass Western governments; nor did the Campaign for Nuclear Disarmament. But the opposition to the war in Vietnam succeeded in breaking President Johnson's will to govern, and the American people's will to continue the war. If we compare it with the 'pro-Boer' opinion in England which opposed Britain's part in the Boer War of 1899–1902, we can see that it is not simply an autonomous and honourable expression of enlightened and morally sensitive domestic opinion about foreign policy, but also an instrument, however involuntary, in the orchestra of a world-wide coalition against the United States. Demonstrations at a Democratic Convention in Chicago or in front of the American Embassy in Grosvenor Square were as much part of the war as troop movements along the Ho Chi-Minh trail. And the most striking reflection of all was that it was impossible for any corresponding expression of public feeling to occur in Hanoi, Moscow or Peking.

There are two traditional laments about the arms race. One is economic, that it is wasteful; the other political, that it is dangerous to the peace. The economic argument used to be summed up in the phrase 'the crushing burden of armaments'. As early as 1710 the Quaker writer John Bellers argued the waste of wealth and labour in war. In his description of the arms race already quoted, Montesquieu went on, with ironical exaggeration, to describe its economic effects:

Thus Europe is ruined so completely that individuals who found themselves in the position of the three richest powers of this part of the world would have no means of subsistence. We are impoverished despite the riches and commerce of the whole world; and soon, by dint of raising troops, we shall have nothing *except* troops, and we shall be like the Tartars.

Not content with buying up the troops of the small powers, the great powers make it their business to pay subsidies for alliances on every side, and almost always lose their money.

The consequence of this situation is the perpetual increase of taxes. Moreover, the powers no longer depend on income but expend their capital on war, which blocks all future remedies. It is not unknown for states to mortgage their funds even in peacetime, and to employ for ruining themselves methods that they call 'extraordinary' – so extraordinary that the most profligate young bloods scarcely conceive of them.[21]

21. *De l'esprit des lois*, Book XIII, Chapter 17, pp. 203–4.

Fifty years later Kant condemned not only standing armies, but national debts also, as part of the mechanism of the rivalries of power politics.[22]

The economic argument swelled through the nineteenth century. Disraeli appealed to Palmerston to 'put an end to these bloated armaments which only involve states in financial embarrassment'.[23] John Bright's love of peace was nourished and tarnished by his concern about 'panic in the funds' and damage to the textile industry. When in 1898 Tsar Nicholas II invited the powers to the first Peace Conference at the Hague, his declared aim was to mitigate the 'ever increasing financial burdens' of armaments, through which economic progress was paralysed or misdirected. Germany attended the conference with reluctance and contempt, and one of the German delegates roundly attacked the prevailing doctrine:

I do not believe that among my honoured colleagues there is a single one ready to admit that his sovereign, his government, is engaged in working for the inevitable ruin, the slow but sure annihilation of his country. I have no mandate to speak for my honoured colleagues, but so far as Germany is concerned, I can reassure her friends completely and dissipate all benevolent anxiety regarding her. The German people are not crushed beneath the weight of expenditure and taxes; they are not hanging on the edge of the precipice; they are not hastening towards exhaustion and ruin. Quite the contrary; public and private wealth is increasing, the general welfare and standard of life, are rising from year to year.

As for compulsory military service, which is intimately associated with these questions, the German does not regard it as a heavy burden, but as a sacred and patriotic duty, to the performance of which he owes his existence, his prosperity, his future.[24]

This was to speak of the arms race as if it were only the prep-

22. I. Kant, *Perpetual Peace*, preliminary articles for perpetual peace, No. 4, pp. 111–12.

23. House of Commons, 8 May 1862 in *Parliamentary Debates*, Third Series, Vol. 166, col. 1426.

24. J. B. Scott, *The Proceedings of the Hague Peace Conferences*, New York, 1920, pp. 308–9.

aration for war, which could be judged apart from the experience of the war it led up to. It is ironical, moreover, that in 1914 Germany was showing signs of financial exhaustion from the naval race before Great Britain. But at the same time as the Hague Conferences a German economic historian, Werner Sombart, was developing the Germany military view into the theory that modern war had actually stimulated economic growth and industrial efficiency.[25] It was a theory that might be adopted by a power that had just completed a century of triumphant industrial growth and rising economic standards without having suffered the devastation of war. Britain had had a comparable experience during the Revolutionary and Napoleonic Wars, and the United States during the two World Wars. The relation of the arms race to economic growth is part of a classic historical controversy, where it is not easy to agree on how to measure the degree of economic activity that may be attributed to preparation for war. But it is clear that economic growth and technical inventiveness have flourished in times of relative peace (as the first half of the nineteenth century) no less than in times of war. However, it is possible that the arms race becomes increasingly interwoven in the process of industrial change, as it becomes qualitative rather than quantitative. The naval race of the mid-nineteenth century was prompted not only by the transition from sail to steam and from wooden ships to ironclad, as we saw, but by the transition also from solid roundshot to explosive shell and from the broadside to the mobile gun in a revolving casemate. The arms race of the later twentieth century, which we loosely call the nuclear race from its dominant feature, was far more diversified, and included almost the whole range of contemporary science and industry: not only nuclear explosives, but nuclear propulsion for ships and aircraft, rocketry, vertical take-off aircraft, electronics, computers, space technology, chemical and biological warfare.

This vast and complex competition, intimately linked to the advance of science and technology, which it both stimulates and

25. Werner Sombart, *Krieg und Kapitalismus*, Ducker & Humblot, Munich, 1913. For a reply see J. U. Nef, *War and Human Progress*.

follows, can give the appearance of an autonomous force, carrying governments helplessly in its embrace towards the logical consummation of war. The classic statement of the theme that the armaments race causes war occurs in Sir Edward Grey's memoirs, when he reflected upon the origins of the First World War:

The moral is obvious: it is that great armaments lead inevitably to war. If there are armaments on one side there must be armaments on other sides. While one nation arms, other nations cannot tempt it to aggression by remaining defenceless. Armaments must have equipment; armies cannot be of use without strategic railways. Each measure taken by one nation is noted and leads to counter-measures by others.

The increase of armaments, that is intended in each nation to produce consciousness of strength, and a sense of security, does not produce these effects. On the contrary, it produces a consciousness of the strength of other nations and a sense of fear. Fear begets suspicion and distrust and evil imaginings of all sorts, till each government feels it would be criminal and a betrayal of its own country not to take every precaution, while every government regards every precaution of every other government as evidence of hostile intent . . .

The enormous growth of armaments in Europe, the sense of insecurity and fear caused by them – it was these that made war inevitable. This, it seems to me, is the truest reading of history, and the lesson that the present should be learning from the past in the interest of future peace, the warning to be handed on to those who come after us.[26]

The doctrine that the arms race is the prime cause of war was widely believed after the First World War, and powerfully shaped the public opinion in the parliamentary democracies that were reluctant to rearm against the Axis powers. It is an example of learning the wrong lesson from history. No arms race played a part in the origins of the Second World War; it was rather an insufficiency of armaments on the Western side. Nevertheless, the right lesson from history is that armaments are the instruments of national wills. To possess armaments without sound policy is as futile as lacking them when there is need for them.

Cobden once argued that there is always a ready excuse for

26. Grey of Fallodon, *Twenty-five Years*, Vol. I, pp. 91–2.

rearmament, but 'when the alleged occasion of the increase has passed away, we never have a diminution'.[27] This is likely to be true of the successive scares that make up a particular arms race. Beyond this, it becomes untrue, inasmuch as arms races are discontinuous, and after wars armaments are usually reduced to correspond with the restored or new-shaped balance of power. But it is of course the case that each successive arms race has been a higher wave in the rising tide of armaments, in volume, complexity and destructiveness, than its predecessor.

John Bright sometimes argued that the amassing of armaments led to the demand to use them. 'What observation has been more common during the discussion upon Turkey than this – "Why are we to keep up these great fleets if we are not to use them? Why have we our Mediterranean fleet lying at Besika Bay, when it might be earning glory, and adding to the warlike renown of the country?"'[28] In the same vein, but more fatalistically, Sir Charles Snow wrote in 1960 of the accelerating nuclear arms race: 'Within, at the most, ten years, some of those bombs are going off. I am saying this as responsibly as I can. *That* is the certainty.'[29] Such misgivings are not borne out by history. It might be truer to say that, since the age of rapid technical innovation in armaments began in the early nineteenth century, fewer weapons have been used in war than have grown obsolete and been scrapped after fulfilling their function of temporarily maintaining or modifying the balance of power. It is interesting to remember that the First World War was fought and won without the Dreadnoughts, supreme symbols of the preceding arms race, being seriously tested in action. Jellicoe conducted the Battle of Jutland in such a manner that the British Grand Fleet never passed over from its

27. Speech at Manchester, 10 January 1849, in J. Bright and T. Rogers (eds.), *Speeches on Questions of Public Policy*, Vol. I, p. 478.

28. Speech at the Peace Society Conference, Edinburgh, 13 October 1853, in T. Rogers (ed.), *Speeches*, pp. 362–3.

29. Address to the American Association for the Advancement of Science, in the *New York Times*, 28 December 1960, p. 14, reprinted as 'The Moral Un-Neutrality of Science', *Science*, Vol. 133, No. 3448, 27 January 1961, p. 255. See Herman Kahn, *Thinking about the Unthinkable*, Weidenfeld, London, 1962, pp. 25–6; R. Aron, *Peace and War*, Weidenfeld, London, 1966, pp. 618–20.

deterrent or throttling role to a conflict that might have been destructive or self-destructive.

But the pressure of continuous technical innovation, added to the native instability of the balance of power, gives rise to certain laws of the arms race, which can be seen in most cases to govern the powers. 1. Technical innovation is in the interest of the weak rather than the strong, since it will introduce change. The stronger power will tend to be conservative, wishing to retain the technical status quo which provides its superiority. Thus, when the Younger Pitt had been showing a favourable interest in submarine experiments, the First Lord of the Admiralty said 'Pitt was the greatest fool that ever existed to encourage a mode of war which those who commanded the seas did not want, and which, if successful, would deprive them of it'.[30] The Admiralty showed the same conservatism in allowing the French to innovate with the ironclad. 2. However, a great power that wants to remain a great power cannot avoid running the race. As the rate of innovation increases, even the stronger power will be compelled reluctantly to take the lead in innovation, for fear of being forestalled. Britain resolved to build the *Dreadnought* in 1905, because other powers had caught up with her in rapidity of naval construction, other powers were known to be contemplating the introduction of the all-big-gun ship, and it was essential not to allow the Germans to gain the advantage. The United States resolved to build the hydrogen bomb in 1950 for similar reasons. The majority of the US Atomic Energy Commission advised President Truman against it, and the chairman of the Commission's General Advisory Committee, Robert Oppenheimer, gave his opinion that the Soviet Union would not make the hydrogen bomb if the United States did not. Had this naïve estimate of Soviet policy prevailed, the Soviet Union might well have acquired the hydrogen bomb first, and with it a crushing preponderance.[31] 3. Nor can a great power that has acquired a

30. Earl St Vincent, quoted by Admiral Sir E. R. Fremantle in his introduction to Herbert C. Fyfe, *Submarine Warfare*, Grant Richards, London 1902, p. xiii.

31. See L. Strauss, *Men and Decisions*, Macmillan, London, 1963, Chapter 11 and p. 274; G. F. Kennan, *Memoirs: 1925–1950*, Hutchinson, London,

lead in the race put an end to the race, by itself crying a halt. Immediately after the first Dreadnought had been launched, the new Liberal government in England in 1906 announced a cut in the naval building programme, in the hope that the second Hague Conference, which was about to meet, might reach agreement on the reduction of armaments. Germany interpreted this gesture as a cynical attempt to consolidate Britain's naval supremacy, and redoubled her own construction. Within two years Britain found that her lead had almost disappeared. Grey then said in the House of Commons:

If we alone, among the great powers, gave up the competition and sank into a position of inferiority, what good should we do? None whatever, no good to ourselves because we cannot realize great ideals of social reform at home when we are holding our existence at the mercy, the caprice if you like, of another nation . . . We should cease to count for anything amongst the nations of Europe, and we should be fortunate if our liberty was left, and we did not become the conscript appendage of some stronger power. That is a brutal way of stating the case, but it is the truth.[32]

The British government resumed the naval race with a new intensity.

To bring an arms race to an end without war requires agreement between the competing powers on mutual disarmament. To the attempts that have been made to do this let us now turn.[33]

1967, pp. 471–6; Dean Acheson, *Present at the Creation*, Norton, New York, 1969, pp. 345–9.

32. 29 March 1909, *Parliamentary Debates*, Fifth Series, Vol. 3, cols. 69–70.

33. This chapter was apparently written in the late 1960s or early 1970s. Eds.

22 : Disarmament

The remedy for the arms race is traditionally thought to be disarmament. This is an imprecise word. It can mean either abolishing weapons, or reducing their quantity, or limiting their increase, or restricting their kinds and uses. The term 'arms control' has come into currency since 1945 to describe the last two of these meanings.

The abolition of weapons altogether has been a futurist's dream since Isaiah's vision of the last days of mankind, when 'they shall beat their swords into plowshares, and their spears into pruning-hooks'.[1] Those who quote these words have not always remembered that they relate to the end of history, and that the desired conditions are to follow upon a disagreeable divine judgement on the nations; nor that the prophecy is exactly reversed by a later (though minor) prophet, Joel, who foresees the nations summoned to a final and fatal tryst of arms before Jehovah.[2] These are variants of apocalyptic, not history; but history contains within itself all the possibilities of apocalyptic. Historical experience so far has pointed towards the second rather than the first alternative.

Disarmament has often been imposed upon or accepted by a power that has lost a war. Compulsory demolition of fortresses is probably the oldest form of it. Kings have imposed it on their vassals in the course of establishing the authority of the state, and it had the advantage that its being carried out was easily observ-

1. The Old Testament, Isaiah, Chapter 2, verse 4, perhaps quoting Micah, Chapter 4, verse 3. They wrote at the time when the Kingdom of Judah was a precarious satellite of Assyria, circa 700 BC.

2. The Old Testament, Joel, Chapter 3, verses 9–10. He wrote probably after the return of the Jews from exile, perhaps as late as 400 BC, when Jerusalem was incorporated in the Persian Empire.

able. Such a disability, imposed on a state by other states, is an example of what is called in international law a servitude. But imposed unilateral disarmament has never been more than temporarily successful, unless when imposed on very weak states, and then it has sometimes been the prelude to their annexation. In the Treaty of Rijswijck in 1697, Louis XIV restored Nancy to the Duke of Lorraine on condition that its fortifications were razed and the duke might not even build a wall round it.[3] Within forty years Lorraine itself was ceded to the French kingdom. But at the Peace of Utrecht Louis XIV himself was required to destroy the French naval base at Dunkirk, which menaced British control of the Channel. Successive French governments managed to evade this obligation, helped by the sturdy self-assertion of the inhabitants of Dunkirk. It was a matter of repeated recrimination between Britain and France, and of attacks by the opposition upon the British government in Parliament. The ban on the fortification of Dunkirk was repeated by the Treaties of Aix-la-Chapelle in 1748 and Paris in 1763; but at the Treaty of Versailles, which ended the disastrous American Revolutionary War in 1783, Britain was compelled to agree to the abrogation of all these articles. In the same way, the Treaty of Paris in 1856 which ended the Crimean War compelled Russia to accept the neutralization of the Black Sea, and therefore to dismantle her bases on the Black Sea coast. The chief aim of Russian policy thenceforward was to free herself from this servitude. In November 1870, when France was succumbing to German invasion and Britain was deprived of her Crimean ally, Russia denounced the Black Sea clauses of the Treaty of Paris in so far as they restricted her sovereignty. 'They were the most inept decisions of the Peace of Paris,' Bismarck (who had encouraged the Russian repudiation) afterwards wrote: 'a nation of a hundred millions cannot be permanently denied the exercise of its natural rights of sovereignty on its own coasts. A servitude in respect of Russian territory of a kind which was conceded to foreign powers was, for a great nation, a humiliation not to be borne for long.'[4] A similar fate befell the demilitarization of the Rhineland by the Treaty of

3. Treaty of Rijswijck, 1697, Article 29.
4. *Reflections and Reminiscences*, Vol. II, p. 114.

Versailles imposed on defeated Germany, in 1919. When Hitler reoccupied the Rhineland in 1936, no power had the will to compel him to withdraw.

There are two instances of a defeated great power adopting a measure of disarmament willingly, in advance of the treaty imposed by the victorious enemy. Both France in 1815 and Japan in 1945 ended a great war in a mood of exhaustion and disenchantment. It is striking that France did not need to be compulsorily disarmed after the Napoleonic Wars: the restored Bourbon king acquired popularity by abolishing conscription in his new constitution of 1814, and the Allies with wise clemency confined themselves to mild indemnities and a temporary army of occupation. They agreed also among themselves, though not requiring French assent to it, on a measure of psychological disarmament: the exclusion of Napoleon and his family for ever from supreme power in France. Within four years France had restored a system of compulsory service; in a generation another Bonaparte was on the throne of France, and the first foreign power to recognize the Second Napoleonic Empire was Britain, the only power that had never recognized the First Empire. After the Second World War, Japan was in a disenchantment with war more profound than France in 1815. Under American supervision the Japanese adopted a constitution which renounced the right of going to war and declared that armed forces would never be maintained. Within five years, this was embarrassing to the Americans, who wanted a rearmed Japan as an ally in the Pacific against Russia, and to the Japanese government, which was alarmed by the Communist triumph in China and by the Korean War. The Japanese Peace Treaty of 1951 accordingly contained an article which contradicted the constitution by recognizing Japan's inherent right of individual or collective self-defence.

It is doubtful whether there is any instance in history of a power disarming unilaterally and voluntarily, although Denmark in the inter-war years came close to taking such a course. In the 1920s successive Danish governments tabled proposals for disarmament, which failed to be passed by the upper chamber. In the 1930s, however, Denmark reduced the strength of its army and navy to such modest levels that the country was without effective defence. But this did not last. The experience of conquest by Germany in 1940 produced a profound change in national opinion, and Denmark became one of the twelve original members of NATO. Her former dependency Iceland had a similar history. Iceland, which had been under Danish rule, became a sovereign kingdom in personal union with Denmark in 1918, and declared herself an independent republic in 1944. She had never possessed armed forces at all. She too became an original member of NATO, with nothing to contribute except a strategic air base. But Iceland had not been educated by a German occupation: neutralist opinion was strong, and there was discontent about American troops on Icelandic soil.

History affords a few examples of successful mutual disarmament between two powers. Obviously a certain comparability of strength between the two parties is necessary for success, but the case of Savoy and France in 1696 shows how a fortunate bargaining position may allow a weak power to negotiate on equal terms with the dominant power. It was the eighth year of the War of the League of Augsburg, and France was exhausted. She still held the two great fortresses which for half a century had assured her power in North Italy: Pinerolo in Savoy, guarding the route from the Mont Génèvre pass down to Turin, and Casale in the duchy of Montferrat, controlling the crossing of the Po between Piedmont and the Spanish Milanese. Louis XIV was ready to pay a price to break up the Grand Alliance; Victor Amadeus II, the Duke of Savoy, decided that he would make greater gains by abandoning the Grand Alliance and making a separate peace with France. He wanted to recover Pinerolo; and he decided that it would be to his advantage to have Casale dismantled, and therefore put at his mercy in the future. The two powers agreed, therefore, that France should surrender Casale, its fortifications be demolished, and the place be retroceded to the Duke of Mantua; and to Savoy herself France surrendered Pinerolo, its fortifications also being razed. The Treaty of Turin of 1696 ended an epoch in French relations with Italy. Although before ten years had passed French troops were again in occupation of most of Savoy, the disarmament of the two fortresses meant that she could no longer hold North Italy. In 1703 Savoy herself acquired the duchy of Montferrat, by the Treaty of Turin which brought her into the Spanish Succession War on the side of the Grand Alliance, and the Emperor stipulated that the fortifications of Casale should not be rebuilt, so that Allied troops might have free access into the duchy from Milan. The Treaty of Utrecht confirmed Savoy in possession of Montferrat, and restored her right to fortify her possessions as she pleased. Victor Amadeus's far-sighted acquiescence in a measure of temporary disarmament had produced a rich territorial gain.

The earliest discussion of a mutual reduction of armaments between two great powers may perhaps be found in the relations between Austria and Prussia after the end of the Seven Years War. In 1766 the Prussian chargé d'affaires reported to Frederick the Great a curious conversation with Prince Kaunitz, the Austrian Chancellor. Kaunitz had talked in a reflective and informal manner of the baneful political effects of human irrationality. The great armies which were maintained everywhere, and which 'we shall sooner or later have to reduce because we shall run out of manpower', were as pernicious to humanity as the monastic system, which in Catholic countries swallowed up citizens who might otherwise be useful to society. Could not the powers find an alternative to this 'guerre intérieure en pleine paix' by reducing their troops? Kaunitz said that he had often pondered the difficulties of the matter, and how to settle the proportion of forces which one power would maintain *vis-à-vis* another. But Prussia and Austria need only accept as a basis their recent Treaty of Hubertusburg. Let them agree to discharge reciprocally three-quarters of the troops they possessed at that time. For verification, let them exchange commissioners to take part in each other's troop inspections. Everything depended on a little confidence and good faith.

The voice of the Enlightenment spoke through the subtle and cynical Austrian Chancellor, but it was not disinterested. The Prussian diplomatist concluded his report with the opinion that Kaunitz had been fishing for information about an increase in the Prussian forces. Frederick commented that Kaunitz' suggestion was unacceptable anyway, since it took Prussia longer to mobilize her troops in an emergency than it did Austria; and that the proposal was clearly prompted by the financial embarrassment of the Austrian government. 'If he returns to the subject, you are to reply to him with due respect that this project seems to you much the same as that of the Abbé de Saint-Pierre; and that, in your opinion, agreement will never be arrived at between powers on the number and quantity of troops that each shall maintain against the others.'[5]

The incident is a diplomatic curiosity, hardly deserving to be called the first proposal for an arms agreement from one government to another.[6] But it is interesting as containing in embryo most of the ingredients and difficulties of disarmament negotiations.

During the Dutch crisis of 1787 France and Britain made a joint declaration about naval armaments. Historians of disarmament, finding this in collections of treaties, have described it as 'the earliest known armaments agreement'.[7] But what happened was this.

France and Britain had been brought to the verge of conflict by an insurgency in the United Provinces. The bourgeois democratic party known as the Patriots, supported by France, had revolted against the Stadholder, supported by Britain, and threatened to carry the United Provinces from its traditional British association into the French camp. The question was whether France would intervene with troops to help the Patriots, at the risk of war with Britain and Prussia. Pitt's government was intent upon peace and retrenchment to confirm the recovery from defeat in the American War, a few years earlier, and only slowly

5. *Politische Korrespondenz Friedrichs des Grossen*, Vol. XXV, Verlag von Alexander Dunker, Berlin, 1899, pp. 225-6. Joseph II returned to the proposal briefly at his meeting with Frederick at Neisse in 1769 (ibid., Vol. XXIX, p. 41, no. 3).

6. Alfred H. Fried, *Handbuch der Friedenbewegung*, 2te Teil, Berlin and Leipzig, Friedens-Warte, 1931, p. 32.

7. Hans Wehberg, *Die Internationale Beschränkung der Rüstungen*, Deutscher Verlags-Anstalt, Stuttgart and Berlin, 1919, pp. 258-60, citing the declarations from G. F. de Martens, *Recueil des traités*, 2nd edition, Vol. IV, Göttingen, 1791, pp. 279, 313-14. Followed by R. Redslüb, *Histoire des grands principes du droit des gens*, Rousseau, Paris, 1923, pp. 241-2; Hosana, *Histoire du désarmement*, Pedone, Paris, 1933, pp. 7-8; M. Tate, *The Disarmament Illusion*, Macmillan, New York, 1942, p. 7.

came to hold that it was worth another war to restore the traditional state of affairs in the United Provinces. On 30 August 1787, on British initiative, the French and British governments signed a declaration that they would not augment their naval preparations above a peace establishment, without giving one another notice. On 16 September the French declared their intention of sending troops into Holland. Pitt's reply was firm and immediate. On 19 September the British Cabinet ordered the mobilization of forty ships of the line. The French government at once climbed down. On 27 October the two powers signed statements of mutual good intentions, agreeing that all military preparations should be discontinued and that their fleets should be restored to a peacetime footing.[8]

The case is instructive in two respects. First, measures of disarmament cannot be understood outside their diplomatic context. The agreement of 30 August 1787 is not so much the earliest agreement on arms limitation, as an incident in an Anglo–French diplomatic conflict in which Britain restored the balance of power without war but by inflicting on France a severe diplomatic defeat. Secondly, the consequences of diplomatic victories are usually unforeseeable. The French deeply resented their humiliation. Napoleon said later that this blow to its prestige had been one of the main causes of the fall of the French monarchy, and it contributed to the revolutionary hatred of England. Within eight years Britain and France were at war again and French armies had triumphantly conquered the United Provinces.

The classic example of mutual disarmament between two powers is the demilitarization of the border between the United States and Canada. The United States proposed the disarmament of the Great Lakes to Britain in 1794, when Britain refused. It then failed to be included in the terms of the Treaty of Ghent in 1814, which concluded the War of 1812. But in 1817, by the Rush-Bagot Agreement, the two powers undertook to confine their armed vessels on the Great Lakes to an agreed minimum, and to

8. See Paul Vancher, *Recueil des instructions*, XXV, 2, *Angleterre*, Vol. III, 1965, pp. 536–8; J. Holland Rose, *William Pitt and National Revival*, Bell, 1911, p. 377; A. Cobban, *Ambassadors and Secret Agents*, Cape, 1954, chapters viii 4, ix 1, pp. 175–96.

build and arm no more. This was the agreement whose spirit was afterwards extended to the whole American–Canadian frontier.

There were two comparable arrangements at the beginning of the twentieth century, between Argentina and Chile, and between Norway and Sweden. Argentina and Chile had been in dispute about their frontier through Tierra del Fuego, Patagonia, and the Andean massif that divides them in the north. In 1888 they agreed to neutralize the Magellan Straits and prohibit the erection of fortifications throughout its length. In 1902, while a British commission of arbitration was settling the Andean frontier at their invitation, they signed a treaty providing that for five years neither power should acquire new naval armaments without giving the other eighteen months notice, and that certain warships then commissioned should not be built. This suspension of armaments seems to have become permanent. In a similar fashion, when Norway separated from Sweden in 1905, the two states established a neutral and demilitarized zone between them.

These instances of mutual disarmament have common features. They were not imposed, but freely agreed between powers of comparable strength or self-confidence. The Rush-Bagot Agreement was the delayed consequence of an evenly contested and moderate war; the Argentine–Chilean treaty put an end to a mild arms race; the Scandinavian arrangement was the result of an amicable dissolution of a dual kingdom. Secondly, the frontiers thus disarmed were wilderness or mountain, with little direct pressure upon them from either side, and remote from the centres of international conflict. In the Scandinavian case, however, Sweden was impelled to come to terms with Norway by her traditional fear of Russia: she faced east across the Baltic, and did not want a hostile state in her rear. It would perhaps be unwise to add that the three pairs of states were distinguished by common history and cultural affinity, since such ties have never prevented conflict when other circumstances have been unpropitious.

Bilateral disarmament is a convenience. Multilateral disarmament has been elevated into a political ideal. In the fifteenth and sixteenth centuries it was not yet an ideal, though it sometimes occurred in fact: it was common for treaties of peace to enjoin the mutual disbandment of armed forces. The predecessor of disarmament as a supreme goal of international politics, something demanded by public opinion and subscribed to, with varying degrees of cynicism, by rulers, was the crusade: the dream of laying aside quarrels and pooling arms with the common purpose of expelling the Mohammedans from Europe. Its only practical outcome was the succession of Holy Leagues, seldom comprising more than four powers, and distinguished from other defensive and offensive alliances only by their enemy.[9] That which won the battle of Lepanto in 1571 is the most famous, but that which reconquered Hungary between 1683 and 1698 was the most successful.

A secularized version of the crusade provides the earliest proposal for arms control. It is found in the Grand Design which Sully, the great minister of Henry IV of France, attributed to his master. He devised a league of states with the purpose of humbling not the Turks but the House of Austria. The military quotas of the states were to be determined by a general council, but Henry himself (according to Sully) made proposals for an armament 'so inconsiderable and so little burdensome, when compared with the forces they usually keep on foot, to awe their neighbours, or perhaps their own subjects', that Sully thought it would be generally acceptable, and moreover it would be capable of reduction when the enterprise against the Habsburgs was successfully completed.[10] Sully's Grand Design was a formative influence on such diplomatic thinkers of the Enlightenment as Penn, Saint-Pierre and Rousseau. Through them disarmament became a regular ingredient in the notion of international order.

The French Revolution made pacifism, for the first time, the official ideal of a great power. 'La nation française renonce à entreprendre aucune guerre dans la vue de faire des conquêtes, et n'emploiera jamais ses forces contre la liberté d'aucun peuple.'[11] This was immediately transformed into its opposite in action.

9. The last general European treaty which paid tribute to the crusading motive was the Treaty of London, 1518, under the inspiration of Pope Leo X.

10. *Grand Design of Henry IV*, Maxwell, London, 1921, pp. 34–5.

11. Constitution of 14 September 1791, Titre VI, in *Select Documents of the French Revolution*, Vol. II, L. G. Legg (ed.), Clarendon Press, Oxford, 1905, Appendix G, p. 242.

Nevertheless, as an indirect result of the French Revolution, disarmament became part of the cant of democracy as the crusade had been the cant of princes. But more important, as a result of the long war against the French Revolution and Napoleon the limitation of armaments became one of the principles of the Concert of Europe, and helped to distinguish the international system of the nineteenth century from that of the eighteenth. The principle had little practical effect, but was regularly appealed to.

The earliest formal proposal for multilateral disarmament came from the Tsar Alexander I, an amiable autocrat who combined a muddled enlightenment with military preponderance in Europe. His was the first of the proposals for disarmament that have been put to the international community by Russia. His descendant Nicholas II issued the rescript of 1898 inviting the powers to a conference on the reduction of armaments, which led to the Hague Peace Conference of 1899. Litvinov proposed the total abolition of armaments to the League of Nations Disarmament Conference in 1927. Khrushchev repeated the proposal at the United Nations in 1959. These initiatives are probably to be explained by the particular role that Russia has played in European history, whether under Orthodox, Pan-Slav or Bolshevist inspiration, as would-be messiah and reformer of the West.

What Alexander proposed in 1816 was 'a simultaneous reduction of the armed forces of all kinds which the powers have brought into being to preserve the safety and independence of their peoples'. The proposal was weakened by Russia's being the only power that had not, since the return of peace, reduced her own forces. In a tactful and practical reply, Castlereagh pointed out the difficulties, which remained constant until partially modified by the pressure of nuclear weapons: 'It is impossible not to perceive that the settlement of a scale of force for so many powers, under such different circumstances as to their relative means, frontiers, positions and faculties for rearming, presents a very complicated question for negotiation; that the means of preserving a system, if once created, are not without their difficulties, liable as all states are to partial necessities for an increase of force; and it is further to be considered that on this, as on many subjects of a jealous character, in attempting to do too much, difficulties are rather brought into view than made to disappear.'[12]

The remainder of the nineteenth century saw no progress in multilateral limitation of armaments. The most respectable attempt was made on the initiative of King Louis-Philippe's government, in order to liquidate the Italian crisis of 1831 in which France and Austria had come to the brink of war. In October 1831 the five great powers signed a protocol which pledged them to reduce their forces to their habitual peacetime footing.[13] It served its purpose by contributing to the détente; once signed, it could be forgotten; and the next year the Italian crisis became acute once more, and was settled only when France occupied Ancona in reply to the Austrian occupation of Bologna. Napoleon III proposed disarmament once or twice, in the desultory way in which he anticipated many future concerns of mankind. The Hague Conferences of 1899 and 1907 made no contribution to this end, for which they were nominally assembled. It was not until after the First World War that reduction of armaments became a matter of serious bargaining between the powers; and the Disarmament Conference of the League of Nations, which together with its Preparatory Commission sat between 1927 and 1934, was a monumental failure. No more effective were the negotiations on conventional disarmament that flickered fitfully for twenty years after 1945, and were eclipsed at last by the discussions of arms control for nuclear weapons.

Yet there was one disarmament agreement, the Washington Naval Treaty of 1922, which has rightly been called the most successful international agreement for limiting armaments ever concluded. Like the League of Nations, it was the product of peculiar circumstances, and they deserve examination. It was a part of the settlement after the First World War, an arrangement between the victors in that war. They were disposed to moderation, and anxious for economies in defence. Great Britain, the

12. C. K. Webster, *The Foreign Policy of Castlereagh 1815–1822*, pp. 97–8; J. Headlam-Morley, *Studies in Diplomatic History*, pp. 255–8.

13. C. Metternich, *Mémoires*, Vol. V, G. W. Smith (trans.), Richard Bentley, London, 1882, pp. 143–6; C. Vidal, *Louis Philippe, Metternich et la crise italienne de 1831–1832*, Boccard, Paris, 1931, pp. 173, 187.

power hitherto navally dominant, was financially overstrained. Moreover, it was part of the settlement in the Pacific, a subordinate theatre of the war, where political disorders were less intricate and political hatreds less intense than in Europe. The two powers that might, before the war, have been most difficult to accommodate in such a gathering were excluded from the affairs of the Pacific by defeat: Russia temporarily, and Germany for good. The treaty settled the growing antagonisms between the victors. The Anglo–Japanese Alliance had fulfilled its main purpose with the defeat in the Far East first of Russia by Japan herself in 1905, and then of Germany in the First World War. Japan was left as conqueror of Germany's former concessions in the Shantung peninsula, and the potential aggressor against a disintegrating China. Hostility to Japan helped to inspire the American navalists' demand for 'a navy second to none', which meant a naval race not only against Japan but also against Britain. The Anglo–Japanese Alliance had become incompatible with Anglo–American friendship, and Britain was pressed to end it by Australia and New Zealand, who feared Japan, and by Canada, who could not be hostile to the United States. It was in these circumstances that the United States convened the Washington Conference of 1921–2.

At the conference four treaties were negotiated. 1. The Four Power Treaty of 1921 (British Empire, United States, Japan, France) decently buried the Anglo–Japanese Alliance and substituted an agreement to confer together about external threats or disputes between the signatories. 2. By the Sino–Japanese Treaty of 1922, negotiated under Anglo–American pressure, Japan agreed to restore Shantung to China. 3. The Nine Power Treaty of 1922 (the four plus Italy, Holland, Belgium, Portugal and China) proclaimed respect for the independence and territorial integrity of China, asserted the Open Door policy, and abandoned the pre-war competition for concessions. This was a classic example of the dependence of successful disarmament upon a political settlement. 'China, in fact, was the stake for which the game of naval competition in the Pacific was being played. In order to stop the game, the stake must be removed from the table; and conversely, in order to save the stake from seizure, the game must be stopped.'[14] 4. On the same day as the Nine Power Treaty, the Five Power Naval Treaty was signed. Britain here accepted parity in capital ships with the United States. Japan accepted a limitation to 60 per cent of the other two powers (their ratio was thus 5:5:3) and France and Italy 35 per cent. Thus, while Britain conceded her old claim to naval supremacy in the world at large, which she was already finding it impossible to make effective when she contracted the alliance with Japan in 1902, she obtained a margin of security over the next two European powers undreamed of in the past two generations.

The settlement meant an immediate reduction of armaments, in the most concrete sense that some seventy capital ships were scrapped by the signatories. This was helped by the obsolescence of the battleship, and the development of naval armaments in the direction of faster and lighter vessels. But the indirect consequence of the limitation in capital ships was the Anglo–American naval race in cruisers and destroyers, which the Geneva Conference of 1927 failed to halt, and the London Conference of 1930 ended just before the Japanese attack on Manchuria began.

More important, Japan only agreed to the 5:5:3 ratio on condition that the other powers agreed not to construct new fortifications in the western Pacific. This guaranteed her against American or British naval bases nearer than Hawaii or Singapore, and gave her regional supremacy, more valuable than general parity in capital ships. Within ten years from the Washington treaties, Japan was beginning her conquest of China, and Britain and the United States lacked both the will to restrain her and the means to apply military sanctions, short of all-out war. Thus this most successful of disarmament agreements, made after the end of the First World War, directly provided part of the conditions for the outbreak of the Second World War.

Throughout international history, multilateral disarmament has been generally unobtainable. Why is this so? The reasons may be grouped under four heads.

1. The simplest reason is national egoism. Every power con-

14. A. J. Toynbee, *Survey of International Affairs 1920–1923*, O.U.P., London, 1925, p. 453.

siders in general that its security would be best served if other powers disarmed while it itself retained freedom to decide its own armaments. Moreover, within every country, even if there are strong influences in favour of economy in defence, there is a Ministry of Defence which rightly speaks for a vested interest in maintaining the customary level of forces. Hence the familiar feature of disarmament discussions, that every power sees the first need as restricting the weapons which its rivals are strong in. When Litvinov repeated the Soviet proposal for the total abolition of armaments at the Disarmament Conference in 1932, the Spanish delegate, Madariaga, asked his permission to relate a fable in reply, which became part of the stock in trade of diplomatic correspondents in the days of the League and the early United Nations. 'The animals had met to disarm. The lion, looking sideways at the eagle, said: "Wings must be abolished." The eagle, looking at the bull, declared: "Horns must be abolished." The bull, looking at the tiger, said: "Paws, and especially claws, must be abolished." The bear in his turn said: "All arms must be abolished; all that is necessary is a universal embrace."'[15] Thus the British, with the memory of the German submarine campaign in the First World War, wished afterwards to have the submarine weapon outlawed; to other powers, submarines were a natural means of counteracting the superiority of the Anglo–American surface navies. Thus the non-nuclear powers of the 1960s held that the first need was to restrict nuclear weapons. The League Disarmament Conference, having explored all the difficulties of quantitative limitation of armaments, came at last to consider what was called qualitative limitation, proposed by the British delegation in 1932: i.e. the abolition of certain forms of armament particularly lending themselves to offensive rather than defensive warfare. But it was soon found quite impossible to agree upon applying the distinction, since each power tended to consider its own weapons as defensive and those of others as offensive.

15. 25 February 1932 (*League of Nations Disarmament Conference*, Series B, Minutes of the General Commission, Vol. I, p. 11). Madariaga had the fable from Churchill. But the animal parallel goes back to Somnino (House, *Intimate Papers*) and no doubt further.

2. A deeper difficulty than national egoism is the difficulty of comparison between powers. They vary greatly in their war potential, vital interests and defence needs. Every power must subordinate disarmament to security, and cannot discuss disarmament without a fair idea of what it may have to defend in the foreseeable future. But every power has security needs that are, objectively, individual and peculiar to itself: being a unique society, with its unique values and weaknesses to safeguard, having a unique frontier or coastline to protect, a unique combination of dangers abroad (or at home) to watch. Moreover, the estimate that every power makes of these objective circumstances is necessarily subjective. Thus it is very difficult to agree on a scale for measuring their needs, and any scale is artificial.

There is an old line of reasoning, going back at least to Tom Paine, that if the powers disarmed proportionately all round their ratio of strength would remain constant, and money and resources be saved (and perhaps the risk of war lessened).[16] Repeated many times through the nineteenth century, it led at last to what was known under the League of Nations as the direct method of armaments reduction. But it was found that it implies conditions which are either rare or unobtainable.

Firstly, it would in theory require a universal disarmament agreement. A single rogue power that stays outside the system (as Bolshevik Russia in the 1920s and Communist China after 1949), a single power that is excluded (as Germany between 1919 and 1926), will preserve the expectations of insecurity for many powers and allow exceptions to the case for proportionate disarmament. Secondly, it implies that all powers have the same margin of disposable armaments. This may not be true, because some powers hold that their defence requirements are absolute, that is, determined by the irreducible nature of their interests, rather than relative to other powers. When Louis Napoleon at the beginning of his presidency proposed to Britain that they should reduce their navies 'upon somewhat the same relative scale', Palmerston replied, not without embarrassment, that it was impossible for England with her world-wide possessions to make her fleet dependent on the size of the fleet maintained by any one

16. *The Rights of Man*, J. M. Dent, London, 1935, Part II, p. 277.

power.[17] When Lord Clarendon argued with Bismarck in 1870 that a proportionate reduction of armaments by the great Continental powers would benefit them all, Bismarck replied that as far as France alone was concerned, Prussia might not feel herself endangered by such disarmament, but that if it were followed by an Austro–French alliance against Prussia, the 20,000 men which might have been dispensed with 'would then be just the balance which might turn the scale against Prussia'.[18] Conversely, the German navy which in British eyes appeared to be, as Churchill indelicately said in 1912, 'in the nature of a luxury', was declared by Bethmann-Hollweg to be 'an absolute necessity for a great power'.[19] And in the 1920s, the French took it ill when Americans said France should pay her war debts rather than keep up so large an army, seeing that the United States itself enjoyed a considerable army without any external danger to occasion it, and the proportionately smaller French army was an essential protection against the deadly danger of Germany.

In the third place, military forces in being are sometimes the only defence of a small power against the greater manpower and war potential of a great power. The small power's forces cannot prevent conquest by the great power; but they can deter pressures and threats short of that, and enable the small power to live in self-respect. In 1922 the Soviet government convened in Moscow the first Disarmament Conference after the end of the First World War, attended by Russia's smaller western neighbours, Finland, Estonia, Latvia, Lithuania and Poland. It was Litvinov's début in European diplomacy. He proposed that each of the powers should reduce its forces by 75 per cent. None of them saw fit to agree.[20]

Fourthly, multilateral proportionate disarmament would imply that the resources so saved would be devoted to peaceful purposes. This again is difficult to ensure. It was generally believed

17. F. A. Simpson, *Louis Napoleon and the Recovery of France 1848–56*, Longmans, London, 1923, pp. 40–41.

18. T. W. L. Newton, *Lord Lyons*, Vol. I, Arnold, London, 1913, p. 271.

19. W. S. Churchill, speech at Glasgow, 9 February 1912, in *The World Crisis 1911–14*, p. 77; E. L. Woodward, *Great Britain and the German Navy*, Clarendon Press, Oxford, 1935, pp. 373.

20. E. H. Carr, *The Bolshevik Revolution 1917–1923*, Vol. III, Macmillan, London, 1950, pp. 440–41.

at the First Hague Conference in 1899 that Russia had taken the initiative in summoning the conference because a reduction in her military budget would enable her to extend and reorganize her railway and canal system to her immense strategic advantage. And this brings us to the heart of the difficulty. What are to be counted as 'armaments'? Should the principle of reduction and limitation be extended to armament potential? How can communications, geographical position, population, industrial resources, be either fairly excluded from the survey of military strength or effectively included? These insoluble problems were wrestled with vainly by the Preparatory Commission of the League Disarmament Conference.

3. To limit or reduce armaments would tend to consolidate the status quo, to petrify the balance of power. It would make it more difficult for weaker powers to challenge a status quo that was unfavourable to them. Agreement to reduce armaments, therefore, is only likely in so far as the powers concerned are ready to acquiesce in the existing distribution of territory and resources, or in so far as the malcontents can be coerced. Prussia was deaf to Clarendon's arguments for disarmament in 1870, because she had not yet fulfilled her master-aim, the unity of Germany. France was unsympathetic to the purpose of the Hague Conferences, because it seemed to ask her to abandon the hope of recovering Alsace–Lorraine. And it was in a spirit resembling that of some Serbs at the time of the first Hague Conference that Dr George Habash said in 1970 that his Popular Front for the Liberation of Palestine would 'accept a third world war if that were the only possibility to annihilate Israel, Zionism and Arab reactionaries . . . Of course we want no peace. Peace means an end to all our hopes. We want a socialist Palestine'.[21]

It was to take account of the need for change, but by peaceful means, that the League Covenant in Article 19 paid lip-service

21. *The Times*, 16 September 1970, p. 6, quoting Dr Habash in an interview with *Der Stern*. 'The one thing Arabs and Israelis have in common is that they do not much care if the world explodes over them, so long as when the nuclear dust clears they come out of it all right,' *The Economist*, 11 July 1970, p. 9. For a discussion of how the new states of Africa and Asia give precedence to asserting human rights over maintaining peace, see A. A. Mazrui, *Towards a Pax Africana*, Weidenfeld, London, 1967, Chapter 8.

to the notion of reconsidering obsolete treaties and international conditions whose continuance might endanger the peace of the world. During the 1950s the Western powers found themselves revisionist on a great issue, the reunification of Germany, believed to be the key to a European settlement, and the Soviet Union on this issue had become a supporter of the status quo. The Western powers therefore made disarmament depend upon prior or concurrent political settlements. 'We have', said the British Foreign Secretary in 1955, 'to go into the question of what political problems need to be settled before disarmament can take place, for it is obvious that a great degree of international confidence is required before it will be safe and practical to begin the disarmament.'[22]

Thus it has usually been the case that proposals for reduction of armaments have come from stronger powers, because they are satisfied with the status quo. Such were the initiatives by Russia in 1816; by France in 1863, to restore her European ascendancy, shaken by the Polish Revolt of that year and the consequent estrangement between France and Russia; by Britain in 1906, as a means of lessening the challenge to her naval predominance by Germany; by the United States when she summoned the Washington Conference in 1921, to keep Japan in check; by the United States again in the Baruch Plan of 1946, which would have put her monopoly of the atomic bomb into commission; and by the United States and the Soviet Union together in proposing nuclear non-proliferation in the 1960s. We may note without false modesty that Britain and the United States have a good record in respect of disarmament proposals, and one of the reasons has been their power, insular security and self-confidence. This is why rival powers have regarded these proposals as self-interested or dishonest, as did Germany in 1906 and the Soviet Union in 1946.

There have been particular circumstances, however, in which a reduction of armaments has been proposed by the weaker power. Louis Napoleon suggested it to the British, as we have seen, when he first came to power, in order to consolidate his regime diplomatically, and he suggested it again through the British to the Prussians at the end of his reign, to offset the military weakness of

22. H. Macmillan in the House of Commons, 15 June 1955, *Parliamentary Debates*, Fifth Series, Vol. 542, col. 607.

which he was acutely conscious. Weakness prompted Tsar Nicholas II's rescript in 1898. Was it weakness that prompted the Soviet proposal for total disarmament in 1927, or a consciousness of strength: 'the interest of the most secure of continental states: a state which had, in every country, its own troops: the local Communist party'?[23] Some states in some circumstances show conflicting aspects to the outer world. Anyway, this was primarily the propaganda of political warfare. Napoleon III's disarmament proposals resembled those of the Soviet government in springing from consciousness of a relative disadvantage in armaments coupled with a restless policy of international change that could only be assisted by an armaments reduction.

4. But if the balance of power is artificial, in the sense that armaments do not correspond to war potential, the temporarily satisfied powers may declare that they cannot disarm without guarantees for security. This was the argument of the French between the World Wars. Germany had been disarmed by the Versailles Treaty, but if the Allies fulfilled their own obligation under the Covenant to disarm, without proper safeguards, the great German preponderance in population and industrial strength might once more put France in mortal danger. Thus France and her allies in Eastern Europe consistently asserted that security came before disarmament; and as guarantees for security they required an international military force and a system of international supervision to ensure that all parties carried out their engagements.

The argument can be made more general. A deeper understanding of the balance of power than the simple desire to perpetuate a favourable status quo does not reveal a more direct path to disarmament. Every balance of power is transient, and a satisfied power, if it is far-sighted, will seek for better foundations of security than the existing ratio of armaments. The French position between the wars was inherited after the Second World War by the United States and Britain, in their debate with the Soviet Union. The United Nations Charter both provided for an international military force and made it impossible through the

23. D. W. Brogan, *The Development of Modern France 1870–1939*, Hamish Hamilton, London, 1940, p. 64.

veto; nuclear weapons made international inspection still more urgent, and this too was unattainable. The relation between disarmament and security is more fundamental than the relation between disarmament and international change, and lies at the heart of international order and of the notion of arms control.[24]

24. This chapter was apparently finished in the early 1970s. Eds.

23 : Arms Control

Between the World Wars the Western powers made an attempt to create a constitutional world order, embodied in the League Covenant, an order in which economic blockade against the law-breaker was intended to have the decisive part. The attempt was half-hearted, and failed. But as the men who tried to win national liberties in 1848 gave way to the men of the next half-generation who succeeded, with modified aims and by different methods, so the League was followed by another attempt at world order a full generation later. As 'blood and iron' followed the Frankfurt Parliament, so nuclear technology succeeded collective security. By 1970 another system of world order had been sketched, harsher and less constitutional in principle, but with some possibility of development and endurance.

The atomic bomb made international supervision and control the central issue in disarmament. The powers that had con-tributed to the bomb were deeply impressed by the urgency of international control. In November 1945 Truman, Attlee and Mackenzie King of Canada jointly proposed that the United Nations should set up a commission to regulate the exchange of scientific information between all nations, control atomic energy to ensure its use only for peaceful purposes, eliminate atomic weapons and other weapons of mass destruction, and find 'effective safeguards by way of inspection and other means to protect complying states against the hazards of violation and evasions'.[1] This provided the main international agenda for the next generation. The Russians, who did not yet possess the atomic bomb, professed to regard the subject as of minor importance. They agreed to the setting up of the UN Atomic Energy Com-

1. Statement of 15 November 1945, Washington DC, quoted in *Survey of International Affairs 1939–46*, Vol. V, O.U.P., London, 1953, p. 710.

mission in January 1946, but that body, like the Military Staff Committee under Article 47 of the Charter, was still-born. Against the Western powers, the Soviet Union resolutely refused to agree to international inspection. She argued that inspection would lead to interference with her internal economic life, and would be equivalent to espionage. Indeed, it was obvious that international inspection would be incompatible with the extreme secrecy of Soviet administration, and with the exclusive authority over its citizens claimed by the Soviet state. Thus the possibility of international inspection receded as the need for it became apparent.

The first sketch of an atomic world authority was the Baruch Plan of 1946. In this the United States, instead of exploiting her monopoly of the secrets of atomic energy in order to force concessions from other governments, proposed constitutional arrangements to bring atomic energy under international control. An International Atomic Development Authority was to be given managerial control of all atomic work throughout the world that had potential military uses, and powers to control, inspect and license all other atomic activities. It was to own or lease the world's stock of the basic minerals (which at that time were mistakenly believed to be limited in quantity). It was to be free of the veto in the Security Council. When its system of international control had been established, the United States would surrender its unique stock of atomic bombs to it, and no more would be manufactured. The American refusal to surrender the atomic weapon until the new system of international control was working effectively resembled the British refusal in 1918 to abandon the power of naval blockade (in response to Wilson's principle of the freedom of the seas) before the League of Nations had been established and proved.

This was a proposal of heroic scope and vision. It was obvious that the International Atomic Development Authority would be an embryonic world government, firmly based on the control of atomic energy. But it was equally obvious that it would be a decent constitutional vesture for American predominance. A majority of the members of the IADA would presumably be friendly to the United States. Though the United States was willing to submit herself to the IADA, like all other powers, her scientists (with their British and Canadian allies) could not be deprived of their forbidden knowledge. Her position in the IADA would have resembled that of Prussia within the German Empire of 1871. The League of Nations was an attempt to build world order on the cooperation of like-minded great powers; the Baruch Plan was an attempt to build world order round one dominant power of great magnanimity. It is probable that this remains the only way in which world order will get itself built, and that the magnanimity will not recur. But the Soviet Union objected to the loss of the veto, to the international ownership of nuclear materials, and to the system of inspection. History does not afford us grounds for believing that a more civilized and less secretive power would have accepted membership of an international order put forward by a more powerful and generous rival. The Soviet Union had stronger political reasons for rejecting the Baruch Plan than the United States herself had had for rejecting the Covenant of the League of Nations.

In 1949 the Soviet Union tested its first atomic bomb. It had thus caught up with the United States, considerably earlier than had been thought possible by Western experts. In 1952 the United States tested its first hydrogen or thermonuclear bomb; in 1953 the Soviet Union followed. The premises of the Baruch Plan had been destroyed. World order, if it was to be built at all, would now have to be built round two dominant powers.

American policy continued to pursue the aim of bringing atomic energy weapons under some kind of international control. But it also acquired a new aim. It became inspired by the optimistic belief that nuclear power was on the verge of becoming cheaper than conventional power and would benefit the world's agrarian nations. This was combined with the hardheaded calculation that the United States herself might gain political goodwill and industrial advantage by exporting nuclear technology. These motives prompted the 'Atoms for Peace' programme, put forward by Eisenhower in a speech to the United Nations in 1953. He proposed an international atom pool to encourage the use of atomic energy for peaceful purposes.[2]

2. *Survey of International Affairs, 1953*, O.U.P., London, 1956, pp. 36–8; *Survey 1954*, O.U.P., London, 1957, pp. 126–8.

The consequences were of two kinds. An international atomic agency slowly came into existence. The Soviet Union at first looked upon the Eisenhower Plan as the Baruch Plan brought in by the back door, but the plan had the support of the agrarian nations. After negotiations between the leading industrial powers, the International Atomic Energy Agency was set up by the United Nations in 1956, and established at Vienna in 1957.[3] Its declared aim was 'to accelerate and enlarge the contribution of atomic energy to peace, health and prosperity throughout the world'.[4]

The United States, however, preferred to conduct most of its atoms-for-peace programmes outside the Agency. It began a series of bilateral aid arrangements with agrarian countries, training scientists in nuclear technology and setting up research reactors. The agreements contained safeguards to ensure that the nuclear materials should only be used for peaceful purposes. Nevertheless the effect of the programme was to spread all over the world the plutonium production and basic reactor technology required for military use, and thus to create, or at least to stimulate, what came to be called the problem of nuclear proliferation. Russia followed suit, making similar bilateral agreements with nine powers in the Soviet bloc together with Egypt, Ghana, Iraq, Yugoslavia and Indonesia.[5]

A parallel development brought the European Atomic Energy Community into being. The six European powers who were negotiating the terms of the Common Market were anxious to encourage the production of nuclear energy, as other energy supplies dwindled, and France wanted to bring Germany's future nuclear industry under international control. Euratom was accordingly set up by a treaty signed in Rome on the same day as the

3. *Survey 1955–6*, O.U.P., London, 1960, p. 217n. The leading industrial powers for this occasion, apart from the four great powers, were Australia, Belgium, Brazil, Canada, Czechoslovakia, India, Portugal and South Africa.

4. Statute of the IAEA, Article II, in *Department of State Bulletin*, Vol. 36, 15 April 1957, pp. 618–25.

5. L. Beaton, *Must the Bomb Spread?*, Penguin Books, Harmondsworth, 1966, pp. 88–9; A. Kramish, *The Peaceful Atom in Foreign Policy*, Harper Row, New York, 1963, p. 84.

treaty establishing the European Economic Community, 25 March 1957.[6]

The International Atomic Energy Agency was originally intended to have the custody of a growing pool of fissionable materials. They were to be transferred to it by its member states, with the secondary purpose of reducing the national military stockpiles. But the aim of an international pool was soon lost and replaced by that of a clearing-house, through which bilateral agreements would be channelled: 'not a bank, but a broker'. This aim too was lost, as the United States pursued its bilateral agreements independently of the Agency. There was however a further aim: to create a system of safeguards ensuring that the assistance granted by the Agency to its member states should be used only for peaceful purposes. Though the Agency had little assistance to grant, the safeguards system began to work. The United States played the principal part in designing it, and the safeguards closely resembled the safeguards in her bilateral treaties for nuclear cooperation. In 1964 President Johnson, as a gesture of internationalism, placed four US reactors for civilian use under the IAEA safeguards. In 1967 he declared his readiness to open to international inspection all US nuclear plants except those with a direct bearing on national defence, and Britain followed suit. But the Soviet Union remained unmoved.

All this was brought about only after much controversy. The nuclear have-not powers at first welcomed the Eisenhower Plan, expecting great benefits from access to nuclear materials. When their hopes receded, there developed the usual conflict of interests between recipient and donor nations. India led the opposition to the safeguards system; it was said to perpetuate the technological gap, and to be a form of industrial espionage. The Soviet Union's policy towards the IAEA reproduced her policy in the early days of the United Nations. She attacked the Director General, Dr Eklund, in the same terms as she attacked his fellow-countryman Hammarskjöld. But in 1963, when her interests were recognized to converge with those of the United States, she began to see the advantages of the system of controls, and became a supporter of the Agency. It was thus preserved, in

6. *Survey 1956–58*, O.U.P., London, 1962, pp. 228–37.

spite of much scepticism, to play a part in the non-proliferation treaty of 1968.

A partial substitute for international control was provided by technical development of military intelligence. Spies began to perform the main functions of international inspectors, in rival corps. The United States tried to offset its disadvantage as a free society, whose governmental processes were largely open to hostile scrutiny, by reconnaissance vehicles with photographic equipment which overflew the Soviet Union and its satellites. It was suggested half-seriously that since the object of all espionage now was to stabilize the deterrent by assuring oneself both of the peaceful intentions of one's opponent and of his capacity to retaliate crushingly against any attack from oneself, it would be sound policy to give one another's spies full facilities for their work.

At the Geneva Conference of 1955 Eisenhower tried to give effect to this by his Open Skies proposal. He suggested that the two dominant powers should 'give to each other a complete blueprint of our military establishments, from beginning to end, from one end of our countries to the other'; and to 'provide within our countries facilities for aerial photography to the other country – we to provide you with the facilities within our country, ample facilities for aerial reconnaissance, where you can make all the pictures you choose and take them to your own country to study, you to provide exactly the same facilities for us and we to make these examinations, and by this step to convince the world that we are providing as between ourselves against the possibility of great surprise attack, thus lessening danger and relaxing tension'.[7] This good-hearted proposal overlooked the fact that good intelligence facilitates attack as well as defence. 'Contrary to the idea of the Open Skies proposal,' as Professor Bull has pointed out, 'the improvement of facilities for intelligence does not necessarily lead to a feeling of greater security; the Russians are made to feel insecure by it.'[8]

When an American U-2 plane was shot down over Russian territory in May 1960, Khrushchev had the opportunity to ex-

7. *Documents on International Affairs 1955*, O.U.P., London, 1958, p. 40.
8. H. Bull, *The Control of the Arms Race*, Weidenfeld, London, 1961, p. 170.

ploit the incident for propaganda, and to wreck the Summit Conference that was about to meet at Paris. The American Secretary of State, Christian Herter, concealed his government's embarrassment in the language of duty: 'The government of the United States would be derelict to its responsibility not only to the American people but to free peoples everywhere if it did not, in the absence of Soviet cooperation, take such measures as are possible unilaterally to lessen and to overcome this danger of surprise attack. In fact the United States has not and does not shirk this responsibility.'[9] Another U-2 plane gave the United States the information about Soviet missiles in Cuba which enabled Kennedy to demand their withdrawal in October 1962. After that, reconnaissance flights in manned aircraft were gradually replaced by the expanding network of reconnaissance satellites, but as late as 1969 a United States navy electronic intelligence plane with a crew of thirty-one was shot down over North Korea.

The Baruch Plan failed to prevent the spread of nuclear weapons among the great powers. Britain exploded her first atomic bomb in 1952 and her first thermonuclear bomb in 1957, France hers respectively in 1960 and 1968, China hers in 1964 and 1967. But having confirmed their independence and dignity and possibly added to their security by acquiring these weapons, the majority of the great powers began slowly to make agreements to limit their use. These agreements slowly emerged as hard and substantial from the wash and surf of the subsiding discussions on conventional disarmament. Let us review them and examine their tendency.

In 1959 the three nuclear great powers and France, together with eight powers with interests in the Antarctic continent (Argentina, Australia, Belgium, Chile, Japan, New Zealand, Norway and South Africa), agreed that Antarctica should be demilitarized and particularly that nuclear explosions there should be prohibited.[10]

In 1963 the United States, the Soviet Union and Great Britain agreed by the Partial Test-Ban Treaty to prohibit nuclear ex-

9. Statement of 9 May 1960 in *Documents on International Affairs 1960*, O.U.P., London, 1964, p. 20.

10. The Antarctic Treaty, *Command Paper 1535*, H.M.S.O., London, 1961.

plosions in the atmosphere, outer space and under water. Nuclear tests underground were excluded, because their detection would require international inspection which the Soviet Union refused to accept.[11]

In 1967 eighty-nine states signed a treaty to demilitarize outer space, including the moon and other celestial bodies. The treaty declared that outer space (including celestial bodies) was free to exploration and scientific investigation by all states, and that it was not subject to annexation or legal occupation. It prohibited the stationing in outer space of nuclear or other weapons, the conduct of military manoeuvres and the establishment of bases. It sought in various ways to encourage international cooperation in exploring and using outer space. The treaty had two lacunae. It did not define outer space. 'There is not a sharp division between the atmosphere and outer space: the outer boundaries of the former are given as anything from 500 to 60,000 miles from the surface of the earth.'[12] And in Article iv it explicitly did not prohibit the use of military personnel for scientific research, and by omission did not prohibit manned military space stations or orbiting laboratories.[13]

Again in 1967, twenty-one states of Latin America (excluding Cuba, but supported by the United States, Great Britain and the Netherlands) signed the Treaty of Tlatelolco, to prohibit nuclear weapons in Latin America. This was the first step, within a single region, towards the non-proliferation of nuclear weapons. The treaty set up an Agency for the Prohibition of Nuclear Weapons in Latin America, to be part of a control system, along with the IAEA, with certain rights of inspection to ensure that the treaty was carried out.[14]

11. Treaty Banning Nuclear Weapon Tests in the Atmosphere, in Outer Space and under Water, *Command Paper 2245*, H.M.S.O., London, 1964.

12. Bull, *The Control of the Arms Race*, p. 175.

13. Treaty on Principles Governing the Activities of States in the Exploration and Use of Outer Space, including the Moon and Other Celestial Bodies, *Command Paper 3519*, H.M.S.O., London, 1968. See L. E. Schwartz, 'Manned Orbiting Laboratory – For War or Peace?' in *International Affairs*, Vol. 43, No. I, January 1967, p. 51.

14. Treaty for the Prohibition of Nuclear Weapons in Latin America, *Command Paper 3615*, H.M.S.O., London, 1968.

In 1968 the United States and the Soviet Union presented to the Eighteen Nations Disarmament Conference at Geneva a draft treaty for securing the general non-proliferation of nuclear weapons. The two dominant powers and Britain sponsored the treaty; France and China took no part in the negotiations. The treaty came into force in 1970, when it had been ratified by the three nuclear great powers and the requisite number of forty other signatories. The treaty divided states into two classes, 'nuclear-weapon' and 'non-nuclear-weapon'. Each nuclear-weapon power signing the treaty undertook not to transfer nuclear weapons nor devices to any recipient; each non-nuclear-weapon power undertook not to receive them from any donor, and moreover not to manufacture or acquire nuclear weapons. But the central provision of the treaty was that each non-nuclear-weapon power undertook to accept the safeguards system of the International Atomic Energy Agency. The nuclear-weapon powers accepted no such obligation. Amendment of the treaty was subject to the veto of any of the nuclear-weapon powers.[15]

The Non-Proliferation Treaty marked the highest point of American–Soviet common interest yet attained. It was moreover an attempt to give legal and institutional effect to the difference between nuclear haves and have-nots. It provided the framework of a technological condominium over international society, by fixing the hierarchy of power. Its main organ of control would be the IAEA, 'the first international organization which has the right to perform inspections in its member states, and is actually doing so'.[16] Like the fight in the IAEA over the safeguards system, the drafting of the treaty 'served to show just how powerful the existing nuclear powers can be if they are sufficiently determined on an objective'.[17]

But this was an unsubstantial condominium: a scenario, not a development. It was not so important that France and China had

15. Treaty on the Non-Proliferation of Nuclear Weapons, as adopted by the United Nations General Assembly Resolution No. 2373 (XXII) on 12 June 1968, *Command Paper 3683*, H.M.S.O., London, 1968.

16. J. A. Hall, 'Nuclear Safeguards', in *Survival*, Vol. 6, No. 6, International Institute for Strategic Studies, London, 1964, p. 250.

17. Beaton, *Must the Bomb Spread?*, p. 100.

no part in the preparing of the treaty. France combined virtue with independence by refusing to sign the treaty, but declaring that she would act as if she had signed it. China was in diplomatic isolation, but was already showing that she too, like the other nuclear powers, held it unnecessary for an outer circle of powers to acquire what had been essential for her own security. The implausibility of the treaty lay not in the absence from it of two nuclear powers who had a common interest with the treaty's designers, but in the conflict of interest between nuclear and non-nuclear powers, and the treaty's lack of effective sanctions.

The treaty sought to create diplomatic and legal inhibitions against the spread of nuclear weapons. It thus reinforced the known reluctance of the leading non-nuclear powers to commit themselves to the vast expense of acquiring a modern arsenal. But most of them were reluctant to accept a permanent military disability without countervailing additions to their security which the nuclear powers were incapable of providing. The 'security assurances' made by the United States, the Soviet Union and Britain in the Security Council in June 1968 were worthless. The American acquiescence in the Russian invasion of Czechoslovakia in August 1968 showed that détente between the two dominant powers was as likely to endanger as to safeguard the interests of middle powers, since the dominant powers put their own common interest in recognizing each other's sphere of influence above all else.

Some middle powers were threatened by their neighbours and not covered by a military alliance: such were India and Israel. They were unlikely to sign the non-proliferation treaty without alternative provision for their security from the dominant powers. Some middle powers were members of a military alliance, like West Germany, and for them the possession of nuclear weapons would have the advantage that it had for France and Britain: of being able to take an initiative in self-defence which would compel the dominant power in the alliance to come to its assistance. Some middle powers were not under threat from abroad and could subordinate their foreign policy to economic development at home. Brazil was the spokesman of those who wished to retain the right to manufacture nuclear explosives for peaceful application. For all these the non-proliferation treaty might bring higher sacrifices than benefits. Above all it discriminated between nuclear powers who reserved the right to continue the nuclear arms race and remained outside any system of international inspection, and the have-nots who were to be put in a lasting condition of technological inferiority and tutelage.

But at the same time the controls of the treaty were weak and sanctions almost non-existent. The existing IAEA system of inspection was agreed to be inadequate; bilateral controls were resented by the inferior partner and distrusted by third parties; controls over its members by Euratom did not command confidence outside Euratom. Therefore a new and more elaborate system of inspection based on the IAEA would have to be built up. When West Germany signed the treaty in November 1969 she made the proviso that she would ratify only if tolerable international controls were devised based on agreement between the IAEA and Euratom. When Japan signed the treaty in February 1970 she made the proviso that if some European signatories were allowed to escape IAEA inspection, she must have the same privilege. Nor were there effective sanctions against violation of the treaty, such as seizure of plutonium supplied under treaty safeguards. The treaty allowed for withdrawal at three months' notice (Article x); the technical barriers between civil and military nuclear power were steadily growing less; and the time that need elapse between denouncing the controls imposed by the treaty and manufacturing nuclear weapons was diminishing too. If the two dominant powers had been wholly agreed, they undoubtedly had the ability to coerce the remainder of the international community; but they lacked the mutual confidence as well as the diplomatic conditions for imposing their joint will. The embryonic world government lurking within the Non-Proliferation Treaty had the same weaknesses as the United Nations itself. Like disarmament, arms control would continue to be discussed and desiderated, but not attained, because it could only follow, not precede, the political unification of the world.[18]

18. This chapter was apparently finished in the early 1970s. Eds.

24 : Beyond Power Politics

In the study of international politics we are dogged by the insistent problem, whether the relations between powers are in fact more than 'power politics' in the popular sense of the term, and whether they can become more. From one point of view, the central question is how far powers can be said to have interests in common. We have seen that the international anarchy is restrained and to some extent systematized in practice by two opposing kinds of common interest, pulling alternately to and fro. The first is the common interest of all powers in their freedom, of which they are faintly conscious in peace, and assert at the eleventh hour in war by an armed coalition against a common danger. The second is the kind of common interest represented by successive dominant powers. For their predominance has generally safeguarded real values, and offered real benefits, for other nations, and sometimes they have wielded an international ideology as their most potent weapon – as the Habsburg powers were the protagonists of the Counter-Reformation, as Napoleonic France was the carrier of the French Revolution throughout feudal Europe, as Britain in the nineteenth century was the champion of liberalism. In the same way Russia in the twentieth century has represented the ideal of socialism. A dominant power that is thus able to give its policies the added momentum of an international ideal becomes a tremendous force, whose limits are reached only if it provokes the counter-interest of general freedom. Nor is it impossible that powers may henceforward increasingly regard their deepest common interest as being the prevention of war and liberation from anarchy, and that this will only prove obtainable by acquiescence in a common government provided by the strongest power.

But the idea of common interest can never have much vitality

T–PP–K

289

if it is separated from the idea of common obligation, and here we touch a more fundamental issue. There has always existed a theory of international relations which asserts the primacy of common conceptions of justice, right and law. There was an ancient tradition, dating back through the jurists and theologians of the Middle Ages to the jurists and philosophers of antiquity, of Natural Law or the Law of Nature. It taught that man is a rational and social animal, that there is a moral order in the universe to which his rational nature bids him always and everywhere to conform, that the true interests of human societies therefore do not conflict, and that they are bound together by obligations of law and morality. This tradition was the source of international law, which was developed in the seventeenth century to restrain the anarchy into which the states of Europe had fallen, and which used to appeal to 'the common standard of right prevailing throughout the Christian world'. But it was eclipsed by the new revolutionary creed of progress at the end of the eighteenth century, just at the time when the European powers, as a consequence of the Industrial Revolution, were beginning to establish a material unification of the world.

The expansion of Europe itself weakened the tradition of Natural Law, by admitting states that had not been schooled in it to the international community. Of the two new great powers of the eighteenth century, Prussia was at the extreme limit of Western Christendom, and had been in many ways scarcely touched by its characteristic culture; and Russia is the heir and champion of the very different traditions of Byzantine Christendom. In the nineteenth century international intercourse was extended far beyond the Christian world, at the same time that Christian political theory was at a greater discount inside the Christian world than it had ever been before. In 1856, at the conclusion of the Crimean War, Turkey was admitted for the first time to the community of nations; but it was a passive and not an active member; and it is from the emergence of Japan as a great power – the first great power that was wholly non-European and non-Christian in its traditions – that we may date the effective transformation of the international community from one based on a common ethos to one whose principle is inclusiveness. Attempts have been made since the French Revolution to find an alternative common ethos in political creed instead of moral tradition. The Vienna Settlement was based on the principle of legitimacy; the Versailles Settlement was based on the principle of self-determination; the Yalta Declaration of 1945 enshrined the principle of 'democracy'. But in each case these formulae have reflected only a transient moment on the surface of affairs, concealing differences rather than expressing 'a common standard of right', and they have soon dissolved and been superseded. It may indeed be asked whether an effective common ethos is likely to grow up again without an effective common government.

Though the tradition of an international community with a common standard of obligation and justice has faded, however, it has not altogether disappeared. It is the main influence that has modified, and can yet modify, the operations of power politics, and it still gleams faintly in the preamble to the Charter of the United Nations. In countries whose culture and politics are favourable to its survival, it can create a 'moral climate' of opinion that will affect politicians who are quite ignorant of any traditional political theories. The extent to which it may do so in practice is highly controversial, and every historical example that may be brought forward in this light will lead to the kind of argument in which there can be no clear-cut and final conclusion, because it depends not on the establishment of facts but on the exercise of moral insight and political judgement.

It is sufficient to instance two statesmen whose beliefs were saturated with conceptions of Natural Law, and whose politics were grounded on its traditions, Gladstone in nineteenth-century England, and Franklin Roosevelt in twentieth-century America; nor is it any accident that each of these men in his generation had a moral ascendancy and a power over the public opinion of the world, evoking a trust and loyalty far beyond his own country, which was unapproached by any other contemporary political figure. (The devotion inspired abroad in the intervening generation by the supreme revolutionary statesman, Lenin, was perhaps more passionate in its quality, but it was limited and sectional by comparison in its range.) This is not to say that Gladstone and Roosevelt were not assiduous, subtle and far-sighted power-politicians. But their politics had overtones that are absent from the politics of a Theodore Roosevelt or a Cecil Rhodes, a Lloyd George or a Clemenceau, a Bismarck or a Cavour. When we consider the foreign policies of the latter we think in terms of patriotism, of grandeur of conception, of brilliance, of virtuosity, above all of success or failure. Most people would agree that Gladstone's Irish policy or Roosevelt's Latin-American policy (like, in another way, Lincoln's Civil War policy) were different in quality from these, the fruit of a richer conception of politics, which made power an instrument and not an end, and subordinated national interest to public justice.

Nevertheless it is always well to be sceptical of statesmen and, as Lord Acton insisted, to 'suspect power more than vice'. It is particularly necessary to guard against the notion that morality in politics is a flower that blooms especially or exclusively in Anglo–Saxon gardens. The first thing to remember about the policies of Gladstone and Franklin Roosevelt is that Gladstone's Britain and Roosevelt's America were dominant powers. This will remind us of the great truth that morality in international politics is not simply a matter of civilized tradition, but is equally the result of security. If British policy in the nineteenth century showed in general perhaps a greater degree of enlightened self-interest than that of any other great power in modern history, it was because Britain then enjoyed perfect security. 'We could afford the luxury of gentleness,' as Harold Nicolson has said, 'because we were completely unafraid.'[1]

Once security is destroyed, all the higher objects of politics are swallowed up in the struggle for self-preservation, a tendency seen in every war. 'A great and civilized power like England', said a distinguished writer before the war, 'should strive for a margin of security big enough to make a certain bias in favour of an ideal policy possible, a bias that may never show itself in any specific political action but will inform the manner or spirit of her international conduct.'[2] Yet since it ceased to be a dominant power, Britain's margin of security has shrunk, and the possibility of an *independent* ideal policy has correspondingly dwindled. This

1. *The Meaning of Prestige*, p. 35.
2. F. A. Voigt, *Unto Caesar*, Constable, London, 1938, pp. 272–3.

is the vicious circle of power politics: morality is the fruit of security, but lasting security as between many powers depends on their observing a certain common standard of morality. The League of Nations in theory transformed it into a virtuous circle, by making collective security a moral obligation. But the solution presupposed a degree of enlightened self-interest among the great powers that did not exist.

The modern substitute for the Law of Nature might be called the Law of Common Material Interest. Contemporary writers on international politics are increasingly driven to place their hopes for future peace on the universal demand for social justice and a rising standard of living, which implies the growth of new economic and social relationships between peoples, and cooperation between powers 'for the planned development of the economies of geographical areas and groups of nations.'[3] The reality of this common interest is profound, but it does not touch the problem of power. The world community is still an anarchy, lacking a common superior, and international politics are still power politics. Every power has an interest greater than welfare, an interest on which it believes that welfare depends and to which welfare must in the last resort be sacrificed – the maintenance of power itself.

It is true that there was equally anarchy in the period when men talked in terms of the Law of Nature, so that its influence upon politics was tenuous and remote. Yet in the long run the idea of a common moral obligation is probably a more fruitful social doctrine than the idea of a common material interest. As the French philosopher Julien Benda has said, mankind has always betrayed its obligations, but so long as it continues to acknowledge and believe in them, the crack is kept open through which civilization can creep. Powers will continue to seek security without reference to justice, and to pursue their vital interests irrespective of common interests, but in the fraction that they may be deflected lies the difference between the jungle and the traditions of Europe. The outstanding contrast between the mood of 1945 and the mood of 1918, which is reflected in the contrast between the United Nations Charter and the League Covenant, is the absence

3. E. H. Carr, *Nationalism and After*, Macmillan, London, 1945, p. 70.

of optimism, the greater realism. Realism can be a very good thing: it all depends whether it means the abandonment of high ideals or of foolish expectations.[4]

4. This is the final chapter of the original *Power Politics*. Contents lists found with the draft of the revised *Power Politics* show that the author intended to conclude the book with a chapter entitled 'Beyond Power Politics', but no draft of it exists. Eds.

Appendix I:
The Grading of Powers

There is broad agreement in diplomatic writing about the nature of a great power. It is a power with general as distinct from local interests; and a power, as Treitschke said, whose destruction would require a coalition of other powers. (The latter criterion is derived from Ranke's celebrated sentence, 'If one could establish as a definition of a great power that it must be able to maintain itself against all others, even when they are united, then Frederick had raised Prussia to that position.')[1] Both criteria have fuzzy edges, but together they provide a workable description.

Are all powers which are not great powers to be classed as small powers? Or is there an intermediate grade of middle powers? The term middle power has been in common use since 1945, and there is a growing literature about it. Can this putative class be described with as much clarity as the class of great powers?

It is generally said that great powers were first recognized at the Vienna Peace Settlement in 1815. But the grading of powers can be traced back to the beginnings of the states-system. It begins in the simple recognition that states are of different kinds and magnitudes. It develops into the doctrine that, according to their size, they have different roles in international society.

When Aquinas is trying to formulate the very concept of the state, he encounters the difficulty that states are heterogeneous. He begins with the Aristotelian description of the *polis* as the perfect community. But this does not fit the Europe of Saint Louis. So he had three classes of political unit: city, province and kingdom. There is a confusing passage in the first chapter of the *De regimine principum*:

1. Leopold von Ranke, *Die Grossen Mächte*, English translation in T. H. von Laue, *Leopold Ranke, the Formative Years*, Princeton University Press, 1950.

In a city [*civitas*], he says, there is a perfect community, providing all that is necessary for the fullness of life; and in a province [*provincia*] we have an even better example, because in this case there is added the mutual assistance of allies against hostile attack. Whoever, then, rules a perfect community, be it a city or a province, is rightly [*autonomastice*] called a king.[2]

What is a *provincia* here? He tries to explain it in 'international' terms, as a member of a kind of league, but I do not believe that he anywhere develops this thought. Two ideas seem to link in his *provincia*, one of the past and one of the future. The fading idea is the Roman imperial political unit, in which sense the word *provincia* was used in early medieval writing, loosely applied, for example, both to Italy and to its internal regions, Calabria, Lombardia, etc. The growing idea is that of the overgrown city-state, like Venice and Florence–Tuscany, or the *pays*, like Anjou or Normandy. This was the true 'state' of the early Middle Ages. In Germany and Italy it developed into the actual modern state of the centuries before unification. In France, Spain and England it became absorbed in the larger national state, but long maintained its separatist claim on men's loyalties against the centralizing monarchies.

There are three kinds of constitution, Aristotle taught, according to whether the sovereign is either One, or Few, or Many. Again, there are three elements or powers within the state, deliberative, executive and judicial.[3] Triplicity was woven into the political tradition that Aquinas adapted to provide the foundations of the modern state. But it was not until the next century that Bartolus fitted the Aristotelian triad of constitutions into a grading of states. He made a *triplicem divisionem civitatum seu populorum*. First, *magna in primo grado magnitudinis*, come city-states, which ought to be ruled not by kings but by the whole people. Next, *major, et sic in secundo gradu magnitudinis*, are states too large by their extent of territory for

2. A. P. d'Entrèves (ed.), *Selected Political Writings*, Blackwell, Oxford, 1948, p. 9.

3. E. Barker (trans.), *Politics*, Clarendon Press, Oxford, 1960, 1279 (pp. 129–30) and 1297–8 (pp. 220–27).

direct democracy, but best governed by aristocracies. He gives Venice and Florence as examples. Last, *maxima, et sic in tertio gradu magnitudinis*, is a people or nation (*gens vel populus*) whose dominion is so wide that its unity and good government require monarchy. He says that the obvious example would be a state that ruled over many other states and provinces, like the Roman Empire.[4]

A constitutional grading of powers emerged in the Holy Roman Empire, that microcosm of international society. From the end of the fifteenth century the Reichstag met in three estates. They were not, as in the French States-General, clergy, nobility, and commons or *tiers-état*. They were the Electors (who were so to say the great powers of the Empire), the princes and prelates, and the free cities. It was an arrangement, not of social class within a nascent national state, but of diplomatic and voting power within a disintegrating international institution. It might be of interest to examine the treatment of this grading of the powers of the Empire in the dreary German constitutional writings of the seventeenth and eighteenth centuries. The most famous of all such treatises, the *Dissertatio de ratione status in imperio nostro Romano–Germanico* by B. P. Chemnitz (1640), is fired by a passionate hatred of the Habsburgs. Its argument that the Empire is properly an aristocratic, not a monarchic body, its sovereignty residing not in the Emperor but in the estates as a whole, is occasionally lifted above constitutional pedantry by this political motive into an atmosphere of realism, where it can discuss the relationship of the three estates of the Reichstag in terms of the balance of power. '*Ipsorum vero ordinum non est aequelis in imperio potestas.*'[5] But it does not pursue the idea far.

In the period of the Renaissance there is a good deal of political writing about what is the best form of the state, rehearsing the Aristotelian classification without taking it further. Bodin, who

4. The relevant extracts are quoted in R. W. and A. J. Carlyle, *A History of Mediaeval Political Theory in the West*, Vol. VI, Blackwoods, London, 1936, p. 78, n. 2.

5. Part I, Chapter IX, section iii, and Chapter XVII, 1647 edn, pp. 71–2, 307–8.

marvelled that after so many centuries' discussion nobody had determined what the best state was, himself is an example.[6] But I have not found anybody before Botero who develops the international grading of powers, and gives substance to the class of middle power. Giovanni Botero (1544–1617) was a Piedmontese teacher of philosophy and rhetoric, Jesuit-trained, who became secretary to St Charles Borromeo, Archbishop of Milan and later tutor to the Duke of Savoy's sons. He purports to refute Machiavelli, but comes near adapting him to Counter-Reformation purposes.

In the second paragraph of his *Ragion di stato* (1589) Botero classifies states as follows. Some dominions (*dominii*) are powerful and some are not, he says; some are natural, based on the will of the subjects or legitimate succession, some are acquired, by purchase, by force, or by treaty. 'Furthermore, some dominions are small (*piccioli*), others are large (*grandi*), others of a middle size (*mezani*), not absolutely but comparatively, and with respect to their neighbours. Thus a small dominion is one that cannot stand by itself, but needs the protection and support of others; such are the republics of Ragusa and Lucca. A middle-sized (*mediocro*) dominion has sufficient strength and authority to stand on its own without the need of help from others; such is the signory of Venice and the kingdom of Bohemia, the duchy of Milan and the county of Flanders. Those dominions are large which have a distinct superiority over their neighbours, such as the empire (*imperio*) of the Turk and of the Catholic King.'[7]

A little later he asks, 'Quali Imperii siano pià durabili, i grandi, i piccioli, ò i mezani.' It is clear that in this chapter he is not speaking of empires in any different sense from states or dominions. He uses the words *stato*, *imperio*, *dominio*, and *potenza* interchangeably. 'Gli stati grandi mettono in gelosia, et in

6. B. Reynolds (trans.), *Method for the Easy Comprehension of History*, Columbia University Press, New York, 1945, Chapter VI; M. J. Tooley (trans.), *Six Books of the Commonwealth*, Blackwell, Oxford (no date), Book VI, Chapter IV.

7. D. P. Waley (trans.) *The Reason of State*, Routledge & Kegan Paul, London, 1956, Book I, section 2, pp. 3–4.

sospetto i vicini,' he says. But 'middle-sized states (*i mediocri*) are the most lasting, since they are exposed neither to violence by their weakness nor to envy by their greatness, and their wealth and power being moderate, passions are less violent, ambition finds less support and licence less provocation than in large states. Fear of their neighbours restrains them, and even if feelings are roused to anger they are more easily quieted and tranquillity restored ... Thus some middle-sized powers (*alcune potenze mediocre*) have lasted far longer than the greatest (*grandissime*), as we see in the case of Sparta, Carthage and above all Venice, for there has never been an empire (*dominio*) in which mediocrity of power went with such stability and strength. Yet although this mediocrity is more conducive to the preservation of an empire than excessive power, middle-sized states (*gli stati mediocri*) do not last long if their leaders are not content but wish to expand and become great, and, exceeding the bounds of mediocrity, leave behind also those of security ... So long as the ruler recognizes the limits of mediocrity and is content to remain within them his rule (*il suo imperio*) will be lasting.'[8]

It will be seen from these passages that Botero gives more attention to middle powers than to the others. He uses two words for them, *mezano* and *mediocro*. He sees them as embodying the moral virtues of the Aristotelian mean. The examples he gives are odd and out of date: neither Bohemia, Milan nor the county of Flanders had in 1589 any longer enough strength and authority to stand on its own without help from others. Probably he had in mind the Duchy of Savoy of which he was a subject, to which there is only one discreet reference in the book.[9] Yet he has been thinking in a Machiavellian way about international politics, about the effect of the size of states on their power or security, and here he is so far as I know a true innovator.

A small power 'cannot stand by itself, but needs the protection and support of others'. A middle power 'has sufficient strength and authority to stand on its own without the need of help from others'. This seems a useful distinction. It is when we come to his great powers that we see the difficulties. Great powers are those

8. ibid., Book I, section 6, pp. 8–9.
9. ibid., Book IX, section 2, p. 174.

'which have a distinct superiority over their neighbours'. This is too vague. But the examples he gives are illuminating: the empires of the Turk and the Catholic King. They are the two powers of his world which today we should be inclined to call super-powers or dominant powers. Their character was a claim of some kind to universal monarchy – as Campanella said a little later, 'aspirano alla somma della cose humane'. Neither could make good its claim (if for no other, more internal reason of resources and organization) because of the restraints imposed by the existence of the other, and international politics were polarized round their rivalry. A few years later, Henry IV restored France to this class. Campanella, writing about 1600, brackets the Ottoman House and the House of Austria as the two universal claimants, but already gives more attention to the Hispano–French rivalry. Sir Thomas Overbury in 1609 says that France is 'the greatest united force in Christendom'. He sees Western Europe as balanced between France, Spain and England, and drops the Turk over the eastern horizon, entertained in 'easy war' by Germany 'while the Persian withholds him in a greater'. The *Discours des princes et estats de la Chrétienté* of 1623 settles the new bipolar description of international politics, between France and Spain, which will serve for a century.

At the turn of the sixteenth and seventeenth centuries the Rankean class of great powers, whose definition came to be that with which this paper began, had not yet fully appeared. Overbury discerned them, as the powers between whom Christendom was balanced. He enumerated them without describing their quality further: France, Spain and England, Russia, Poland, Sweden and Denmark. Botero does not in this way see the developments working within his own historical situation. But his attempted definitions show for the first time the difficulty of distinguishing between middle, great and dominant powers. His prize example of a middle power, in the second passage quoted above, is Venice. But Venice, by all our later notions, was undoubtedly a great power both in respect to the Italian system and to the wider Mediterranean–European system. And his definition of a middle power resembles later definitions of a great power. 'After the great upheaval of 1870', says Taylor, 'neither France nor Austria was a truly great power, capable of standing on its own feet.'[10] 'A great power', says Duroselle, 'is one which is capable of preserving its own independence against any other single power.'[11] How are we to measure the several degrees of power and independence that we are concerned with?

Leibniz gave the first effective definition of international sovereignty, as Bodin had done of internal sovereignty. Leibniz distinguished between sovereign states (*suprematus*), which might be 'free cities, or lords of tiny territories which even a wealthy merchant might easily buy for himself'; and powers (*potentatus*), 'those larger powers which can wage war, sustain it, survive somehow by their own power, make treaties, take part with authority in the affairs of other peoples . . .'[12] This is a simple distinction between great powers and small. He did not take his political analysis further. He gave rise to the legal theorists of the eighteenth century, like J. J. Moser and G. F. von Martens, who classified states according to the degrees of sovereignty they enjoyed.

It seems that the line of thought that Botero had begun is not taken up again until the middle of the eighteenth century, by the Abbé de Mably. Mably distinguishes between powers of the first, second and third orders. But it is during the Napoleonic reorganization of Germany between 1797 and 1803, and the subsequent reorganization of Europe in 1814–15, that the class of middle powers in international society first became much discussed.[13]

10. A. J. P. Taylor, *The Habsburg Monarchy*, Hamish Hamilton, London, 1948, p. 220. He qualifies the idea in *The Struggle for Mastery in Europe*, p. xxiv.

11. S. D. Kertesz and M. A. Fitzsimmons (ed.), *Diplomacy in a Changing World*, University of Notre Dame Press, 1959, p. 204.

12. 'Caesarinus Fürstenerius', in P. Riley (ed.), *The Political Writings of Leibniz*, C.U.P., Cambridge, 1972, Chapter X, p. 116.

13. This unfinished draft, which was found together with the draft chapter on 'Minor Powers', was apparently written in 1972. Eds.

Appendix II:
International Doctrines

It is worth remembering that international society appears as an organic unity, not only when riven by an internal schism, but also when threatened from without, and that this situation too introduces doctrinal passions into power politics. It was not until the twentieth century that Western international society came to embrace the whole world. Before then it was in relationship with an outer world of alien societies which it had not yet absorbed. These alien societies had different principles of existence from Europe, and there was possibility of conflict. The closest, longest and most equal of these relationships was that between Europe and the Ottoman Empire. When in 1453 the Ottoman Turks captured Constantinople and finally took over the inheritance of the Byzantine Empire, Western Christendom for a moment became acutely conscious of its unity. The politics of the defence of Europe against the Turks were religious politics. The Ottoman Sultans on their side believed it was their mission to conquer the world for Islam. The rulers of the West regarded the Turks with fear and disgust as a barbarian intruder, and revived the idea of a crusade to deliver the Balkans and the Near East from the infidel. Until the early seventeenth century the ultimate aim of conferences and peace treaties was said to be cooperation against the Turk as today it is said to be cooperation to improve the world's economic condition.

In this relationship between Europe and the Ottoman Empire religious motives overrode political ones and political grievances found ideological expression. Whole populations, like the Bogomils of Bosnia, 'turned Turk' rather than be rescued by Catholics; in order to escape papal oppression the Adriatic inhabitants of the Papal States threatened to do the same; in 1521, when the Hungarian defenders of Belgrade had resolved to blow up the citadel, their plan was betrayed to the Turks by the Orthodox clergy; and as late as the beginning of the seventeenth century the Spanish government deported the Moriscoes, who were descendants of the Moors, in order to rid itself of a Turkish fifth column. The Russians, on the other hand, who were the only surviving independent representatives of the Orthodox East, regarded the Ottoman Empire in Europe as a Christian *terra irredenta*. The same view gained ground among the Western powers, especially after the middle of the eighteenth century, when Turkey was in decline and had become known to the cabinets of Europe as 'the Eastern Question' – that is to say, no longer a mortal threat, but a problem which the West could formulate in its own diplomatic terms even if it was not agreed upon the answer. But even after Turkey had been admitted to the Western society of states at the end of the Crimean War in 1856 (in order to protect it against Russian encroachments), the Eastern Question was still discussed with overtones of doctrinal passion; and the struggles of the suppressed peoples against Turkish domination attracted the 'transferred nationalism' of Western individuals, especially the British, like Byron in Greece and T. E. Lawrence in Arabia. The Turk remained 'the unspeakable Turk' in the West until the collapse of the Ottoman Empire and the genius of Kemal Atatürk transformed him into a sober, reliable and admired recruit to the Western way of life.[1]

1. This fragment, which relates to the draft chapter on 'International Revolutions' (see the editorial footnote at the end of Chapter 7 above), was apparently written in the late 1950s, or early 1960s. Eds.

Index

heartland, 73ff.
Henry II, 213
Henry IV, 92
Henry V, 36
Herter, C., 284
Hiroshima, 68, 249
Hitler, 37f., 76, 93, 140, 181, 189, 171
  expansionist aims, 59
  and Czechoslovakia, 77–8, 178
  use of threats, 78–9, 118
  and Austria, 162, 198
  and Rhineland, 260
Hoare-Laval Plan, 214
Hobbes, T., 90, 101f., 138, 142, 157
Holy Alliance, 83–4, 85, 197, 237
Holy Roman Empire, 297
House, Col., 33–4, 246f.
Hudson, G. F., 139
Hume, D., 168–9
Hungary, 152, 193, 214
  1956 revolt, 51, 114
  nationals in Yugoslavia, 131–2, 133
  see also Little Entente
Hydrogen bomb, see nuclear weapons

Iceland, 65, 261
ideology and fanaticism, 83, 85f., 88
imperialism, 93–4
India, 26, 28, 64, 83, 149, 164, 180, 231
  and Goa, 52, 147
  and nuclear energy, 282, 287
Indo-China, 50, 57, 164, 170, 228
Indonesia, 147, 154
Industrial Revolution, 56, 290
International Atomic Development Authority, 279–80
International Court of Justice, 109
international law, 66, 107–10
  system of, 102, 105
  Natural Law as source of, 290
interests, 96–9, 289

of great and minor powers, 43, 50–52
of dominant powers, 287, 289
  vital, 95–7, 104
  common, 289
intervention, 186, 191–9
  in Russia (1918), 188
  definition of, 186, 191
  and coercion, 191–2
  great powers and, 192–4
  to preserve balance of power, 194, 196
  defensive, 194, 197
  in Latin America, 195–6
  collective, 196, 237
  offensive, 197–8
Iran, see Persia
Ireland, 155, 213
Iroquois, 172
isolationism, 172, 209
Israel, 149, 158, 164, 287
Italian states, 30, 160, 170, 196
Italo-Abyssinian War, 47, 66, 100, 132, 208–9, 214

jackal states, 169, 181, 214
Jackson, Pres. A., 153
Japan, 55, 57–8, 65, 100, 188
  as great power, 47f., 208, 231, 290
  in the Second World War, 77, 79, 221
  and USA, 92, 139, 224
  peace treaties, 220, 229, 260
  and armed force, 260, 288
  see also Korea; Manchuria; Port Arthur; Russo-Japanese War; Sino-Japanese War; Washington Naval Treaty
Jefferson, T., 33, 56, 58
Jellicoe, Adm., 255
Jerusalem, 158
Johnson, Pres. L. B., 282
just war, 109f., 138, 142

Kahn, H., 249

Montesquieu, C. de, 242, 251
Montferrat, duchy of, 261–2
Montreaux Convention, 58
Moore, Sir J., 70
morality, and League Covenant, 213
    in international politics, 290–92
    relation to security, 292–3
Morgenthau, H., 18–19
Morley, J., 84
Morocco, 58, 154, 237
Moser, J. J., 301
Munich crisis and Treaty, 133, 135, 213–15
Mussolini, B., 47, 96, 118, 142, 149, 181

Nagy, Imre, 114
Namier, Sir L., 159
Naples, kingdom of, 192
Napoleon III, 39, 48, 51, 56, 86, 187, 268, 272, 275
Napoleon Bonaparte, 36, 45–6, 74, 93, 186, 204, 264
    belief in land power, 71–2
    invasion of Russia, 145
    and defence of Rhine, 150
    refusal to relinquish territory, 151
    and balance of power, 178, 185
    inventor of artillery barrage, 243
Napoleonic Wars, 31, 33, 55
Nasser, Gamal Abdul, 64, 76
'nation', meanings of, 27–8
national self-determination, 27, 85, 201, 203
    in Asia and Africa, 216, 230
naval armaments, Anglo-Dutch declaration (1787), 263–4
Nazi-Soviet Pact, 93, 215
Nazism, 86ff., 90, 92f., 135, 198, 212f.
Nelson, H., 69
neutralist states, 160f.
New Zealand, 269
Nicholas I, Tsar, 153, 193
Nicholas II, Tsar, 252, 267, 276

Nicolson, Sir H., 99, 292
Nkrumah, K., 147
non-intervention, 198–9
Non-Intervention Agreement, 199, 214
Non-Proliferation Treaty, 283, 286–8
non-self-governing territories, 234–6
North Atlantic Treaty and alliance, 103, 133f., 157, 167, 219, 222–3, 261
Norway, 146, 265
nuclear energy, see atomic energy
nuclear weapons, 11, 42–3, 59, 80, 223, 268
    hydrogen bomb, 49, 137, 224, 229, 256, 280, 284
    international inspection issue, 120, 278–80
    US-Soviet rivalry, 243, 248
    atomic bomb, 278, 280, 284
    agreements to limit, 283–8
Nuremberg War Crimes Tribunal, 111

Olmütz, Treaty of, 192
Oppenheimer, J. R., 256
Ottoman Empire, 83, 155, 164, 180
    Russian policy on, 153
    Western powers and, 302–3
Outer Mongolia, 164–5
outer space, demilitarization of, 285
Overbury, Sir T., 173, 300

Pacific, War of (1879–84), 150
pacifism, 242, 250, 266
Paine, Tom, 272
Pakistan, 149f., 165, 229f.
Palestine, 148, 274
Palmerston, H. J. T., 124–5, 154f., 176–7, 243, 252, 272–3
Panama, 195
Paraguay, 110f.
Paris Peace Conference (1919), 38, 40, 43, 46, 60; (1946), 220

315